The Complete Idiot's Reference Card

Romantic Do's

- ➤ Say "I love you" when it isn't expected.
- ➤ Make your partner number one.
- ➤ Give without expecting anything in return.
- ➤ Send your partner love notes.
- ➤ Passionately kiss in public.
- ➤ *Want,* not *have* to be romantic.
- ➤ Have a sense of adventure.
- ➤ Take the initiative in romance.
- ➤ Listen well, ask questions, and be interested in your partner.

Romantic Don'ts

- ➤ Wait for the holidays to be romantic.
- ➤ Show affection only during sex.
- ➤ Put friends and business ahead of your partner.
- ➤ Expect your partner to initiate romance.
- ➤ Show more interest in your life than your partner's.
- ➤ Complain about, criticize, or condemn your partner.
- ➤ Look for the bad, instead of the good, in your partner.
- ➤ Invest little in your relationship.
- ➤ Neglect to take time to look good for your partner.

7 Common Romantic Myths

- ➤ Romance is expensive.
- ➤ Only women and effeminate men like romance.
- ➤ Romance is only for new love.
- ➤ If your partner knows you love her, you don't need to tell her.
- ➤ Being romantic is time-consuming and will take away from your career.
- ➤ Romance has nothing to do with sex.
- ➤ Romance wanes; commitment endures.

alpha
books

How to Say "I love you" in Other Languages

Arabic	*Nhebuk*	Italian	*Ti amo*
Bulgarian	*Obicham te*	Japanese	*Kimi o ai shiteru*
Cambodian	*Bon sro lanh oon*	Korean	*Tangsinul sarang ha yo*
Cantonese	*Ngo oi ney*	Latin	*Te amo*
Chinese	*Wo ie ni*	Navaho	*Ayor anosh'ni*
Creole	*Mouin rinmim ou*	Norwegian	*Eg elskar deg*
Croatian	*LJUBim te*	Polish	*Kocham Cie*
Czech	*Miluji te*	Russian	*Ya vas lyublyu*
Danish	*Jeg elsker dig*	Slovak	*Lubim ta*
Filipino	*Mahal ka ta*	Spanish	*Te amo*
French	*Je t'aime*	Swedish	*Jag a'Iskar dig*
Gaelic	*Tha gradh agam ort*	Thai	*Ch'an Rak Khun*
German	*Ich liebe Dich*	Welsh	*'Rwy'n dy garu di*
Greek	*S' ayapoh*	Yiddish	*Ich libe dich*
Hungarian	*Szeretlek te'ged*	Zuni	*Tom ho' ichema*
Indonesian	*Saja Kasih saudari*		

The Meaning of Flowers

Azalea (pink)	Temperance, love, romance
Baby's breath	Fertility, gentleness, everlasting love
Buttercup	Flirtation
Cardinal flower	Distinction
Carnation (red)	Betrothal
Carnation (striped)	Refusal
Carnation (yellow)	Disdain
Chrysanthemum (red)	I love you
Chrysanthemum (white)	Truth
Chrysanthemum (yellow)	Doomed love
Daffodil	Regard
Dahlia	Treachery and danger
Gardenia	A secret love
Foxglove	Trickery
Heather	Betrothal
Honeysuckle	Lovers entwined
Jasmine (Indian)	Attachment
Jasmine (Spanish)	Sensuality
Jonquil	Affection returned
Lavender	Distrust
Lilac (purple)	Love's first emotions
Lily (Arum)	Eagerness
Lotus	Discovery of an illicit affair
Marigold	Grief, despair
Morning Glory	Affection
Orchid	Beauty
Pansy	Hopeful
Poppy	Vanishing pleasure
Tulip (red)	Declaration of love
Tulip (variegated)	Beautiful eyes
Tulip (yellow)	Hopeless love
Violet (purple)	You occupy my thoughts

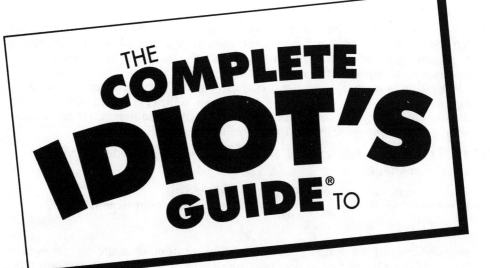

THE COMPLETE IDIOT'S GUIDE® TO

Romance

by Nancy Fagan

alpha
books

Macmillan USA, Inc.
201 West 103rd Street
Indianapolis, IN 46290

A Pearson Education Company

Copyright © 2000 by Nancy Fagan

International Standard Book Number: 0-02-863657-0
Library of Congress Catalog Card Number: Available upon request

02 01 00   8 7 6 5 4 3 2

Interpretation of the printing code: the rightmost number of the first series of numbers is the year of the book's printing; the rightmost number of the second series of numbers is the number of the book's printing. For example, a printing code of 00-1 shows that the first printing occurred in 2000.

Printed in the United States of America

Publisher
Marie Butler-Knight

Editorial Director
Gary M. Krebs

Product Manager
Phil Kitchel

Acquisitions Editors
Jessica Faust
Randy Ladenheim-Gil

Development Editor
Amy Bryant

Production Editor
Mike Thomas

Copy Editor
Heather Stith

Cover Designers
Mike Freeland
Kevin Spear

Illustrator
Jody P. Schaeffer

Book Designers
Scott Cook and Amy Adams of DesignLab

Indexer
Nadia Ibrahim

Layout/Proofreading
Svetlana Dominguez
Terri Edwards
Mary Hunt
Donna Martin
Gloria Schurick

Contents at a Glance

Contents

Appendixes

Foreword

In my practice as a relationship counselor and on my Web site, www.loveadvice.com, one of the most frequently asked questions is, "How can I get my mate to be more romantic?" We all want romance, but until *The Complete Idiot's Guide to Romance*, nobody was telling the unromantic how to become romantic. Romance isn't taught in school, so there's a mystery about how romance is achieved.

Women and men both think romance is supposed to just happen in some magical way, like in the movies. They believe that intentional romance isn't romantic. So nobody does anything. They just sit around yearning for romance to drop in on them by accident.

Women want romance from the men in their life. Men want sex, and to get it they've discovered they're supposed to be romantic, but they don't know how. Women think romance should be a surprise, a spontaneous unexpected gesture, so they can't tell their man exactly how to be romantic. Then it wouldn't be a surprise.

I remember a distraught man who came to me wondering how to be romantic enough to make his lady happy. He told me, "I tried to be romantic. I brought her red roses every day. So one day she says, 'Oh no, not more red roses.' So I stopped bringing them, and then she says, 'You don't bring me flowers anymore.'" He didn't understand that a routine is not romantic. *The Complete Idiot's Guide to Romance* has so many romantic gestures that you'll never get stuck in a romance rut.

Recently a woman came to me with a romance problem. Her boyfriend had sent her a bouquet of flowers to mark their six-month anniversary. She sent him a ticket to a concert by his favorite musical group—one she didn't particularly care for—along with the surprise news that she would be visiting her mother that weekend. When he got upset and said he wasn't going to go because he didn't want to go alone, she couldn't understand what she had done wrong. "He's an independent person. Why couldn't he go to the concert alone?" she wondered. Her liberated outlook made her forget that being romantic means being together and sacrificing your comfort for your lover's, like a knight of old laying his cape across a pool of mud for his loved one to walk across. This woman obviously needed *The Complete Idiot's Guide to Romance* to make sure her surprises were romantic.

Many people believe that they're either romantic or they're not, as if being romantic is innate, a quality that you're born with. Nothing could be further from the truth. You can learn to be romantic. *The Complete Idiot's Guide to Romance* is filled with so many ideas to help you be more romantic that if you just did one or two a week, you'd have enough romance for the rest of your life.

Tracy Cabot, Ph.D., is the author of five books on relationships, including *How To Make a Man Fall in Love With You, How To Win the Woman You Want,* and *Letting Go: How To Get Over a Broken Heart,* which was made into an ABC Movie of the Week starring John Ritter and Sharon Gless. Worldwide, Dr. Cabot's books have sold over a million copies and have been translated into French, Spanish, German, Dutch, Italian, Japanese, Hebrew, Korean, Czechoslovakian, Portuguese, and Albanian. In addition, Dr. Cabot's articles on relationships have appeared in *Cosmopolitan, Bride's, New Woman, Savvy, Family Circle, Ladies Home Journal, Playgirl,* and others. She is a contributing editor to *American Woman* and *Honeymoon,* where her columns "Just Between Us" and "The Sensuous Honeymoon" appear in each issue.

Throughout the ages, some of the most successful lovers were those who seemed the most unlikely. Great love and great lovers are not dependent on money, good looks, or superior intelligence. Any of these characteristics might be a plus in a relationship, but great lovers know that it takes romance to win the heart of a lady fair.

Now you can sharpen your skills and learn from the greatest lovers throughout the ages courtesy of "Dr. Romance." If you learn nothing more from this book, you'll learn that romantic gestures can be as simple as a wink at the right time, to the right person. You'll learn how to develop your own romance tools, using your personal resources, and you'll find you won't have to reinvent yourself in the image of someone else to be a success at the game of love.

Tempted to bypass the history lesson in Part 1 and get right to the "how to" of romance? Don't. History is a great learning tool, especially when it comes to the whys and hows of romance. History gives us an understanding of why we do what we do, and the mistakes we should avoid. You need this little bit of history to fully comprehend the many ways in which romance has developed over the ages. Your perceptions of romance, relationships, love, and sex are colored by the historical actions of others. Dr. Romance provides just enough insight into ancient and not so ancient love before getting down to the basics so you can rev up your romance rating.

Did you know that non-sexual romantic gestures become more important when sex is prohibited, geographically difficult, or otherwise impossible? Consider that the next time you decide a long-distance romance can't cut it, or circumstances keep the two of you apart.

Is boredom turning your long-term relationship into a ho-hum chore? Dr. Romance tells you how to use sexual and non-sexual romance to keep the flame of love from turning into a mere flicker.

Whether you're a fledgling at the game of love or you've been on the merry-go-round for a while, *The Complete Idiot's Guide to Romance* has tips to smarten you up to win and keep the lady of your dreams!

Pat Gaudette, Publisher
FRIENDS & Lovers, the Relationships Guide
http://friends-lovers.com

Introduction

W. Somerset Maugham defines love as "the dirty trick nature played on us to achieve the continuation of the species." Many people view romance almost as an enemy. I'm here to show you that it is the greatest ally you can have. All you have to do is reacquaint yourself with it.

Romance means adventure! So the next time you complain that your relationship is boring, know that what you're really saying is that you need to add excitement to your love life. This book is devoted to teaching you how to add that excitement to your relationship.

How This Book Is Organized

The Complete Idiot's Guide to Romance is divided into five parts that take you from discovering what romance is to becoming a romantic person.

Part 1, "What Is This Thing Called Romance?" will introduce you to well-known characters who had an impact on the art of romance. Through their trials and tribulations, you'll discover concrete techniques guaranteed to help you capture the heart of the one you love.

In **Part 2, "A Romantic Gesture a Day,"** you'll learn all about the makings of romantic sex! You will learn the tricks and secrets from the great lovers through history who perfected the art of seduction. You'll learn to use what they used, plus mix in what they didn't have: your sexy partner! Get ready, because the most sensual aspects of good sex come way before the action begins!

Part 3, "Becoming a Modern-Day Romeo and Juliet," introduces a smorgasbord of romantic tools to impress your partner with. You'll have enough ideas at your fingertips to spend a lifetime romancing your partner.

In **Part 4, "Going for the Gusto,"** you get to travel down the golden path of love as you discover how to romance your partner in the most exquisite lifestyle (complete with big dollar signs).

In **Part 5, "Romance Forever,"** you'll bring together all you've learned and apply it to your partner. Dating the one you love will never be the same. You will be armed with the strategies you need to keep romance alive on your journey through "ever after."

Extras

Throughout *The Complete Idiot's Guide to Romance,* you will find four types of boxes that contain special information about romance:

An Affair to Remember

Romance leads to great relationships, and these boxes tell the stories behind some of the best-known love affairs throughout history.

Cupid's Report

These boxes contain resources, facts, research, and general knowledge related to love and relationships.

Dr. Romance

These boxes contain romantic tips and exercises that will bring you closer to your partner.

Words of the Heart

In these boxes, you will read a range of emotions expressed by others.

Acknowledgments

Writing the acknowledgments is always my favorite part of writing a book; it's the cherry on top of the cake! It's a time for me to give thanks to everyone I've come across in the path to this book. Yes, the next few paragraphs are going to sound like an Academy Awards acceptance speech, so skim the list until you find the section you either fit into or have an interest in reading and leave the rest behind.

Love of my life: Like always, my son Brandon is top on my list. He's the best kid in the entire world. I only have one Brandon and that makes him twice as special. Okay Brandon, just like before, with each new book sold you get to have a shopping spree at Toys "R" Us. Surprise! Have fun! I love you.

Family: Of course, I have to say thanks to my mom and my five brothers: Doug, Stuart, Craig, Kip, and Garrick. Through you, I've been socialized in the world of men, which is a great gift for any woman. I know you guys are tired of romance, but I appreciate your opinions and feedback ever since Dr. Romance was born.

Clients: There is no way I could have come up with the material for this book if it hadn't been for all the people who confided in me regarding the issues that affected your relationships.

Readers: If I can continue to provoke thought in my readers, I am doing my job well. Your letters and e-mail help to shape my writing. They give me a guideline to help others with similar issues. So you see, your pain has served a purpose because it's helping others.

Boaz Rauchwerger: What can I say about you except you are the best friend a woman could have! Your 24-hour phone line, continued support, and positive messages have helped me immeasurably. You are the best thing that ever came from you know who! Yes, him!

Evan Fogelman: Of course, I'm getting to you, Evan. How could I ever forget about you? Thank you very much for putting up with my little worries and finding this book deal.

Editors: First of all, thanks to Jessica Faust who patiently guided and shaped my writing into a form perfect for "idiots." Thanks also to Amy Bryant. You're amazing! You made a tedious process an enjoyable learning experience. Your suggestions and feedback were wonderful, and I appreciated all of it. You are a wonderful editor, and I hope our paths cross in the future.

Others: You guys have been great: Rosemary, Melissa, Beverly, Laura, Angelica, Iris, Becky, Dr. Brett Thomas a.k.a. Dr. Love (My body loves you!), and, of course, my Grandma Brown (I love you Grandma!).

Get in Touch with Me

Getting letters from readers has to be the greatest reward for my work. If you have any questions, comments, feedback, or ideas you would like to share with me, please write to: Dr. Romance, P.O. Box 503566, San Diego, California 92150-3566. You can also contact me by e-mail at AskDrRomance@aol.com. I'd love to hear from you.

Trademarks

All terms mentioned in this book that are known to be, or are suspected of being, trademarks or service marks, have been appropriately capitalized. Alpha Books and Macmillan USA, Inc. cannot attest to the accuracy of this information. Use of a term in this book should not be regarded as affecting the validity of any trademark or service mark.

Part 1

What Is This Thing Called Romance?

There is no way to keep people apart. From the very beginning, there has been an unmistakable magnetism that draws them to each other. This lure goes beyond lust or chemistry. It's a basic need people have for each other. Without it, they are incomplete.

Although pairing off sounds natural and uncomplicated, getting a couple together is anything but simple. Depending on the era, there has always been an emotional, societal, or moral force that makes becoming a couple difficult.

In this section, you'll read about how various characters throughout history learned to come together in romance by using the tools they had at their disposal. Learn from their mistakes by not repeating them in your relationship. By doing this, you'll set the stage for a great relationship.

Chapter 1

Romance: A Retrospective

In This Chapter

➤ Biblical romance

➤ Mythological romance

➤ Medieval romance

Romance is one of the most precious things we have as humans. Romance allows us to be intimate with another person in a way that we aren't with others. Romance helps men and women to connect with each other.

If you think being romantic is a difficult thing, then you are not alone. Since the beginning of time, men and women have struggled to discover exactly what it means to be romantic. Even the White Knight from the Middle Ages and Victorian women struggled with the romance dilemma. As you will read in this chapter, they discovered that the complexity behind romance was actually very simple: It just meant putting forth extra effort to show their partners they cared.

All Roads Lead to Romance

Have you ever wondered where romance came from or how it started? (Some of you may even wish romance had never started at all.) Romance developed during many periods throughout time. Some periods, however, are remembered more than others because they are portrayed on television and in film and continue to be written about. The following three romance themes are quite common:

1. Early humans' experiences with love, such as that between Adam and Eve

2. The mythological times with Cupid's sense of adventure

3. The romantic ways of the knights and maidens

Romantic tales are present in art, science, and folklore, and romance continues to thrive in our culture. As one philosopher, Kahlil Gibran, put it in 1923:

> *The moment you have in your heart this extraordinary thing called love, and feel the depth, the delights, the ecstasy of it, you will discover that for you the world is transformed.*

An Affair to Remember

In the Judeo-Christian belief, God created man in the beginning. But God realized something was missing. Man was incomplete, like the seas without fish or the earth without animals. So God took a rib from Adam's side and created the first woman, Eve. She was the one who could perfectly complete Adam, the one who would provide what was lacking in him, the one who would do what the male was unable to do alone. As stated in the Bible, when Adam first laid eyes on Eve, he said, "This is now bone of my bones, and flesh of my flesh." (Genesis 2:23) The woman was made from man, made for man, given to man, and named by man. During the first sexual union, Adam and Eve became one flesh.

We may imagine that even in the simplicity of Adam's romantic ways with Eve, he learned that the amount of effort he put forth was what attracted Eve the most. Mythology, with all of its energy, showed that all people want is to be with the one they love. Lastly, the knights showed the world how satisfying romance can be when you use what is available in your environment. These qualities thrived in the past and will continue in the future because they are the essence of romance.

The Origin of Romance

If Cupid didn't invent romance, who did? To find the answer, you have to go back to the stories of the first humans to exist on the planet. Depending on whom you talk to, the idea of the first humans varies widely. In this chapter, I will refer to one of the most well-known early couples: Adam and Eve.

If Adam's romantic ways were so tremendous, then why doesn't anyone associate his name with romance? He should be considered the Father of Romance, but he isn't. Let's examine why.

Some may argue that it wasn't Adam's courting but circumstances that made Eve so receptive to his advances. True, as the story goes, Adam and Eve lived in the utopian land of Eden. Adam didn't have to worry about competition because he was the only existing man at the time. And, the Bible says Adam and Eve were both naked, so something was bound to happen!

But things are never as perfect or as easy as they appear. Eve likely had needs that Adam didn't know about. How often have you had a partner who seemed to get emotional for no apparent reason? Usually, it's because romance is missing. If you give her romance, she'll light up like a bright summer's day.

When God created Eve, Adam never realized the work that he would have to put into wooing her. The challenge was discovering how to win her heart. Adam, like all men and women, realized that creating romance isn't a natural talent for most—it takes a little extra effort. However, the work is well worth it when you reap the benefits.

> **Words of the Heart**
>
> "When the devil cannot reach us through the spirit, he creates a woman beautiful enough to reach us through the flesh."
>
> —from the 1927 movie *Flesh and the Devil*

Adam and Eve's First Date

According to the Bible, at the beginning of time, there were seven days. During the week, Adam went to work and kept himself busy doing whatever it was that he did back then. By the end of the week, he became lonesome. This bothered God, so God created "date night" and gave Adam a beautiful companion by the name of Eve. She was "all that"! Unfortunately, Eve had no interest in going on a date with Adam.

"God," Adam asked, "give me the ways to be romantic so that I can have Eve for my wife." God answered all right, but not in the way Adam was hoping for. God informed Adam that he was on his own. It was up to him to figure out this thing called love. After all, God had given him a brain to figure it all out.

> **Dr. Romance**
>
> If you lived in a world where the humans lacked the sense of sight, what five qualities would you choose in a partner?

So Adam sat down one Saturday morning and analyzed the times when Eve was her most attentive. Up to that point, he'd learned that some things pleased Eve more than others. He decided to call those behaviors *romantic gestures*, and do more of

5

Cupid's Report

The heart is the symbol most associated with love. The original meaning of the heart was a person's emotional core. A flaming heart signifies devotion between two lovers, but a heart broken in two pieces means heartache.

Cupid's Report

The planet Venus is named after the Roman goddess of erotic love, beauty, and the arts. Its astronomical symbol of a circle with a cross coming out of the bottom side is believed to represent either her necklace or mirror.

Dr. Romance

Create a romantic fantasy with you as a Greek god's love interest. What titillating stories would you have to share with your friends about the experience?

them to win her heart. "I'll name all the animals to suit her; she'll be pleased by that," Adam thought. He continued his list of what Eve liked him to do: draw hearts in the dirt, give her unexpected surprises, brush her hair with his fingertips, sing to her at dusk, bathe her in the sea, hold her close when they danced, flatter her, and most of all, take time to go out of his way to catch her interest.

Adam needed help. (He sure could have used *The Complete Idiot's Guide to Romance*.) He knew all the answers could be found at the Tree of Knowledge, but he resisted the temptation. He believed that he could find the answers on his own.

Adam was astute with his observations of women or, in his case, woman. He learned precisely what Eve needed just by paying attention to her reactions. His effort paid off, because Eve wouldn't let him out of her sight.

When was the last time your partner couldn't get enough of you? If you behave the way Adam did, you will see a connection between what you give and the emotional dividends you receive.

A Few Myths About Romance

Adam and Eve may have been the first to experience romance, but the ancient Greek and Roman gods and goddesses made it desirable for all to have. The stories of the mythological gods and goddesses added the fire that made romance unforgettable.

About 3,000 years ago, the ancient Greeks and Romans came up with stories to explain life on earth. They believed that a family of gods ruled the land. These gods were eccentric and possessed the emotions of humans to an exaggerated degree. For instance, when a god was embarrassed, he didn't just blush; he flew to the sky and hid behind a cloud. Or when he was in love and wanted to give his partner flowers, he had the power to make flowers blossom along every step his partner took.

These exaggerated expressions of emotions were exciting to hear about. Interestingly, most mythological stories had an element of love. This is one reason mythology is easy to relate to, even today. People love stories of passion, intrigue, and romance.

Mount Olympia, the Birthplace of Mythological Romance

Let's look at romance for a moment as though it were a person rather than a thing. Because it was born in the Garden of Eden, it took on certain tame characteristics that only Adam and Eve could have given it: love, honor, and commitment. Although these traits are important in love, other qualities are needed.

After romance was born, it was taken in by the gods on Mount Olympia. As you know, genetic influence is an important part of a person, but what is just as significant to a person's development is the environment in which that person is raised. Romance was raised by the gods, who were anything but conventional. Imagine what Romance's home life must have been like: gods running around half-naked most of the time, arrows being shot into people to make them love, affairs, out-of-wedlock children, half-animal/half-human beings, flying creatures, people being turned into inanimate objects, and so on. This kind of chaos could make a child go crazy.

But romance not only survived its childhood, it thrived. The influence of the Greek and Roman

Cupid's Report

Bows and arrows are some of the more common symbols of love in the United States. However, bows and arrows symbolize different things in different cultures:

➤ In Buddhism and Hinduism, they signify the mind and the five senses and willpower.

➤ In China, they are a fertility symbol and can represent the Tao.

➤ In Christianity, the bow symbolizes temporal power, and the arrows symbolize martyrdom.

➤ In Islam, the bow signifies Allah's power and his arrow is his wrath.

➤ In Japan, they symbolize a shedding of the ego during meditation.

➤ In Shamanistic cultures, they are a birdlike flight to heaven.

gods and goddesses shaped its personality into all the characteristics that make up romance today: energetic, adventuresome, whimsical, exciting, intense, playful, passionate, determined, and creative. As William Wordsworth said in 1843:

Love is the immortal flow of energy that nourishes, extends, and preserves. Its eternal goal is life. What a gift we are blessed with all because romance was born!

Dr. Romance

Take inventory of your romantic behaviors. Have you been more romantic with some partners and less with others? Did you find yourself more romantic because your partners were more responsive to your romantic gestures? It's always rewarding when someone thanks you for being romantic, even if it's just to say thank you for calling. So reward your partner the next time you like what he does. It's a guaranteed way to increase more of the same type of behavior in the future.

Cupid's Report

A bow and arrows are Cupid's tools and symbols of romantic love. The tension of a bow's strings symbolizes male prowess, vigor, and vitality—all qualities associated with love. The arrow is a purely masculine sign that signifies penetration, virility, and speed. It is often associated with lust in both men and women. Cupid fires two kinds of arrows: those gold-dipped will rouse passion, and those with lead will kill passion.

The gods were mischievous and brimming with lust and adventure for all things and people. To entertain themselves, they would sit on their mountaintop and create romantic scenarios that they wanted to see acted out between mortal men and women. To them, it was almost like writing a play and then casting actors in the roles to play out the scenes. The mortals had no idea that this play was going on. Instead, they just thought it was the fate of life's experiences.

You Can Point an Arrow at This One

Cupid has played a role in the celebration of love and lovers for 3,000 years. In Greece, he's known as Eros, the young son of Aphrodite, the goddess of love and beauty. To the Romans, he's Cupid, the son of Venus. Cupid is often portrayed as a mischievous little boy, and the human heart is his playground.

Cupid personifies the uncontrollable nature of love and sexual attraction in people. His primary role in eternity is to bewitch the hearts of men and women by causing them to fall in love. He does this with his bow and arrow. All he has to do is shoot his arrow at someone and the person instantly falls in love with the first person he or she sees.

Can you imagine the fun you could have with that tool? Just for kicks, you could shoot an arrow at Judge Judy and make her fall passionately in love with her bailiff! Cupid's personality was just like this. He made the most unlikely people fall in love just for his own amusement.

Plato described Cupid as

> ... a demon halfway between god and man. He made his home in men's hearts; but not in every heart, for where there is hardness he departs. His greatest glory is that he cannot do wrong.

If Cupid has been ignoring you, look to see which stage your heart is in. Your heart goes through cycles, just like the four seasons. After difficult times, such as a heartbreak, your heart will be cold, or hard, making it difficult for you to open up to another person. Just recognizing this cycle will help you to know that your heart is in the healing stage and won't be there forever. As you begin to heal, your heart will feel like spring again, with new life growing inside.

Even today Cupid's presence remains strong. All you have to do is look around to see his influence. He's on Hallmark cards, stationery, trinkets, furniture, tattoos, Harley bikes, jewelry, and the Internet. He's tied so closely with Valentine's Day that you'd think the holiday would be named Cupid's Day.

People no longer consider Cupid to be a god. Instead, he's evolved into a symbol of love. He's referred to more in reference for love than in serious prayer as he once was.

Words of the Heart

"The lover regarded himself as a martyr subject to the whims of the person whom he adored. She was the sole arbiter of his destiny, endowed with the power to kill or save. This religion of profane love demanded patience, humility, abnegation, obedience, and fidelity."

—*from Theories on the Origin of Courtly Love* by C. Stephen Jaeger

An Affair to Remember

Cupid had his own intense love affair with Psyche, a beautiful mortal. Psyche's beauty made Cupid's mother, Venus, the beautiful goddess of love, jealous. She ordered her son to make Psyche fall in love with the ugliest creature in the land. But when Cupid saw Psyche, he fell in love with her. The gods ordered Psyche's parents to leave her alone on a mountain where her husband, a fearsome creature, would take her away. Unexpectedly, the wind took Psyche to a house that appeared vacant. As she walked through the house, a male voice introduced himself as her husband. He warned her not to try and discover his identity, but she couldn't resist. One night while he lay sleeping, she brought a lamp to the bedside. It was Cupid. He awoke and flew away into hiding. Venus heard of her son's marriage and was enraged. She announced a reward for anyone who could find Psyche; she was found and sent to the underworld. If she survived, she would be free to stay with Cupid. In the end, she fell into a fatal sleep and Cupid pleaded with the gods for forgiveness. They honored his request and made Psyche immortal so that they could marry and spend eternity together.

It All Changed One Knight

Romance evolved significantly in the fourteenth, fifteenth, and sixteenth centuries. During this time, the archetype of the knight in shining armor, or as some refer to him, the White Knight, was developed. He was the gentleman found in every woman's fantasies, past and present. He'd be the equivalent of Prince Charming or Mr. Right in today's terms. The woman he pursued was commonly referred to as a maiden, such as Maid Marian from the Robin Hood story.

The White Knight of the Middle Ages had many advantages over Adam, as well as more tools at his fingertips for encouraging romance to burst forth:

➤ Horses to ride great distances in order to court a maiden

➤ Musical instruments and lyrics for love songs to sing to his lover

➤ Written language to express his love or books to read from that spoke of endearment

➤ A snazzy wardrobe of provocative leotards that left very little to the imagination, but did a fine job of catching a maiden's interest

➤ Capes that a knight could lay over a mud puddle so his maiden wouldn't get dirty

➤ Castle windows that made romantic interludes exciting and challenging for the knights who attempted to sneak through them

During this time, people of higher socioeconomic status married for utilitarian purposes. Basically, this meant that the man with the most money married the woman of his choice! Women had no say in the arrangement; a woman's duty was simply to bear heirs. Love was a separate issue from marriage. Out of this unhappiness grew courtly love—the most profound addition to romance ever!

Cupid's Report

Wolfgang Mozart, the musical genius, at one time had romantic feelings for his pretty cousin, which, at that time, was considered taboo. The mutual feelings led to an exchange of love letters over an extended period of time. Mozart ended one letter to his cousin by writing, "Good-bye, for now. I kiss your hand, your face, your knees and your—in a word, wherever you permit me to kiss. I am with all my heart your very affectionate nephew and cousin, Mozart." Realizing the relationship couldn't work, he later married a proper wife, Contanze.

White Horses, Maidens, and Courtly Love

Courtly love can more accurately be defined as adultery; however, it was something that was an accepted and expected part of marriage in the Middle Ages.

Surprisingly, the White Knight was welcomed to the home for courting while the husband was home. This practice lasted for nearly three centuries.

The goal of the courtly interaction was not for sexual pleasure. Instead of sexual relations, the focus was on verbal expression and pursuit. The more difficult a woman was to catch, the more valued she was. A man measured his romantic success in terms of how much time his love interest allowed him to spend with her. Of course, the more time she gave him, the stronger he interpreted her love to be.

For a man to be competent in courtly love, he had to possess two things:

1. A high level of skill in courtly talk

2. A feeling of being overwhelmed by the woman's presence

Words of the Heart

"... to be love for its own sake, romantic love, true love, physical love, carefree love, with the aim of love only—apart from real-life responsibilities. 2. Humility, courtesy, adultery, and the religion of love."

—C. S. Lewis's description of courtly love in *The Allegory of Love: A Study in Medieval Tradition*

Women, on the other hand, were objects of desire to men who faithfully pursued them through romantic actions, word, and song. Think about the relationship that you're in. Would you be considered competent in courtly love by those standards? In the Middle Ages, it was a knight's duty to be familiar with the ways of romancing the one they loved.

The Rules of Courtly Love

Rules enable people to know what to expect and how to behave. Courtly love was no exception. The rules were not written in a book for people to follow, they were just known. Imagine the maiden who wasn't made to blush by her knight. The knight who followed the courting rules the closest was the most desired man in the land.

There were nine typical rules that applied to courtly love:

➤ One must constantly, without intermission, think of his lover.

➤ One must religiously devote his love to her.

➤ One should not desire to embrace anyone else.

Dr. Romance

So many myths surround romance that sometimes people get confused about just how simple it is. Here is a list of the seven most common myths that surround romance:

1. Romance is expensive.

2. Only women and effeminate men like romance.

3. Romance is only for new love.

4. If your partner knows you love her, you don't need to tell her.

5. Being romantic is time-consuming and will take away from your career.

6. Romance has nothing to do with sex.

7. Romance wanes; commitment endures.

➤ One should not deny jealousy—it is a sign of love.

➤ One should be steadfast during good times and bad.

➤ One should desire one's current lover more than any from the past.

➤ One should be so courteous he would rather die than offend her even in thought.

➤ One should be courteous at all times.

➤ One should suffer for love.

I admit, these rules seem a little obsessive and extreme. It's a good thing the rules of romance have changed, or else no one would want to have any part of it. Romance does not have to be a full-time job the way it was in the Middle Ages. Today, if you spend even five minutes a day toward developing the romance in your relationship, you're the envy of everyone.

Take a minute to calculate how many minutes you spend, on average, doing romantic things for your partner. If it's less than five, you need to put some serious thought into reprioritizing your time so that your partner considers you to be the best knight in her life!

The Least You Need to Know

➤ Romance is stronger if you show a genuine interest in your partner.

➤ Courting your partner comes with practice. When in doubt, use the ways of the knights. They work well for both men and women.

➤ To make your relationship the most incredible love affair, you need to make it your number-one priority.

➤ Mischievousness is always a way to enhance romance. Follow Cupid's lead.

Chapter 2

The Changing Nature of Romance

In This Chapter

➤ Calling and courting

➤ Parking and petting

➤ Hanging out and shacking up

➤ Cruising the classifieds and surfing the Net

Cupid became very active at the end of the nineteenth century. He knew that singles were ready for a change, so he gave it to them. People began to advertise in the newspaper for a mate. Then Cupid saw the opportunity to move courting out of the parlor (and the paper) and into the city with advancements in travel. Because of increased ease of travel, courting couples were no longer under watchful eyes at home. Next came the car (and along with it the back seat of sin). Most recently, Cupid's work has shown up on the Internet.

Each era introduces more romantic tools to make wooing the one you love an easier task. In this chapter, you'll read about all the romantic developments that have come about in recent history. Although in the past romance has ebbed and flowed like a teenager's moods, romance now seems to be more of a focus in relationships.

Victorian Secrets Come Out of the Closet

The Victorian era (1830–1901) brought two new characters to our romantic history: the gentleman and his lady. Boy, were they an improper fit! The gentleman had two sides to his character. On the one hand, he was well-behaved, especially when in the company of a lady. On the other hand, he was wild with testosterone and eager to sow his oats. The gentleman's disposition depended on the situation and the company he kept.

Dr. Romance

Romance gives a relationship a sense of meaning and excitement. Being romantic involves being generous with your concern, interest, and affection.

Throughout history and in many cultures, women have hidden their desires, pretending not to have passion the way men do. Proper Victorian ladies were taught to want nothing to do with sex. Women of today still struggle with the conflict of "Is it okay to do it?" Learning the impact that the Victorians had on our psyches will help to shed this nonsense in our romances today.

An Affair to Remember

Queen Victoria became the queen of England at the age of 16. She also briefly met Prince Albert, her first cousin, at this age. She didn't think much of him beyond a platonic relationship until she met him again three years later. At that time, she described him as, "accessibly handsome, such beautiful eyes ... my heart is quite going." Within a year, she proposed marriage to him, and he accepted. They were extremely happy and had nine children together. It all came to an end when Albert died of typhoid fever at 42. Queen Victoria was so devastated over her loss that she lived in seclusion for many years and wore black the rest of her life. She even maintained his rooms as though he was still alive, ordering the servants to bring hot water to his room for shaving each morning. She eventually remarried, but she never stopped mourning for Albert.

In the Victorian period, ladies were idealized as benevolent, chaste, mother figures. Any lady who didn't interact with gentlemen according to this ideal was frowned upon. Can you imagine the frustration the poor ladies felt? The logic of this ideal lady didn't make sense. Remember, brothels were very popular at the time, and if the paid ladies liked sex, why wouldn't all ladies? Unfortunately, it took many decades before it was acceptable for women to admit they enjoyed sex.

The romantic gestures used by the ladies of the Victorian era are almost obsolete in today's world. Ladies used charms like singing, playing an instrument, reading aloud, and writing words into poetry and beautiful letters to reel men in. Just think how romantic it would be to have someone entertain you in this fashion today!

By this point in history, the gentleman had the biggest advantage over the men in the past. He now had additional means for romance: calling cards, brimmed hats for tipping, houses to call on, and etiquette manuals to teach him, as well as the ladies, how to do everything properly. Together, the lady and gentleman brought the rituals of romance back into popularity.

Mates Here, There, and Everywhere

The ladies and gentlemen of the Victorian era were not limited to the boy next door or the girl down the lane in their romantic pursuits. They were born in a booming time in history when the advances in technology brought a large population influx to the cities. With this inflow of new people, different classes mingled together, and the middle class grew.

With all the new partners available, mate searching became complicated. Cousin Tori was no longer the one in charge of matchmaking for Mr. Sean's second cousin, who would be coming for a visit. Instead, for the first time, there was a sense of anonymity and great possibilities for partnering up with an attractive new stranger from a faraway land.

Cupid's Report

In the Victorian period, it was very common behavior to avoid any action that was associated with sex. Ministers and doctors preached against masturbation during the Victorian era. They claimed it was a demon practice of self-abuse that was killing thousands of young people by turning them into feeble, pale, and drooling idiots.

Cupid's Report

The changes that resulted from the Industrial Revolution brought with them a confusion about proper behavior. Etiquette books brought clarification to the new social interactions between people who had never socialized together previously. They instructed people how to behave properly in all the new situations. Separate books were written for men, women, children, and teens. The subjects covered in these books ranged from courting to ballroom dancing. The goal of the etiquette books was to give people a standard reference for improving their behavior against a proper standard for all people to live up to.

Dr. Romance

Believe it or not, the graham cracker was invented in order to reduce sexual interest. The religious fanatic Sylvester Graham (1794–1851) believed that a bland cracker would decrease sexual drives in those who ate them. Research has not proven this theory to be true; however, research has shown that a person's sexual interest decreases slightly after eating a full meal. So if you don't want your libido to decrease after a meal, keep your intake light.

Words of the Heart

"Men are rewarded and punished not for what they do, but rather for how their acts are defined."

—Thomas Szasz, 1973

This new way of thinking was illustrated by the introduction of the personal ads. The personal ads were originally intended to help people locate lost friends, but quickly the section evolved into what we know as the mate-searching personals today. To lure mates, men and women used the same bait you see today: financial stability for men and beauty for women. In one typical ad, dated 1893, a woman stated, "Handsome young woman with nice figure looking for husband to cook, clean, and care for." As you see, she advertised her attractiveness and talents to attract a man.

Court, Courtship, and Marriage

During the Victorian era, one of the most valued characteristics was respectability. For a woman, respectability was defined as behaving in a proper fashion that was worthy of respect by others. Accordingly, women were taught to showcase this quality as a way of attracting a suitable mate.

Young girls were schooled in the arts of blushing and fainting in public. This kind of behavior demonstrated that a lady was truly shocked whenever faced with any sort of impropriety. For instance, if a gentleman spoke to a lady in an improper way, she would faint to show that she was put off by the statement.

In the days before telephones and electronic media, people went "visiting"—that is, they went to people's homes. A gentleman caller would specifically visit as a way to spend time with the lady he was attracted to. Such gentlemen callers were limited to one or two visits with the lady a week, during the daylight hours. The visits were extended to longer hours and increased frequency as the couple became more serious about their relationship.

To facilitate good visiting, both ladies and gentlemen carried calling cards at all times. In the Victorian times, a calling card was a business-size card printed with the person's first and last name and home address. It was called a calling card because, if the card was given to someone, it gave that person permission to call on or visit the card giver.

A calling card was used in courting to signify romantic interest in a person, but cards could not be given to strangers. A man had to be formally introduced to a woman by a third party before he and the woman could speak to each other. At that time, if the two people were interested in each other, calling cards would be exchanged. If, however, the woman was not interested, she would not give the man her card.

In order to adhere to proper etiquette for calling, a lady was always properly dressed in her bonnet, shawl, and gloves when a gentleman came calling. Likewise, the gentleman removed only his hat and held it in his hand or on his lap if he was seated during the visit. The constant presence of the lady's mother or sisters helped to keep the visit proper.

Dating Etiquette

The main meeting ground for Victorian single people was in town on the walking paths that took them from place to place. The etiquette books instructed each sex specifically on how to behave on these walking paths.

A gentleman could not initiate contact with an attractive lady unless she first smiled or bowed at him. Regardless of how attracted a lady was to a gentleman, she could not look back once he passed her. This rule forced the lady to be forward with her intent before the gentleman passed and initiate contact on the spot. It's too bad there are no such clear rules of contact today. If there were, getting together would be much easier.

According to the gentleman's etiquette book, it was proper to acknowledge each person who passed him on the path, regardless of sex, by tipping his hat. This gesture could become awkward from time to time, because if a lady was not interested in him, she could choose to ignore him. Today, people no longer consider it necessary to acknowledge each stranger who walks past them. Instead, it's more customary to avoid eye contact. However, just think of how many new people you would meet if you started greeting new people as you passed by them. What do you have to lose? It could be the best dating service ever known.

Not Tonight, Dear

Who do you think originally told the public that ladies didn't feel sexual pleasure? If you guessed that it was parents, you're wrong. It was Victorian doctors! These doctors informed the public that the act of sex was only for the purpose of producing offspring. Little girls and boys were indoctrinated with this belief as they grew up; consequently, they believed it.

Cupid's Report

The term **hooker** comes from General Joseph Hooker (1814–1879), who in 1864 frequented the "ladies" at a row of boarding houses in Washington D.C. so much that eventually the row of houses was referred to as "Hooker Row."

Dr. Romance

For many years, sexually active people have been concerned with sexually transmitted diseases. During the Civil War (1861–1865), for instance, there was a wave of transmitted diseases in the United States. According to the Kinsey Institute of Research, half of 531,000 soldiers, combined North and South, had venereal diseases. Reports like this one have taught lovers to engage in safe sexual practices.

When a woman married, she was instructed to lie still like a dead fish during sex and let the gentleman do his thing. Because men believed that women did not get physical pleasure from sex, they thought nothing of her unresponsiveness during the act.

Prudery is still affecting us some 150 years later. The Victorians passed on guilt and archaic guidelines for modern-day romance to adhere to. If we can learn to leave the guilt of the lady and take the lessons of courting from the gentleman, our love lives will be better for it. Understanding the past can open your eyes to understanding the confusion in your relationships, especially where gender roles are concerned.

The Twentieth Century: A Stage for Rapid Confusion

The twentieth century began with the ending of the Victorian era in 1901. The ending of this period was not abrupt; instead, society gradually deviated more and more from the behaviors described in the etiquette books. By 1901, the majority of Victorian ways were no longer practiced because new ways of living were considered acceptable. Gone were the restrictions, clothing, and attitudes of the Victorians.

An Affair to Remember

Humphrey Bogart was not initially seen as a Hollywood sex symbol, and no one expected that he would last. He was short and skinny, spoke with a lisp, and had a receding hairline. His upper lip was paralyzed from a World War I injury, which caused him to have a perpetual scowl on his face. When Lauren Bacall was cast opposite Bogart, it became clear that the couple had great onscreen chemistry. For the first time, Bogart was viewed as a romantic lead. After a brief period of time, their onscreen love affair branched off into real life. Bogart divorced his third wife and married Bacall. They had a fairy-tale romance offscreen, and the tabloids captured every public moment of it on film. The love affair ended when Bogart died of throat cancer at the age of 57.

The first noticeable change in romance in the twentieth century for men and women came in the '20s. This decade was full of roaring good times and free-spirited fun. World War II in the '40s brought with it short courtships and quick marriages. In the '50s, male and female roles were clearly defined.

A new kind of romance flourished in the '60s, '70s, and '80s with the invention of the pill and a woman's increased ability to control her reproductive life. Finally, near the end of the '90s, seeds of romance began to spring up when they were least expected to.

Words of the Heart

"The past is the only dead thing that smells sweet."

—Edward Thomas, 1917

The Car Gives the Green Light to Romance

With the invention of the car early in the twentieth century, courting in the home was out, and parking was in. This change did not occur overnight. It began very gradually in the upper class and worked its way to the lower class over the years as cars became more affordable.

The car was a young person's way to escape the watchful eyes of the parents. This means of escape was the beginning of sexual awakening for women because it gave them an environment that was conducive to physical experimentation with men. Without chaperones, petting was commonplace and so was the awareness of physical pleasures.

The Roaring '20s

The 1920s was a time when the United States began to shine as the land of opportunity. The whole nation felt this sense of prosperity, and it showed in the free-spirited actions of the people. Men and women developed a lively new style of dance, and the dance hall was a common place for men and women to meet. Women gained a new confidence, which showed up in their revealing new flapper fashions and uninhibited lifestyles. Having fun for both sexes was more evident on a large scale. Although alcohol was outlawed, bootlegging (selling and distributing liquor illegally) was a common practice. Life was one big celebration for men and women.

The Downtrodden '30s

The 1930s were anything but a romantic period in history. The depression was in full swing, the era of Hitler was beginning, and overall things looked bleak. This was a time when people had very little, so they stayed close to the ones they loved. The emphasis was on the family because love was one of the few things that was free.

The Jitterbug '40s

Relationships took on a serious tone in the '40s. World War II was raging, so couples found security in marriages. As the men went off to war, they were unsure whether they would ever return again, so they married the women they loved. For couples, it was a time when hardship, turmoil, danger, and distance made the heart grow fonder. Often, their only way of communicating to each other was through love letters and telegrams.

During the '40s, the nation was working together for a common cause: to end the war and bring the men home. While the women waited, they became part of the working force for the first time in history. When the war ended, men were reunited with the partners they loved. The result was a significant increase in the birth rate, known as the Baby Boom.

The Popularity of Marriage in the '50s

The couple of the '50s created the "traditional" male and female romantic roles. The man was seen as the leader and provider, and the woman as the follower and care-taker. Together, they made dating an important part of romance as well as an activity-based pastime. "Parking" became more popular as more people had cars.

The Kinsey sex report was published in 1948. Kinsey's view of female sexuality was quite different from doctors of the Victorian era. Alfred C. Kinsey discussed women's orgasms, and people wanted to hear more.

Cupid's Report

Real-life couple Ozzie and Harriet Nelson played the traditional roles of husband and wife on television in the '50s. The actors portrayed an average, white, middle-class, suburban couple. She was the stay-at-home wife who spent her life taking care of her husband. He was happy being the apple of her eye and the provider who left her without a care in the world.

The '60s and '70s: A Romance Shift

Relationships between men and women took on a new, more casual style with the invention of the birth control pill. Men and women no longer considered marriage the only context for sexual relations between two people. It was socially acceptable for couples to enjoy each other physically without the expectation of a serious relationship.

Sexuality was at its peak. The motto of '60s and '70s romance was, "Don't forget to take your pill." This era was a time of experimentation and total social freedom. Inhibition was out, and "going for it" was in.

Up to this point in history, the lack of birth control was a motivating factor behind the chastity of women. Women played it safe and waited for marriage before any serious hanky panky took place. In the '60s and '70s, living together was no longer reserved only for married people. Relationship choices were not based on the fear of unplanned pregnancies. Couples in this era had a lot of latitude that others in history had never experienced.

Advertising for Romance in the '80s

In the 1980s, the increasing number of AIDS cases frightened couples into examining how they handled their relationships. People decided that they needed more out of a relationship than just sex. They wanted bonding, closeness, and traditional love, meaning dating and courting. However, the roles in relationships had changed with the feminist movement, which caused confusion for each sex. Neither sex knew quite how to interact with the other.

As a result of this confusion, couples eventually learned to be flexible and become more androgynous in their interactions with each other. What was important in a relationship was to find a partner who respected you and who you could share life and love with.

One thing that grew out of the '80s was a proactive approach for getting what you want. Finding a partner was no exception. People took an active, self-directed method to meeting others. Women, in particular, no longer felt the need to wait for men to ask them out. Women were no longer financially dependent on men and thought nothing about picking up the tab or splitting the cost of dating when out with a man.

Dr. Romance

Each person in a relationship brings with them bits and pieces of all the times they have lived through. Depending on your age and your partner's age, you will find that each of you has been influenced differently. The next time you sit down with your partner, bring up this subject and compare your backgrounds. You will be surprised by how much of an impact certain times had on your views regarding relationships.

Cupid's Report

Within three years of the pill being released, more than 2 million women were using it. For the first time ever, women had the luxury of sampling sex without the fear of pregnancy.

The personal ad, which seemed to have been forgotten for many years, resurfaced during this time as a common way to find partners. Ironically, in a time of equality, research showed that men and women continued to advertise themselves similarly to the way they had since the development of the personal ad: Women advertised their attractiveness, and men advertised their financial stability.

Virtual Romance in the '90s

Doug@Internet.com meets Diana@Internet.com, and the whole world of virtual romance explodes. Welcome to the newest way of finding love. The virtual love scene is where partners are meeting over a computer screen and living happily ever after when they log off. Not everyone is doing this, but sizable numbers of people are experimenting with it as a viable way to find romance. For instance, on any given day, love@aol, has an average of over 325,000 personal advertisements posted, and it's just one of hundreds of online dating sites.

What starts online continues offline with communication being a big part of romance today. Couples are back to expressing their love in writing by typing romantic e-mail messages.

Lovers in the twentieth century have rebelled against Victorian values and gained new understanding about their sexuality. With that understanding comes the recognition that sex is only part of the love equation. Romance is also important, and the past has much to teach us about the rigors of romance.

The Least You Need To Know

➤ In the twentieth century, society learned that women could experience sexual pleasure just as men did. This fact was confirmed by the *Kinsey Report* in 1948.

➤ The invention of the birth control pill led to a new age in sexuality. It gave women and men the freedom to enjoy sex without the concern of unplanned pregnancies.

➤ The car and the classified ad played important roles in the development of romance.

➤ Today you have the luxury of romancing the one you love in the privacy of your home. Take advantage of the romantic edge you have that people in the past weren't afforded.

Modern-Day Romance

Can you imagine marrying someone you didn't love or a partner that someone else chose for you? These were the facts of life before the Industrial Revolution and Romanticism.

The American dream was born from the idea of achieving goals apart from the goals of the family unit. This idea nourished the trait of individualism in men and women. This new individual uprising affected relationships, too. No longer were partners chosen in terms of how the family would benefit from a union of husband and wife. Instead, choices became based on the individual's needs apart from the family. This is when the idea of romantic love as a condition for marriage started. The society was changing rapidly, as was the idea of romance.

Words of the Heart

"Sure there is music even in the beauty, and the silent note which Cupid strikes, far sweeter than the sound of an instrument. For there is music wherever there is harmony, order, or proportion; and thus far we may maintain the music of the spheres; for those well-ordered motions, and regular paces, though they give no sound unto the ear, yet to the understanding they strike a note most full of harmony."

— Sir Thomas Browne, 1643

Dr. Romance

Do you take your relationship for granted, or do you continue to rework it? Sometimes people think their relationships are set in stone and can't be changed. Not true! The dynamics of all relationships, old and new, can change. You can discover what will make you happy; all you have to do is keep trying.

You may be saying to yourself, "Okay, this is interesting, but why do I need to know the history of romance?" In this chapter, you will learn about the three main reasons it's important to be familiar with romance history:

1. You can benefit from the mistakes others have made in romance so that you don't repeat them in your relationship.

2. History teaches you which tools in romance convey love most effectively. You don't end up trying to reinvent the wheel.

3. It helps you to understand the strong underlying historical messages in sexual relations that may affect your present-day relationship. It illuminates and answers some questions you may have about women and sexuality.

Learning from the Past

Although relationships are always important, the intensity of romance increases and decreases in popularity throughout romantic history. It increases during times, such as the Victorian era, when sexual urges are denied. The sexual energy is then redirected into other forms of expression such as letter writing, reading aloud, and other romantic gestures.

The emphasis on romantic gestures lessens when society views sex as an acceptable means of expressing the feelings of attraction between partners. This way, the demonstration of love is mostly physical and not so concentrated on romantic gestures.

Nonsexual Romantic Gestures

The nonsexual expression of love is emphasized more during times when sex is either impossible or frowned upon. During these times, men and women have had to demonstrate their love in other ways. For instance, during World War II when the geographic separation of men and women made sex impossible, there was a surge in nonsexual romantic gestures, in particular, letter writing and care packages.

Another example of when sexual romance was not practiced often was prior to the invention of birth control. Sex outside of marriage was risky; couples did not want to deal with the possible consequences of a pregnancy before they were ready for it. Accordingly, they also placed a high value on nonphysical romantic gestures.

Couples today sometimes find it necessary to place more importance on nonsexual displays of romance. Even in the days of effective birth control are factors that encourage this kind of expression. For example, the partners may be far away from each other, or the couple may have concerns about contracting AIDS or other sexually transmitted diseases and choose not to express their feelings sexually.

Sexual Romantic Gestures

The sexual expression of love was once reserved primarily for married men and women. The introduction of the birth control pill in the '60s meant women no longer had to worry about unwanted pregnancy and led to the dramatic addition of sex to the twentieth century list of romantic gestures. More and more unmarried partners commonly use sex to show they care.

Romantic Archeology: Tools from the Past

Romantic tools have been in existence since the beginning of time. What are these tools? They are the use of various behaviors, words, or items to express loving feelings to your partner. Romantic tools vary from person to person, decade to decade, and culture to culture. These tools have been handed down throughout time as lovers consider them to be an important part of showing their love for each other.

For instance, Tim uses a care-taking way of being romantic with Beverly. He loves to show he cares by cooking nightly dinners for Beverly as well as taking on household chores exclusively. He knows that Beverly dislikes both cooking and cleaning, so he does these things to show his affection for her.

As Tim's example demonstrates, romantic tools don't have to be expensive. Just use what is available to you. Some people may use poetic thoughts to express their feelings, some may get

Words of the Heart

"Said Sir Ector, 'Sir Launcelot ... thou wert never matched of earthly knight's hand; and thou wert the courteoust knight that ever bare shield; and thou wert the truest friend to thy lover that ever bestrad horse; and thou wert the truest lover of a sinful man that ever loved a woman; and thou wert the kindest man that ever struck with sword; and thou wert the goodliest person that ever came among press of knights; and thou wert the meekest man and the gentlest that ever ate in hall among ladies; and thou wert the sternest knight to thy mortal foe that ever put spear in the rest.'"

—Sir Thomas Malory, *Le Morte D'Arthur*, 1470

matching tattoos. The key to handling a romantic tool correctly is simply to start using it. The thing that makes a tool romantic is the intent behind it. It shows your partner that you have the desire to show her you love her and that you think she's so special that you go the extra mile to show her so.

A Shopping List of Romantic Tools

Part of the enjoyment of loving someone is showing your love. When people are excited about the people they love, they are eager to demonstrate that feeling in all sorts of ways. Romantic tools evolved as men and women experimented with different ways of showing their love to each other.

Looking back through the history of romance can give you many ideas about how to romance your partner. And you may not have to look back very far because some romantic tools of the past were so effective that they have continued to the present day. Some tools seem so commonplace that it's hard to believe that at one point in history they never existed.

If you are out of ideas on how to show your partner you care, just pick a tool from the following list:

> Wink
>
> Blow a kiss
>
> Fax messages of love
>
> Hold hands
>
> Give gifts
>
> Serenade
>
> Send e-mail
>
> Write poetry
>
> Curtsy
>
> Date
>
> Talk on the phone
>
> Page him or her
>
> Carve your names in a tree
>
> Send telegrams
>
> Dance cheek to cheek

Kiss his or her hand

Make love

Cook

Make a toast

Read poetry

Wear lingerie

Place a personal ad

Scratch notes on cave walls

Send flowers or candy

Cover a puddle with your coat

Tip your hat at the one you like

Call on your love at home for a surprise visit

Massage him or her with bath oils or gels

Use calligraphy to write notes

Write notes on scented stationery

Making Tools Work

The previous list demonstrates the variety of tools you have to work with. Everyone has different tastes, so what works for one person may not work for another. If you notice that your partner isn't responding to your romantic gestures, it could be because your partner doesn't view them as romantic. In this situation, it's best to experiment with different tools until you find one that your partner responds to.

Words of the Heart

"Whether they give or refuse, women are glad they have been asked."

—Ovid

For example, Garrick thought it was very romantic to write letters to his long-distance girlfriend, Jennifer. However, he noticed that she never wrote back. He assumed it was because she lacked the proper supplies for writing. He put together a special stationery present for her. It was equipped with all the supplies she could possibly need including self-addressed, stamped envelopes. He made the erroneous assumption that she would think the gift was romantic simply because she was a woman. He couldn't have been more wrong because the simple fact was that she hated to write. When she didn't write back, he thought it was because she didn't love him as much.

If you aren't having much success in romance, maybe it's because you have been using tools that your partner isn't responding to. One very simple way to remedy this problem is to learn what your partner considers to be romantic.

Discover Which Tools to Use

The only way to find to rout what your partner considers to be a romantic gesture is by asking. In this section, you will learn a simple exercise to use with your partner that teaches both of you which tools to use based on personal preferences.

The object of this Romantic Tool List exercise is to create immediate romance by using one romantic tool each day. Utilizing romantic tools makes each partner more receptive to giving and receiving love, because romantic tools are a way to make a relationship a place that fosters intimacy.

To begin the exercise, both you and your partner need to sit down with writing paper and follow these steps:

1. Write five things that you would like your partner to do for you to show he or she cares. Be very specific with each item. Make sure you describe it in clear terms: who, what, where, when, why, and how.

Dr. Romance

What kind of arrows would you want Cupid to shoot at you and your partner? You know what? You have the kind of relationship you want *without* Cupid's arrows. All you have to do is deliberately go after the goals you want your relationship to achieve. It doesn't take magic arrows to do it, either.

2. After each item, also write how you would like your partner to respond to the request. For instance, if your request is to be kissed before he leaves for work, specify what kind of kiss you would like (that is, peck kiss, French kiss, cup your face in his hands and kiss you, and so on).

3. Take turns reading your list to your partner. Ask your partner whether each item is clear. If not, rewrite it until your partner understands specifically what you would like for him or her to do.

4. Post each list on your refrigerator or somewhere that each of you will be reminded of the exercise.

5. Do one item off the your partner's list each day. Your partner should do one thing off your list as well.

The key is to make sure that the items on the list are very specific and simple enough to be done daily. Here is a list of examples to help you generate your list:

➤ Ask me about the details of my day.

➤ Be home for dinner at 6 P.M.

➤ Put the kids to bed by 8 P.M. and spend one hour talking to me.

➤ Give me a massage for 30 minutes.

➤ Let me go out for drinks with my friends.

➤ Go to a ball game with me.

➤ Go away for a weekend with me without the kids.

➤ Kiss me passionately before I go to work.

➤ Call me at work and tell me you miss me.

➤ Surprise me with a home-cooked meal.

➤ Meet me for lunch.

This exercise is the best way to make romance a part of your daily life by developing new habits. This exercise also teaches you how to expand your romantic tool list according to how your partner wants to be romanced. What better way to shop for tools than to have the expert with you!

Past and Present Sexuality

Sometimes even the best relationships are plagued by outdated Victorian belief systems. A perfect example of this reared its head recently when a 35-year-old man asked me if women truly liked sex or if they only pretended to like it. Unfortunately, his question is a common one and proof that we have not quite escaped the past and the message that men like sex, and women don't.

Good Girl and Bad Girl Images

Sure, women like sex as much as men do, but the uncertainty about sex for some women is still there. Young, single women, in particular, have to deal with good-girl, bad-girl images of women. The good girl is pure, chaste, and moral and strives toward upholding the good mother image. She is not interested in sex. The

Cupid's Report

Throughout history, people have always given advice about sex. In his book *History Laid Bare,* Richard Zacks tells of a monk named St. Jerome, who in C.E. 370 gave men the following advice: "Men ought to keep away from [menstruating] wives because thus is a deformed, blind, lame, leprous offspring conceived: so that those parents who are not ashamed to come together in sexual intercourse have their sin made obvious to all."

bad girl is soiled, selfish, and immoral and loves sex. What a strain for men and women to have to decide between these two images.

Married women are somewhat exempt from this labeling because women throughout history have been expected to have sex with their husband in the context of a marriage. However, both single and married women have had to face the lingering question of whether they should enjoy the act.

Although our society still believes this good girl/bad girl dichotomy of women, the split is somewhat minimized when sexual behaviors take place within a committed relationship. Romance is the bridge that connects the two images and makes it socially more acceptable for women to give in to their desires without feeling dirty.

Good Sex and Trust Go Hand in Hand

From the beginning, men have been depicted as sexual animals driven by their hormones. All this really means is that men have been given positive messages about sexuality. As a result, the majority of men have a positive opinion of sex in relationships.

Dr. Romance

Don't forget the basics of romance: patience, kindness, no envy, no boasting, no rudeness, and no self-seeking. Don't be easy to anger, don't keep records of wrongdoings, and don't delight in evil but rejoice in love because love protects, trusts, hopes, and never fails. If you stick with the basics, you'll be a winner in romance. Romance works if you work it.

When the sexes have such different attitudes about sex, it may seem like a stretch to get the them together to participate in an act that they were designed to enjoy together. Yet there are some romantic tools that can come to the rescue. One tool that's particularly effective is to make positive statements about sexuality. As the saying goes, if you want to get rid of a bad thought, you have to replace it with a good one. This is exactly what this tool does.

Remember, the key to replacing old beliefs with new ones is repetition. This means that you need to tell your partner over and over how positive making love is. Pretty soon, you will hear your statements coming out of your partner's mouth. As a result, your relationship will be all the happier.

If you are looking for some positive statements to say to your partner, just select a few from the following list:

"Being so close always feels so right."

"Nothing is more exciting in a relationship than two people who follow up their talk of love with actions of love."

"You make me feel like the luckiest person in the world when you snuggle up to me that way."

"You always smell so nice."

"This is the most pure form of love there is."

"You make me feel so special when we make love."

"I value the commitment we share."

The Least You Need to Know

➤ Relationships are happier if you show a genuine interest in your partner. The way to show this interest is by being romantic. You have a lot of romantic tools to use, so don't hold back.

➤ To make your relationship the most incredible love affair, you need to make it your number one priority.

➤ If you are familiar with the romantic ways of the past, you will have more tools to use on your partner in the present.

➤ Knowing what your partner considers to be romantic is the easiest way to get the response you want from the romantic gestures you make.

ROMANCE + RELATIONSHIP = ?

Chapter 4

Romance and Your Relationship

In This Chapter

➤ Keeping the romantic fantasy alive

➤ Creating the greatest love story ever

➤ Making your relationship an affair to remember

➤ Fairy-tale fantasies: role models for love

One of the most enjoyable parts of having a relationship is being able to fulfill your romantic fantasies. You know, the one about being swept off your feet by a knight in shining armor or rescuing the damsel in distress?

Knights and damsels are a thing of the past, but romantic fantasies still exist. A romantic fantasy is something important to you that is missing in your love life. It's what you think about in your quiet time. If only you had it, your life would be more complete.

In this chapter, you will learn how your romantic fantasies can come true by learning how to make them happen. All dreams need work to become realities. Whether you are in a relationship or not, you can still formulate your plan of action to make your romantic dreams come true.

Cupid's Report

In the novel *Gone with the Wind*, Scarlett O'Hara's romantic fantasy grew out of her desperate situation: "I'm tired of it all. I've struggled for food and for money, and I've weeded and hoed and picked cotton ... There must be some way out. There must be someone somewhere who has money I could borrow ... Only one person, Rhett Butler ... I'll marry him," she thought coolly, "and then I'll never have to bother about money again." Practical as Scarlett was, she not only dreamt of a rich man to save her from poverty, she also made a plan of action and followed the path to fulfill her dream.

Bringing Romantic Fantasies to Life

Romantic fantasies are different for everyone. Each fantasy takes on a life of its own with a unique feeling, tone, and theme. Some people have simple fantasies; other people's fantasies are very detailed. One thing that is common with all romantic fantasies is the element of desiring something that you don't already have in your life and that can only come through a romantic partner.

Sharing Your Fantasy

Many times, both partners in a relationship have fantasies that they would like to share with their partners, but they don't reveal them. Sharing a fantasy can make you vulnerable. Fantasies also can evoke strong emotions. For these reasons, fantasies are usually kept private. To present your secret thoughts to someone can take courage.

To demonstrate how sharing fantasies can improve your love life, let's take a closer look at two modern romantic fantasies. The fantasies come from a married couple, Randy and Melissa, who have no idea the other entertains a fantasy that could bring them much closer together.

Randy is a businessman who lives his life traveling the world looking for companies to buy while his wife stays at home. Although this lifestyle may sound exciting, it's also very lonely for him. Instead of enjoying the places he travels to, he typically just orders dinner in his hotel room and attends to his business. In his fantasy, he dreams of having his wife join him in his travels, but he doesn't believe it will ever happen because he thinks she's too busy to go.

Melissa, Randy's wife, also has a romantic fantasy. She longs for a man who will make her his top priority. A man who wants to spend endless hours with her because he can't get enough of her. She wants to feel needed and desired. Unfortunately, she thinks that Randy loves his career more than her. She believes this because he's always traveling and never asks her to go.

As you can see from this scenario, one of the biggest barriers to sharing a fantasy with your partner is erroneous assumptions. No one can read another person's mind. Yet it's easy to come up with many reasons why you think your partner would not want to live out a fantasy with you.

An Affair to Remember

King Hussein met Lisa Halaby, the future Queen Noor, due to his passion for flying. When they met, Lisa, a Princeton-trained architect, was working on an airport design project in Jordan. Her father, the president of Pan-Am, was invited to the king's palace for a party. Lisa went along, uninvited. At the party that night, love unexpectedly appeared when the 5'0" king met 5'10" Lisa. At this point in the 43-year-old king's life, he had been married three times and had eight children. One year prior to meeting Lisa, his much beloved wife of 10 years died in a helicopter crash. The night he met Lisa was the beginning of a new love for him. He pursued her ardently for six weeks, at which time they became formally engaged.

Then there's Raymond. He wanted so much to take his girlfriend to the neighborhood he grew up in. She was important to him, and he wanted to share this with her. Unfortunately, he never asked her to go, and his fantasy went unfulfilled. He assumed she would say no because it was an unsafe area and was sure she'd be uncomfortable going there. Remember, the only way to fulfill your romantic fantasy is to let your partner know what it is.

Telling Your Partner What You Want

How do you tell your partner about your romantic fantasies? It's easy. All you have to do is be clear about what you want and then tell your partner. Randy, Melissa, and Raymond knew what they wanted, but they never asked their partner to be a part of it. I know it sounds easier to do than it is, but what do you have to lose? If you have someone who loves you, that person may be more eager to make you happy than you think.

The first step to telling your partner about your romantic fantasy is to think about what you want. Then write the fantasy down in one sentence. Have your partner write his or her fantasy down, too:

I would like my partner to fulfill this fantasy:

Partner 1:_____.

Partner 2:_____.

Cupid's Report

Through the seventeenth century, lovesickness was considered to be both a physical and a mental affliction that doctors regularly offered treatment for. One fourth of *Eratomania*, a seventeenth-century medical book, was dedicated to the cure of lovesickness, which was called Anatomy of Melancholy.

Do you see how easy that was? Now that you have written it down, you should be clear about what you want. The next step is to share the fantasy with your partner. Go ahead, she won't bite! I promise!

Keeping the Romantic Fantasy Alive

Being in love can be the most beautiful and memorable time in someone's life. Falling in love elevates a person's mood to an unparalleled level. It makes your body hurt with longing. Sleep is no longer possible. You spend all your time imagining your love's touch and kiss. You can't wait to get to know your love better. You want to be as close to the person as possible. You want to know the person's every thought, hear the person's every laugh, and look at him or her until sleep takes your sight away.

Soon enough with love, the stars begin to fade, the growl in your stomach returns, sleep is once again sound, concentration is undisturbed, cloud nine dissipates, and priorities get reprioritized. This is the time in a relationship when romance falls by the wayside. People become complacent and no longer do what they did during the courtship phase. They don't think it's necessary, but they couldn't be more wrong!

Romance is the most important aspect of a relationship because it makes each person long for the other. The basis of romantic fantasies is the care you feel for your partner. Sharing fantasies is a great way to continue a strong loving bond with the one you love. When you stop exploring romance, your fantasies will soon dry out or turn to someone else. To stay satisfied with your love life, fill up your relationship with real-life romance.

Creating the Greatest Love Story Ever

It's easy to be fascinated by other people's love affairs and desire to have what they have, especially if the relationship is intense, happy, and seemingly problem-free. These great love stories epitomize an ideal that everyone would love to attain.

However, keep in mind that you are seeing only the public image of the relationship. You don't see the work that goes on behind closed doors. All relationships take effort to be successful, especially great love stories.

Would you like to make your relationship the greatest love story ever? Of course you would; everyone would. If you would, just keep reading along and learn how to do it. Before you know it, you will be transforming your good relationship into a great one.

Learn from Happy Couples

The best way to learn about how to have the greatest love story ever is to listen to how other happy couples do it. All you have to do is ask or read about happy couples, and you will learn the tricks. For instance, in the book *The 30 Secrets of Happily Married Couples*, author Paul Coleman tells how happy couples stay happy. His findings are based on many research studies on marital happiness. Basically, his 30 secrets can be summarized into three main goals that all couples should have:

Words of the Heart

"Don't assume that another person doesn't need you because they appear overly involved in other areas. Save your judgments and perceptions for yourself. Many times people overindulge in endeavors because they do need another. Don't be confused by the contradiction between their needs and your perceptions."

—Ellen Nelle, American poet, 1995

1. **Practice good communication.** Communication skills include considering the part you play in the problem, trying not to be defensive, and seeing the issue from your partner's perspective.

2. **Have realistic expectations for a long relationship.** Realize that change involves ups and downs and appreciate the effect that major changes, such as having children, will have on your relationship.

3. **Make time for each other.** Make regular dates, have fun together, and take every opportunity to be affectionate.

These three goals sound like such a simple recipe for living happily ever after, but they require something that many people forget: daily commitment.

Daily Commitment Is a Privilege

How many times have you heard someone say any of the following: "I have to remember to get her a card," "I must buy him a present," "I should take her out for dinner," or "I need to call him"? Couples commonly say these phrases. Having the greatest love story ever is not built on things you "have to do." Rather, it's based on feeling privileged to be able to do them. This difference in perception is the difference between a happy couple and a super-happy couple.

Dr. Romance

Sit down with your partner and make a list of the qualities the other possesses that keep you interested. Then switch lists.

A key step to making the transition from a good relationship to a great relationship is to first reframe your perspective on the things you do for your partner. In great relationships, closeness is based on small daily acts of kindness, such as making your partner a cup of tea before your partner asks you to do it. An important aspect to doing these small acts is that you consider it an honor to do them rather than a duty.

Building the greatest love story ever is work that is never complete. Love is a living, breathing thing that requires daily attention to keep it alive. Just remember, if you put in the minimum work, it will be reflected in the degree of happiness and satisfaction you feel in your relationship. If you put in 100 percent, you will have a relationship that gives you 100 percent fulfillment. This is the kind of relationship others admire and strive for. Taking part in the greatest love story ever requires a lifetime of privileged work—and what an honor that is to take on!

An Affair of the Heart, Mind, and Soul

A romantic relationship is an emotionally intimate bond between two people. Such a relationship is best when it is with someone who knows you, understands you, and accepts you. It is enhanced through talking intimately about feelings, thoughts, and needs.

Sometimes when the qualities of a romantic relationship are not met, one or both partners seek them outside the relationship in an affair. An affair can be as exhilarating as it is destructive to the relationship. When a person in a relationship feels the temptation to have an affair, it's usually because the romance in the relationship has stopped being important. Keep this thought in the back of your mind as you search for ways to inject more romance into your relationship.

Words of the Heart

Cleopatra: "If it be love indeed, tell me how much."

Antony: "There's beggary in the love that can be reckon'd."

Cleopatra: "I'll set a bourn how far to be belov'd."

Antony: "Then must thou needs find out new heaven, new earth."

—William Shakespeare, *Antony and Cleopatra* [I.i]

Make Your Relationship an Affair to Remember

When you think of an affair, what comes to mind? Passion? Romance? Attachment to another person? That's exactly what an affair is; however, the downside is that it is typically associated with a limited duration. What if you could extend an affair and make it an everyday and lifelong occasion with your partner? You can do it; it's just a matter of decision.

The way to make this happen is to turn your relationship into an affair. The first step to doing this is to know just exactly what needs are met by an affair:

➤ Feeling desired

➤ Being loved

➤ Feeling needed

➤ Sexual fulfillment

➤ Being understood

➤ Close friendship

➤ Intellectual stimulation

➤ Feeling complete

➤ Attachment

➤ Being listened to

Look over the preceding list and ask yourself which of these characteristics you provide for your partner. The ideal way to use this list is to sit down with your partner and take turns putting this list in order of which characteristics you feel the strongest, down to those you feel the least.

Use the following space to rank each characteristic from most felt to least felt. Remember that you and your partner should both do this exercise.

Most Felt

1.

2.

3.

4.

5.

6.

7.

8.

9.

10.

Least Felt

When each of you has completed your list, compare notes with your partner to see the order you put the characteristics in. Pay special attention to the last few items because they will tell you the areas that you need to work on with your partner. The goal of this exercise is to identify the areas that are holding you back from having an affair with your partner.

Dr. Romance

The difference between a selfish partner and someone who truly loves you is simple. A selfish partner gives to you only when it benefits him. Someone who loves you gives to you simply to give and has no ulterior motives.

Cupid's Report

If you are having difficulties, the quickest way to fix them is to focus on tools. Tools are skills that you use with your partner when confronted with difficulties. The more skills you develop, the more equipped you will be to successfully handle problems. If you are looking for a good book to begin with, start with *The Complete Idiot's Guide to the Perfect Marriage* by Hilary Rich and Helaina Kravitz (Macmillan General Reference, 1997). This book covers every aspect that could possibly affect any romantic relationship.

When Kerry and Joe did this exercise, Kerry saw that Joe was not feeling needed. This observation led into a discussion about what she could do to make him feel needed. As it turned out, all Joe wanted was for her to ask him for help now and then. Kerry was very independent and had learned to do everything for herself. She realized that this was her way of never having to rely on others. Talking about this exercise allowed her to take Joe up on his offers to help her with things that he was good at.

You can do the same with your partner. Look at the feeling that he put on the bottom of the ranking list. Then ask him what he needs that would help him get a stronger sense of that feeling. You'll be surprised at how this simple exercise will illuminate important feelings that your partner has been experiencing. This exercise many times reveals feelings that are new to both partners. When you are able to strengthen your weak areas, your relationship will be the love affair you always wanted.

Mixing Oil and Water

People have many ways of expressing and perceiving love. Most commonly, they communicate in either words or actions. Knowing your partner's style of loving makes it easier to communicate in his language.

Partners who express love in the same style communicate feelings much easier than those who have different styles. The goal of this section is to teach you how to express your love in your partner's style so that your partner feels your love more fully.

The Words and Actions of Love

Francisco and Anne have two different styles of showing their love for each other. Francisco shows his love through his behavior; Anne shows hers with words, both written and spoken. Last year, this difference in styles caused quite a bit of misunderstanding between them. Each partner didn't feel fully loved although they were. The problem was that they were demonstrating love in their own style, and the other person didn't understand the message.

Francisco showed Anne he loved her when he made love to her. Because Anne didn't know this, she felt unloved and refused his sexual advances. This refusal, in turn, caused Francisco to feel unloved. What Anne needed was for him to tell her he loved her. He didn't feel loved, so he didn't tell her. This misunderstanding was a vicious cycle until they learned how to know how the other person expresses his or her love.

The following list is broken into two sections for each style of love: words and actions. Look at each item and put a check next to each one that describes how you show your partner you love him or her. Have your partner do the same thing.

Words

- ❑ Saying affectionate things
- ❑ Calling your partner when you two are apart
- ❑ Writing love notes or letters
- ❑ Telling your partner how you feel about things
- ❑ Telling your partner you miss him or her
- ❑ Complimenting your partner

Actions

- ❑ Buying gifts
- ❑ Making love to your partner
- ❑ Initiating affection
- ❑ Sitting quietly with your partner
- ❑ Participating in your partner's activities
- ❑ Exercising with your partner

When you learn your partner's style of loving, try out that way of expressing love. Pretty soon, your partner will feel just as loved as you want her or him to feel. That's exactly what happened with Francisco and Anne. They learned how different their styles were and were surprised by how many messages of love they were each missing from each other. Not only do they now understand their partner's way of communicating love, they also each have a new way to express it. I suppose this could be considered bilingual romance because they now have expanded their expression of love to two languages.

Fairy-Tale Fantasies of Love

Fairy tales have become a part of our image of what romance is supposed to be like. This image not only deceives women, but also men. One of the definitions of the term "fairy tale" in Webster's is "a made-up story, usually designed to mislead."

On one hand, everyone knows that fairy-tale romances are make-believe. On the other hand, fairy tales inspire us to believe in happy love stories. For this fact alone, they have given us something we need for building our own love affair: hope. Many people have lost hope, and it's time to get it back.

An Affair to Remember

Ariel was a young mermaid who lived under the sea. Her father warned her to stay away from humans because they were bad. She was curious and disobeyed him one day when she swam to the surface of the ocean to observe humans on a ship. She fell instantly in love with Prince Eric, who stood on deck. A fast-approaching storm caused lightning to strike the ship, setting it on fire. Ariel rescued the prince and brought him to shore safely. In order to win Eric's love, Ariel traded her beautiful voice to the sea witch for a pair of legs. Part of the trade was the condition that the prince must fall in love with her in three days or she would lose her voice forever. On day one, the prince found her on the beach high on a rock trying to escape his dog, which was playfully pursuing her. He rescued her and brought her back to his castle. The next two days were filled with romantic walks and a horse–drawn carriage ride through the countryside. On day three, he was fully in love. The prince kissed Ariel, and they both lived happily ever after.

Modeling Love on Fairy Tales

Some people think that fairy tales create a false image for a real partner to live up to. The next time you read a fairy tale about a love affair, look to see the characteristics that form the foundation of these stories. What you will find are characteristics such as the following:

➤ Looking for unconditional love

➤ Wanting to be loved by someone

➤ Seeking understanding

➤ Looking to be accepted by another

These stories also show that life is happier *with* someone as opposed to being *without* someone. What they show is the humanness in having a mate. People innately gravitate to others for a sense of completeness. We are relational beings, with a need to relate to others. In a fairy tale, these themes are conveyed simply in a fantastical setting. In fact, fairy tales serve as wonderful models to use when deciding on what you want in your relationship.

Regaining a Belief in Fairy Tales

How can we make romance just as magical as it is in the fairy tales? All you have to do is create your own love story, the greatest love story ever known. This means cherishing the one you love as though he were a prince or she were a princess. It means making your relationship a priority by including romance as one of its basic ingredients. An apple a day may keep the doctor away, but a kiss a day keeps others away!

The Least You Need to Know

➤ When it comes to passion, all relationships, at one time or another, go through cool spells. When you feel this happening in your relationship, you must make the decision to rekindle it.

➤ Don't become complacent in your relationship.

➤ You don't just have to dream about a fairy-tale relationship—you can create it by sharing and living out your romantic fantasies with your partner.

➤ Nothing worthwhile is ever acquired easily. If you love your partner, you will have to put the work into keeping him or her happy by treating your partner just as special as you'd like him or her to treat you.

Part 2

A Romantic Gesture a Day

If you want to have really satisfying sex, there are a few things you need to do to make it happen. This section shows you how to introduce romance into your everyday world to create an atmosphere of seduction.

Seduction needs to start in the home and in the mind. This means that you can have great sex if you set the stage for it to happen. All you have to do is create a tempting bedroom that your partner will never want to leave, as well as titillate his mind with provocative thoughts. By doing this, when you and your partner finally get down to it, it will be incredibly fulfilling both emotionally and physically. Isn't that what romantic sex is all about?

Chapter 5

The Romantic Bedroom

In This Chapter

➤ Making your bedroom suit your romantic mood

➤ Finding the perfect lighting for love

➤ Using color to make you feel romantic

Jim and Debbie had outgrown their small two-bedroom home two years ago when they turned Jim's office into a nursery. The only logical place to put Jim's work area and computer was in the already crowded bedroom. They managed, though, by squeezing his work console into the corner between the bed and the bookshelf. After everything was arranged, they barely had enough room to open the closet door, but at least it fit.

Problems cropped up eventually when Jim began sleeping on the couch because the bedroom reminded him of the anxieties of work. Jim and Debbie eventually had to move Jim's office out of their bedroom to put their love life back into their bedroom.

You spend one-third of your life in your bedroom, so how it looks has a significant impact on your psyche. When a room looks romantic, you feel romantic. It encourages touch, tenderness, and passion. You want a bedroom that feels like a getaway from life. The bedroom should make your mind relax and bring a warmness to your heart. Making a bedroom romantic isn't necessarily about redecorating. It's more about the details that encourage romance.

In this chapter, you will learn the importance of having a romantic bedroom. You will discover the essentials of how to put romance into your bedroom by making it a place for only love and rest. You'll learn to accomplish this by decorating it with elements that encourage romance: lighting, accessories, fabrics, scents, and color. After reading this chapter, you will no longer consider your bedroom just a room to rest your head. You will consider it an intimate adventure that you can't wait to get home to.

The 12 A.M. to 8 A.M. Room

If you want to create romance in your relationship, the bedroom is the place to start. The first step is to eliminate all activities in that room except for sex and sleeping. Too often, people make the bedroom a multipurpose room. The bedroom is used for many things that have nothing to do with romance, such as exercising, office work, paying bills, or storage.

Look around your bedroom and take inventory of all of the things that might be distracting to love. These items cause anxiety or stress when you see them. When Steve looked around his room, he saw his weight bench, the classified ads to find a new job, and his list of things to do. Each time he saw one of these things, his mind was instantly filled with stress. Steve isn't different than the average person. He uses his bedroom for things other than relaxing activities that are conducive to romance.

Words of the Heart

"It should make any one go to sleep, that bestead would, whether they wanted to or not."

—Charles Dickens

It's All Based on Your Mood

Romantic bedrooms need to have an overall mood. Look at the following list, find one mood that appeals to you, and assign that as the mood for you to build your bedroom around. Base your decision on something that you consider romantic:

➤ Whimsical

➤ Tranquil

➤ Nurturing

➤ Traditional

➤ Contemplative

➤ Dynamic

➤ Romantic

➤ Sensuous

The romantic mood will be different for everyone. For instance, Jewel may consider a whimsical mood to be romantic, but Bruce may view a traditional mood as romantic.

John and Ellen spend their lives giving to other people, which depletes them emotionally. When they come home from work, they need nurturing, so they created a bedroom that fits this need by adding irresistibly soft pillows and covers to their bed, soft rugs on the floor, and gentle lighting that soothes them. In the next section, you will learn how to make your room fit your needs.

It's Your Creation

When a room looks romantic, you feel romantic. Making a room look romantic means you have to make some effort to create the environment. The easiest way to do this is to come up with a schedule of when you will do certain activities, such as paint the bedroom walls, hang curtains, stencil the ceiling, and look for a rug. Just thinking about something will get you nowhere except fantasyland. Scheduling something makes it real and, therefore, likely to get done. Fill in the following chart, and you will be well on your way to a romantic bedroom.

Goal	Activity to do	Scheduled date
_____	_____	_____
_____	_____	_____
_____	_____	_____
_____	_____	_____
_____	_____	_____

Different Strokes for Different Folks

You can find romantic inspiration just about anywhere; it's just a matter of what your tastes are. For some, the colors of nature inspire their decorating taste. They learn soothing color combinations by looking for them in nature.

One of the first things you need to discover is what you find romantic. This is different for everyone. Is it lace? Fur rugs in front of a fireplace? Silky red fabrics? Ornate Victorian antiques? Animal prints? Simple whites? Candles? Discover what you find exciting, and bring it home to your room just like you did when you were a child.

Cupid's Report

Once when Cleopatra prepared a romantic dinner for Mark Antony, she had the floor covered with bright red roses 18 inches deep.

Variety in the Bedroom Doesn't Always Mean Sex

A bedroom without variety is a lifeless room. Variety is the spark that renews interest in things that have become routine. If you want to have a good relationship, the last thing you want is for your bedroom to be predictable. Humans are creatures that crave newness because it stimulates us. Shouldn't your bedroom cause stimulation and cravings?

Variety in a bedroom comes from accessories and pieces of furniture, big or small. These include the bed, sheets and fabrics, scents, pillows, and carpets. Not all of these accessories are mandatory: You'll have to see what suits you.

Lights, Candles, Action

Nothing is less romantic than a 100-watt bulb blazing from an overhead light. Lighting can be flattering or unflattering, and this type of harshness is unflattering to everyone.

An Affair to Remember

Josephine's 14-year-old son was responsible for bringing Josephine and Napoleon Bonaparte, the great military commander, together. Her son went to Napoleon with a request of keeping his father's sword after his death in the war. Because he was a military commander, he was the only one who could release the sword to the boy. The widow, Josephine, sought out Napoleon the next day to thank him for his deed. The instant Napoleon saw Josephine, he fell madly in love with her gentle charm and grace. He passionately pursued Josephine, and within a year they married. She sought security and stability but found neither with Napoleon. Financially he cared for her in the lifestyle she was accustomed to, paying her enormous bills for clothing, shoes, jewelry, and art. However, Napoleon was often away at war for months at a time. He pleaded with her to stay near him so he could see her during his breaks from fighting. As a mother of two from her former marriage, this was difficult for her. Eventually, the great commander desired an heir to rule after him. Josephine, by this time, was 46 and past the age of fertility. Although passionately in love with Josephine, Napoleon requested an annulment and ended their marriage. Letters of sorrow from a heartbroken Napoleon followed their separation. Five years later, Josephine died, and Napoleon wrote, "Josephine is the only woman I have ever truly loved. She reigns in my heart and I mourn for her."

Think of all the romantic places you've been. Were these places brightly lit? Would a romantic restaurant table be the same with bright lights? Of course not.

You have a lot of options when it comes to light sources. How many light sources can you think of that can be used in a bedroom? You can have light coming in the windows from the stars, moon, city, and streetlights. You can have playful lights that come from colored bulbs, strobe lights, and black lights. And there's nothing like the light that pours over a room from a roaring fireplace.

Are you beginning to see the romance in all of this? Well, the ideas don't stop there. One trip down the lighting aisle of a large hardware store is guaranteed to give you a vast assortment of choices to help you create just the right lighting for your romantic bedroom.

The Flicker of a Candle

The most romantic lighting of all is the flickering candle. A candle has a way of transforming the mood of everyone within the reach of its rays. With the strike of a match, its flame begins to burn, and within moments, the flames of romance ignite in the people nearby.

A great way to tell your partner that you're feeling romantic is to have a few candles lit around the room when he comes to bed. Pretty soon, your partner will begin to associate burning candles with intimacy.

Creating a Theme

Not only does your bedroom need a mood, your bedroom also needs a theme. A theme is the subject of your room. Babies' rooms often have a nurturing theme and are decorated with soft pastels. In a teenager's room, the theme is often rock bands. Here are some theme suggestions for your romantic bedroom:

➤ Ancient Greece

➤ Twentieth-century art deco

➤ Roman baths

➤ Renaissance era

➤ Mayan temples

➤ Five-star hotel suites

➤ Polynesian islands

➤ Arabian harem tents

➤ Victorian parlors

➤ Eighteenth-century rococo

➤ Nineteenth-century neoclassical

Cupid's Report

Candles come in unscented and scented forms. A few of the more popular fragrances are cinnamon, lavender, rose, peach, and vanilla. If you or your partner has allergies or are sensitive to smells, it is best to stick to the unscented kind.

Don't feel limited to these themes. They are intended to help your mind think outside of its normal ideas. Once Bridget and Michael settled on an oriental theme that appealed to both of them, they began to see theme items in every store they walked into. Prior to having a theme, they had no idea what to decorate their bedroom with, but now, they saw oriental items everywhere: rugs, lamps, and trinkets. You will find that this will happen to you, too. But first, you need to decide which theme you want for your bedroom.

Come to Bed, Darling!

The bed is the central feature of the bedroom. It's not only a place to sleep, but also a place to be close to the one you love. A bed can take on many faces. It can be as simple as a futon on the floor or as elaborate as a canopy bed with incredible fabric flowing to the ground. Beds can be decorated expensively or inexpensively. What's important is that it's inviting to you and your partner. The goal is to create a bed that entices lovemaking and meets your rest needs at the same time.

An Affair to Remember

In the *Odyssey* by Homer, Odysseus and his wife Penelope were separated for 19 years. When he returned home, Penelope wanted to make sure it was her husband. She knew that he was the only one who would know the details of their bed, so she tricked him into describing it in great detail: "A great secret went into the making of that complicated bed; and it was my work and mine alone. Inside the court, there was a long-leafed olive tree, which has grown to full height with a stem as thick as a pillar. Round this I build my room of close-set stonework, and when that was finished, I roofed it over thoroughly and put in a solid, neatly fitted, double door. Next, I lopped all the twigs off the olive, trimmed the stem from the root up, rounded it smoothly and carefully with my adze, and trued it to the line to make my bedpost. This I drilled through where necessary and used as a basis for the bed itself, which I worked away at till that too was done, when I finished it off with an inlay of gold, silver, and ivory and fixed a set of purple straps across the frame." With this description, Penelope knew it was her husband and embraced him with open arms.

If It Doesn't Feel Good, It Isn't Romantic

Nothing thrills the senses more than luxurious fabrics, such as silk, fur, satin, and velvet. They can be used to create a romantic mood or feeling in the bedroom. If you've never slept between satin sheets, you're missing out. Fabrics don't have to be reserved just for the bed, however. They can also be used on the walls, windows, and floors. The more fabric you use, the stronger the statement. Some additional fabrics that emphasize romance in a bedroom are lace, cheesecloth, and brocade.

Flowers and Scents

Flowers are associated with romance. When a man sends a woman a dozen long-stemmed red roses, the message is love. When a woman picks a daisy and launches into "He loves me; he loves me not," she is performing a classic romantic ritual.

All romantic bedrooms should have flowers in them. Flowers in the bedroom are a continuation of romance carried on from outside the bedroom. You can use fresh-cut flowers or dried potpourri. The fragrance they release is pleasing, not to mention arousing. So the next time you see a flower, pick it and place it on your partner's pillow. You'll be surprised by how much pleasure it brings.

The Colors of Love

Colors are intertwined with emotions. This connection is even reflected in our language: We can feel blue, be tickled pink, see red, be green with envy, have black moods, and be mellow yellow. Color is central to your bedroom's rebirth, too, because the shades you choose will affect the overall feel of the room.

Colors can bring out an emotional reaction. For some, black is a color of mourning and makes them feel sad. For others, black is sexy, powerful, and artsy. Look at the following table to help you determine which feelings you would like to feel when you spend time in your bedroom. After you determine the feeling you would like, make that color a part of your bedroom.

Cupid's Report

Do you remember the TV show *I Dream of Jeannie*? If you recall, the pretty Jeannie had a bedroom in her bottle that was covered from top to bottom in fabric. This fabric gave her a room that she could be comfortable in for thousands of years. Unlike Jeannie, you will never have to worry about being locked in your room for millennia. However, fabrics can make your bedroom so comfortable that you won't ever want to leave it.

Dr. Romance

A great side product of a romantic bedroom is relaxation. If you don't feel relaxed in your bedroom, you haven't made it romantic enough.

If you want to feel	Use this color
Animalistic	Prints
Artsy	Red
Classy	Blue
Comfortable	Greens
Dynamic	Red, black
Earthy	Browns
Exciting	Red
Feminine	Pastels
Fresh	White
Masculine	Black
Mysterious	Purple
Nurturing	Pastels
Passionate	Red
Playful	Primary or bright colors
Powerful	Red
Restful	Blues
Romantic	Pink
Sensuous	Red
Serious	Dark green
Sexy	Red
Stimulating	Red
Tranquil	Blues
Warm	Oranges

In particular, your bedroom walls are the frame to the romantic picture you have created in your bedroom. The walls can be a single favorite color that serves as the backdrop for all the other elements in the bedroom, or they can be the main focus of the room. There are several colors you can use on your walls to enhance its romantic appeal. The following sections explore the possibilities of red, pink, blue, green, and white.

Flaming Red

Red is associated with many things that are passionate such as excitement, power, strength, fire, blood, seduction, temptation, and magic. Although red is associated with love, I don't recommend painting all four of your bedroom walls red. Red creates too much stimulation when you are surrounded by too much of it. In a bedroom, it is better to use red sparingly in the accents rather than excessively on the walls. This way, just a touch of passion will be added to spark your fire.

Sweet Pink

Pink is a romantic color with a soft, approachable feel. When you spend time in a pink room, you begin to take on its characteristics: mellow, inviting, intimate, and comfortable. Pink brings images of

➤ Blushing.

➤ Innocence.

➤ Sweetness.

➤ Tenderness.

The shades of pink range from dusty rose to magenta. The softer the shade of pink, the more romantic a feel it will have. As far as painting goes, the softer the color, the more wall space you can cover. For instance, if you are using a pastel pink, you can paint all four walls with the same color. But if the pink is a very hot pink, you may want to paint only one wall with that color so that it isn't overwhelming to your senses.

Cupid's Report

Every item in your room has a potential for creating an emotion, whether it's a lamp, bedspread, rug, or table. Keep this in mind when you are decorating so that you can make every element of the room work to help you set the mood you want.

Gentle Blue

The color blue is a favorite color for bedrooms because it gives you a sense of relaxation. Blue is also associated with people who are conservative, dependable, traditional, and confident. Whether a soft blue or dark, blue brings a serene, peaceful feeling to a bedroom. When painting in blue, there is no minimum or maximum space to color because the shades are pleasant to the senses. The coverage depends on your taste.

Relaxing Green

Dark green naturally sets up a bedroom for a feel of relaxation and comfort. Green gives a sense of stability and safety to a room that has a calming effect on the people who surround themselves by it.

The shades of green range from pastel greens, which give a spring feeling, to dark, traditional greens like hunter green. Because of this range, when you paint your walls, you'll want to determine the mood you want. For instance, if you

Words of the Heart

"Man is so made that he can only find relaxation from one kind of labour by taking up another."

—Anatole France, 1881, *The Crime of Sylvestre Bonnard*

A favorite color says a lot about a person's personality. People who love red are confident, secure, risk-taking, trend-setting, stimulating, happy, dynamic, provocative, passionate, intense, dramatic, and energetic.

paint all four walls pastel green, the room will have a fresh, light feel to it. If you paint all four walls dark green, the room will be very dark, yet soothing. Green is always a relaxing color, so you can't go wrong with a little paint or a lot of it.

Light White

White is by far the most common color you will see on walls, because it's the easiest color to match out of all the other colors painted on walls. White creates an open, fresh feel that makes you feel relaxed and calm. You can't go wrong with white on all four walls, but for some, it may seem boring. Because of this boredom factor, you may want to add an additional color.

The Least You Need to Know

➤ The bedroom should be limited only to activities that promote romance, such as sleeping and sex. Otherwise, the bedroom will lose its ties to romance.

➤ If you don't think your bedroom communicates your feelings of romance, then you need to go to work to transform it.

➤ Candles transform a bedroom into an instant romantic getaway.

➤ Romantic fabrics such as satin give your bedroom an inviting touch.

➤ The color you use in your bedroom is important. It allows you to set the mood you want in order to get your needs met.

Chapter 6

The Ultimate Seduction

In This Chapter

➤ The truth about seduction

➤ Brain stimulation

➤ Seductive behavior

➤ Fun with flirting

Seduction is a two-headed coin. On one side, the word *seduction* is robust with images of romance and lust. On the other side, seduction is seen as something bad that hurts others. Even Webster's descriptions of the word depict it negatively:

1. To lead away.

2. To persuade to disobedience or disloyalty.

3. To lead astray usually by persuasion or false promises.

4. The act of seducing to wrong.

This chapter sticks to the romantic aspects of seduction. Seduction thrills anyone who experiences it and creates a craving for more. At no other time does a person feel as embraced by love and romance as when his partner seduces him. After all, it's a time when complete attention is given him. If the feelings are mutually intense, the experience can be addictive.

In this chapter, you'll learn all about being seductive. I've based the seduction techniques you'll learn about in this chapter on the methods the master seducers have used throughout history. (You know these people have to be good at seduction if people are still talking about them thousands of years later.)

Words of the Heart

"The average man is more interested in a woman who is interested in him than he is in a woman—any woman—with beautiful legs."

—Marlene Dietrich

Myths About Seduction

Myths about seduction come from all sorts of things, especially the media. We build our ideas about seduction by watching the seduction that takes place through the advertisements that bombard us on a daily basis. We begin to associate only those characteristics with the act of seduction. What we forget is that the media represents our ideals and our dreams. The media does not represent reality, yet we base our ideas about seduction around the images it presents.

As you read through the following common myths about seduction, take note of how many you believe are true. Don't be discouraged if you believe most or even all of them. Just realize that our minds are influenced by what we expose them to.

➤ **Myth 1: You have to be pretty or handsome to seduce someone.** The truth is that there is such a range of attractiveness that what isn't attractive to one person is attractive to another. To convince yourself of this truth, all you have to do is look around at all the different kinds of couples.

Dr. Romance

People who accept "facts" about love too easily may be accepting myths in place of truths. If you are unsure about a fact of love, do a little investigating to find out the truth. This way, you won't let myths hold you back in love.

➤ **Myth 2: If a man wants to seduce someone, he'd better have a lot of money.** People fall in love with people, not bank accounts. Enough said.

➤ **Myth 3: If you wait long enough, eventually you'll get the courage to seduce someone.** The truth is that if you wait to approach someone, your opportunity may be lost. Don't let shyness overcome you: Make your move now!

➤ **Myth 4: Overweight people aren't attractive enough to seduce someone.** Wrong again. Seduction has very little to do with the physical size of another person. It has much more to do with attitude and confidence.

Cerebral Seduction

A lot of people disregard cerebral seduction in favor of physical seduction. However, all seduction begins with the mind. That's right, the mind. The brain is the biggest sex organ, so if you learn how to stimulate that part of your partner, romance becomes easy.

Before I teach you how to perform cerebral seduction (also known as mental commands) on your partner, let me explain how and why it works. First of all, mental commands are not a new concept. All of us have been receiving them since the day we were born. They are the messages others plant in our heads to shape our behavior.

Words of the Heart

"There's language in her eye, her cheek, her lip. Nay, her foot speaks; her wanton spirit looks out at every joint and motive of her body."

—William Shakespeare from *Troilus and Cressida* [I.i]

Advertisements give such commands all the time when they show, for instance, two women in a singles club. Both women are in jeans; however, one is the advertised designer jeans. The ad says, "Buy our jeans," but the picture shows a group of handsome men around the woman in the advertised jeans and none around her friend. This command is a mental command. The advertisement is saying, "If you wear these jeans, you will be popular." This implied message makes more of an impact than the spoken words.

The same principle applies to romantic relationships. You try to shape your partner's romantic behaviors by planting ideas in your partner's head that will stay there for him or her to think about again.

What's Behind a Mental Command

Mental commands work very well on couples who want to feel more romantic with each other, whether the couple has been too busy to spend time together or isn't as happy in love as they would like to be. Either way, mental commands work well by taking a couple's past romantic experiences and bringing them to the present day.

For example, Jim and Fritta's children have grown up and left home, and now they feel like strangers living under the same roof. For years, they had the children in common, and now they feel as though they don't share anything. Jim noticed that Fritta wasn't physically affectionate with him anymore, and he missed that. He knew that the only way the affection would come back would be if she felt close to him again. To help the two of them grow closer again, Jim used mental commands. All he did was use these three steps:

1. Say to your partner, "Do you remember that time when … " (think of a romantic time that each of you shared).

2. When she remembers the time, begin to discuss the details of the time. You might want to say things such as, "Do you remember how close we felt when we danced?" or "When you kissed me on the deck, do you remember when I told you I loved you for the first time?" Continue to reminisce about that wonderful time. Doing this will bring back the strong loving, romantic feelings from the past into your present moment.

3. Bring that good feeling to your relationship again by scheduling a date. You can say, "It can be that wonderful again. Let's go back to that restaurant next week."

As soon as Fritta and Jim began to relive their warm times, she was more affectionate with him. He knew the feelings were buried inside of her, and this exercise brought them to the surface again. Mental commands are nice because they quickly bring back that loving feeling. The trick is to stay on Step 1 long enough for your partner to feel the feelings she or he once felt.

An Affair to Remember

Jean Harlow was sultry and startlingly sexy. As for Clark Gable, it was said that every woman he met fell in love with him. As an on-screen couple, Harlow and Gable were so convincing that people wondered if the romance carried over off-screen. However, no off-screen affair was ever verified. Their last film together ended prematurely when she became sick and died unexpectedly. She was only 26. The cause of death still remains unknown. It was rumored that Gable provided $25,000 worth of flowers at her funeral.

How to Mentally Seduce Your Partner

In romantic relationships, mental commands are ideas you want your partner to think about. When you give a mental command, you are in essence planting ideas in his or her subconscious mind.

For instance, do you want your partner to call you more often? Start by reminiscing about a past romantic phone call by saying something like, "Do you remember that time you called me in the middle of the day from work? I'd just stepped out of the shower, and we had that arousing conversation?" Saying this helps your partner to reexperience the intensity of the feelings he or she once felt.

Because your partner is presently feeling the same feelings that he or she felt from the past, your partner will want to call you again. Encourage this action by saying something like, "You just never know what might happen if you call me from work this week. You may catch me getting out of the shower again!" You can bet your partner's going to be calling you from work.

Now it's your turn. You can mentally seduce your partner by planting ideas in his head. All you have to do is tell your partner the thoughts you want him to have. Practice your commands before you try them out on your partner. This way, when you are ready to mentally seduce your partner, the words will flow smoothly.

Words of the Heart

"She did not seduce; she ravished."

—George Meredith, *Diana of the Crossways*, 1885

Casting Call: Seducers Wanted

It's human nature to assume that your partner wants to be seduced the same way you do. Boy, has this assumption caused some problems with couples! Before you can properly seduce your partner, you need to know what kinds of behaviors are commonly considered seductive. The *Kama Sutra* suggests the following:

➤ Be well-dressed.

➤ Conduct yourself as if love were natural.

➤ Tell your partner you love him.

➤ Be beautiful.

➤ Have versatility.

➤ Like the good qualities in others.

➤ Take delight in sexual unions.

➤ Have a firm mind.

➤ Be anxious to acquire and obtain experience and knowledge.

➤ Do not be greedy.

➤ Enjoy social gatherings and the arts.

➤ Be intelligent.

➤ Have a good disposition with good manners.

Cupid's Report

The *Kama Sutra*, better known as the Lover's Bible, is an ancient Indian guide to erotic love. It discusses everything from orgasm-delaying techniques to an endless variety of kisses and anything sexual you can imagine.

➤ Be straightforward in behavior.

➤ Be grateful.

➤ Think before acting.

➤ Be active.

➤ Have consistent behavior.

➤ Know the proper time and place for doing things.

➤ Do not speak with madness, loud laughter, hate, anger, dullness, or stupidity.

➤ Have knowledge of the *Kama Sutra* and be skilled in the arts connected with it.

As you look through this list, you will see that many of the behaviors have nothing at all to do with sex. Instead, they are characteristics of a good companion. That's what's so simple about seduction: it just comes down to being pleasant to be around.

To rate your own seductive skills, just look through the list again and place a mark next to all the behaviors you have. If you have a lot of checkmarks, then pat yourself on the back because you are an expert seducer already. If, however, you lack a lot of these qualities when you are with your partner, then it's time to start improving your seductiveness.

When Sandy looked at this list, she realized that the characteristics she didn't check off were pretty significant. She found that she was not grateful, was greedy, and did not have a good disposition around her husband. She realized that she was always in a bad mood around her husband. This was her way of venting her frustrations about her life, so she let it all out on him. He'd complain that all she did was gripe. Of course, this wasn't very romantic, and she wanted to change it. She became more careful of griping to her husband, focused on the positives more, and used her friends as sounding boards when she needed to vent.

Dr. Romance

This love potion from the *Kama Sutra* may help with seduction:

"If you crush milky chunks of cactus with sulfur and realgar, dry the mixture seven times, powder it, and apply it to your penis, you'll satisfy the most demanding lover."

How to Improve Your Seductiveness

Many people don't realize the great value of seduction. Instead, they want to go straight to sex. However, when you do this, you miss out on one of the greatest pleasures of intimacy.

The best way to improve your seductiveness is with just a few things: thoughtfulness, time, patience, and gentleness. These characteristics will take good sex to superb sex. Seductiveness, in terms of these characteristics, allows a person to change gears and get ready for intimacy.

Thomas and Liz discovered the value of seduction a few months after their baby was born. Liz had become irritable and not in the mood for intimacy. One day, the two of them drove to the mountains for a day alone. During the two-hour drive, Thomas gently stroked Liz's leg to help her unwind from her stressful new duties in motherhood. By the time they arrived at their destination, Liz was not only relaxed, but also aroused from all of her husband's caresses.

Words of the Heart

Casanova was a notorious seducer. Born in Venice in 1725, Casanova was said to be able to seduce any woman he chose. According to biographer John Masters, Casanova's gift was "in keeping his wits and his erection when all about him were losing theirs."

Sometimes life can cause so much stress that partners lose interest in intimacy. When this happens, seduction is a great way to relax your partner. One of the best acts of seduction comes when you acknowledge your partner's hard work. Monica did just that to James one night. She had decided to treat him like a king that night and pamper him with seduction. When he walked in the door, she took him to the big bathtub and told him she'd be back with dinner after his bath. The bath looked very inviting to James after his hard day. The tub was warm and bubbly and lit with candles. He climbed in and felt like a new man. A little while later after he was already in his pajamas and in bed, Monica walked in with dinner on a tray.

As you can see, seduction doesn't always have to begin with a glass of wine. Sometimes just nurturing your partner is the biggest turn on a person can have.

The Don Juan School of Seduction

A man who successfully seduces is a man who has mastered the art of romancing a woman. A man who is a master of romance is a man who takes time to listen to a woman, talks with her, enjoys her company, and makes her feel important. When a man does these romantic things, he is a man who has a happy relationship.

Don Juan was known for his seductiveness because he knew how to make a woman feel special. Any person, man or woman, can be a graduate of the Don Juan School of Seduction. All it takes is learning how to develop the skills Mr. Juan was known for: listening well, enjoying conversation, spending time with his partner, and knowing how to make his partner feel special.

To see where you stand on these skills, see how many of the following Don Juan Seduction questions you can answer. "I don't remember" doesn't count as an answer. Be honest with yourself when you read each one.

1. When was the last time you really listened to your partner?
2. When was the last time you sat down with your partner and enjoyed a conversation?

3. What do you enjoy about your partner's company?

4. How do you make your partner feel special? List four things that make him or her feel special.

Now it's time to take inventory of your seductive skills. If you answered all four questions in a way that suggests you are a winner at seduction, you graduate and are deemed a master Don Juan graduate. However, if you didn't pass this test, all you have to do is work to improve the areas you missed. For instance, if you can't remember the last time you really listened to your partner (question one), ask yourself what you can do to give her your undivided attention. This might mean turning off the TV or not bringing your work home with you. Becoming a Don Juan with seduction is all about giving your undivided attention in the present moment. You can do it!

The Art of Conversation

A good listener is very exciting. Just imagine a time when someone genuinely took an interest in intently listening to what you had to say. Do you remember how good it made you feel?

One of the key elements to seduction is having good communication skills. These six characteristics are essential for good communication:

1. Give your partner your full and undivided attention.

2. Make eye contact while your partner talks.

3. Do not interrupt when your partner is talking.

4. Do not finish your partner's sentences.

5. When you don't understand your partner, ask him or her to clarify what he or she said.

6. Confirm what you heard your partner say to show you're listening and understand everything that was said.

Playful Come-Ons

Flirting is a way of being playful with someone. When you focus your flirting on your partner, it makes him feel special because you are giving him a special kind of attention. And what's more fun than having a person respond to your flirtation?

You don't have to be single to flirt. Flirting is something that you can do whether you're married, single, engaged, separated, very young, or very old. It's a way of joining with someone in the spirit of fun.

Even though Katie and Martin have been together for eight years, he still loves to kiss her hand in public. It began the night they met when instead of just shaking hands with her, he drew her hand to his mouth and kissed her gently as he stared into her eyes. Her blushing each time he kissed her hand is what made him do it again and again.

Flirting with your partner adds a bit of fire to the time you spend together. If unexpected, it can add a thrill that rides up your spine and gives you goosebumps. It keeps a sparkle in your partner's eye and a smile on his face. It's something you have the power of giving him on a whim, just because you love him.

An entire book could be written on flirting, but it boils down to three essential things: verbal flirtation, eye contact, and touch. These three essentials to flirting are already programmed into your DNA, so they will happen naturally when you feel an attraction to someone. Nonetheless, you do have control over increasing their occurrence.

Dr. Romance

Flirting is one of the first behaviors to die down after a couple has been together for a while. It's also the best behavior to use to give your relationship a charge when it needs it the most.

Using Body Language

In her book, *Reading People*, Jo-Ellen Dimitrius compiled a list of body language signs that indicate sexual interest. Here are a few items on that list:

➤ Making eye contact
➤ Exaggerated smiling
➤ Laughter
➤ Staring
➤ Winking
➤ Wetting lips
➤ Crossing and uncrossing legs
➤ Flipping of the head or hair
➤ Entering someone's personal space
➤ Touching oneself (smoothing nylons or playing with shirt buttons)
➤ Touching the object of one's affection
➤ Listening intently
➤ Intently looking the other person up and down
➤ Blinking
➤ Thrusting out the chest or hips
➤ Walking with a swagger or wiggle

➤ Primping

➤ Lounging back

➤ Smiling coyly

➤ Wearing revealing clothing (particularly if not appropriate for the occasion)

➤ Wearing excessive makeup, perfume, or cologne

➤ Whispering or other attempts at intimacy

➤ Trying to isolate the target of one's affection by getting him or her alone

Being Emotionally Attractive

The only way to make your partner want to flirt with you is to be emotionally attractive. This means that you have these characteristics:

➤ You smile a lot.

➤ You laugh easily.

➤ You are interested in others.

➤ You are a good listener.

➤ You focus your attention on your partner when you are together.

➤ You are relaxed around your partner.

➤ You don't dwell on your miseries.

➤ You don't interrupt your partner when he is talking.

➤ You are sympathetic to other people's problems.

➤ You have a sense of fun.

Words of the Heart

"To talk of honor in the mysteries of love is like talking of Heaven or the deity in an operation of witchcraft just when you are employing the devil: it makes the charm impotent."

—William Wycherley

The next time you are with your partner, pay attention to your behavior to see how many of these emotionally attractive characteristics you have. Don't be discouraged if you lack a few. Many times, just the awareness of these criteria will make you alter your behavior to include more of them.

Verbal Flirtation

Stuart looked across the table at Susan and said, "You are the most beautiful woman (pause) I've ever known." They'd been married 11 years at the time, but the compliment made her heart pound excitedly. That's exactly what flirting with words does to a person.

Verbal flirting involves compliments and teasing words said in various tones, such as in whispers. Try these flirtatious lines on your partner:

➤ "You look so handsome."

➤ "I just can't get enough of your eyes."

➤ "Your touch is electrifying."

➤ "I just love the way you look at me."

➤ "You sexy thing, you."

➤ "Flex your muscles for me. I just love to look at them!"

➤ "You look fabulous in that negligee."

➤ "I could just get lost in your eyes."

➤ "I love your touch."

➤ "You have such a sexy voice."

➤ "I think you're incredible."

Just remember that when you verbally flirt with your partner, it makes more of an impact when you have direct eye contact. You'll know you're affecting your partner every time you see a blush or a smile. This reaction is your reward for loving your partner.

Look Deep into My Eyes

You can send messages to your partner in several different ways with just one look. There is nothing more intense than sustained eye contact, even with someone you've known for many years. One of the most difficult things to do with your partner is to keep your eyes focused on him or her at the time you ordinarily break away. After all, if you keep your eyes there, you become vulnerable.

For the sake of flirting with your partner, let's keep it simple. When you are feeling amorous and looking at him or her, keep holding your look until you feel so much tingling that you want to run out of the room. At that instant, you'll know that your partner has already received your message, read it fully, and is about to respond. Now the fun begins!

Dr. Romance

Flirting involves eye contact, and sometimes that's uncomfortable for people. To improve your comfort level, all you need to do is sit down with your partner and practice looking into each other's eyes for intervals of 10 seconds, 25 seconds, and then 45 seconds. Expect to have lots of giggles, because prolonged eye contact can be an intense thing to do. If you are nervous, just remember that the eyes looking back at you are eyes that love you.

Reach Out and Touch Someone

A flirting touch is one that lets your partner know that you like to touch him or her. It can be a sexy touch or a loving touch to show you care. Other touches along this line are the kind you do when you first begin to date. These are the touches that excite you to no end: walking hand in hand, bumping knees under a table, sitting side by side, having your hair brushed away from your face, resting your head on his shoulder, or simply hugging good-bye. A sexy touch is anything that is racy and scrambles your hormones. I'll leave this kind to your vivid imagination.

Touching is a difficult thing for many people to do. This is precisely why it creates an impact when you do it. Some people are naturally affectionate, and touching comes easily to them. If you are not one of those people, don't fret. If you go the extra mile to touch your partner to emphasize a point, it will be noticed.

Studies show that a touch significantly alters someone's perception of you. The one who is touched views you more warmly. There are all kinds of touches to try when you are flirting with your partner or someone you'd like to know better. Touching while you sit in front of the television is a good place to start. When he is watching a show, you can reach over and massage his neck. You can gently caress his face, you can brush his hair back, or you can delicately rub his hand with yours.

Remember, true flirting is about connecting. All you have to do is act naturally. Go with your gut and follow it through. This is the secret to flirting.

The Least You Need to Know

➤ Seduction is a great way to help your partner make the transition from work mode to intimate mode.

➤ Seduction titillates the mind and soothes the soul.

➤ Don't believe everything you hear about seduction; sometimes the myths just put a stop to seductive behavior.

➤ Flirting is the quickest way to incite romantic excitement in your partner.

Uncovering Your Fantasies

For two years, Cindy had no idea that her boyfriend Randall had fantasies until one day she finally asked him. "Sure I have a fantasy, and you're in it," he said. He went on to tell her about how much he would love to make love in a Jacuzzi on a warm summer night. She looked at him and said, "Well, I know just the Jacuzzi. Let's do it!"

Everyone has sexual fantasies, but the only way to find out what your partner's fantasies are is to ask. Sometimes you'll find that your partner's fantasies align with your fantasies, and sometimes they won't. What's important is that you feel comfortable in exploring them together in a way that satisfies both of your preferences.

Fantasies act as a sort of mental preparation or warm-up for the act of lovemaking. In this chapter, you'll learn how to merge your sexual fantasies with your partner's to find some that are mutually satisfying. You will also find many sexual fantasy scripts to use on your partner that will send him or her over the edge in lust for you.

The Scoop on Fantasies

Both men and women have sexual fantasies, but do the fantasies of men and women really differ that much? Sure, there are some differences, but male and female fantasies have one important similarity: sexual content.

That's what makes fantasies so exciting: Partners can explore them with each other because they deal with the same basic subject matter. Who else is better equipped to talk about sexual fantasies with you than a partner who knows you sexually? Just think of how much fun you'll have in doing so.

What's in a Man's Mind

Men's fantasies are generally very broad and cover as many areas as there are thoughts in someone's head. Some of the earliest fantasies men have are very simple: They might begin as just a fantasy of having a naked woman in the same room. As men grow up and experience that fantasy as a reality, their fantasies become more complex and involve women swallowing semen, anal sex, fetishes, women with women, virgins, and all sorts of sexy scenes.

What Women Fantasize About

Nancy Friday has been researching and writing about women's sexual fantasies since the 1960s. This is hard to believe nowadays, but she had a difficult time getting her first book about women's sexual fantasies published because no one believed women had them! The truth is that women do have sexual fantasies like men do, just not generally the same kind of fantasies.

Women's fantasies fall into three categories, according to Nancy Friday's findings: women in control (seductress, sadist, and exhibitionist), women with women, and the sexually insatiable women. What's nice about these three categories is that it simplifies the selection of a fantasy to live out. To help you narrow it down even further, you might want to ask which of the three categories your partner finds more arousing, and then develop your fantasy from there.

How to Turn On a Woman

In her book, *Light Her Fire*, Ellen Kreidman teaches the male reader how to ignite passion, joy, and excitement in the woman he loves. She advises men to look at their traits to see what turns a woman off and on. Read the following two lists and see how many traits you have in each column. The more turn-ons you have, the more aroused your partner will be around you. If you have a lot of turn-offs, then it's time to make some changes in yourself if you want to turn her on.

Turn-offs	*Turn-ons*
Low self-esteem	Confidence
Lack of humor	Sense of humor
Negativity	Intelligence
Laziness	Support
Self-centeredness	Sensitivity
Insecurity	Sense of self-worth
No ambition	Goals
Suspicion	Imagination
Dependence	Independence
Extreme jealousy	Desire
Lack of tenderness	Courage
Lack of understanding	Compassion
Self-pity	Decisiveness
Smothering	Dignity

Who Ever Said It Was Perverse?

Can you comfortably tell your partner what turns you on? Can you openly talk about your fantasies? If you can, then consider yourself very lucky, because discussing this subject is difficult for many people.

How would you feel if your partner said to you, "Honey, I think the maid is so sexy, how would you feel about having her join us tonight?" I don't think this statement would go over too well for most people. Whether your partner wants to actually act out the fantasy or not isn't important. What is meaningful is that your partner feels safe enough to invite you into his or her world of sexual thoughts.

We grow up hiding our sexuality. Unfortunately, for many people, shame and guilt dictate how they behave in the bedroom. For example, many teenagers are ashamed to masturbate in the privacy of their beds. Think of all the negative propaganda surrounding masturbation: "You'll go blind if you touch it!" "Warts will grow all over your hand if you go near it!" "It's a sin."

I can recall as a teenager listening to the pastor of my church give a sermon on how wrong masturbation was. At the end of the service, he asked for all of the masturbators to come to the front of the church and be forgiven. I still remember the shock on all the teenagers' faces as our youth pastor stood and made his way to the front of the church. Talk about shaming a person for sexuality! Messages like these make it difficult for many people to relax and enjoy their sexuality.

Negative messages about sex come from many sources throughout a person's life. As a result, in adulthood, many people have learned to avoid the subject matter all together. It not only becomes a taboo subject to talk about, but also a desired act that hides in their minds in various fantasy forms.

It's time to open your mind a little and shed some of the Victorian beliefs that surround sex. Women like sex; men like sex. Now let's like it together.

Getting Down to Business

Before you can bring your sexual fantasies to life, you and your partner must communicate with each other about them. No one can read minds, so you must discuss your fantasies.

Also, keep in mind that just because your partner may have an image in his head, it doesn't necessarily mean that he wants to act it out. Only you and your partner can decide where to draw the line. Sometimes merely telling your partner about a fantasy is just as spine-tingling as trying to act it out.

To get started, you and your partner write down five of your sexual fantasies and tell each other about them:

My Sexual Fantasies

1. _____
2. _____
3. _____
4. _____
5. _____

My Partner's Sexual Fantasies

1. _____

2. _____

3. _____

4. _____

5. _____

Mental Positioning

Who can forget the bar scene in *When a Man Loves a Woman*? Meg Ryan sits at a bar appearing to be a single woman, all alone. A man tries to pick her up and fails miserably. Then in walks Andy Garcia, a pilot, using the corniest lines a woman could hear. Before you know it, she climbs into his lap and kisses him passionately. The audience soon learns that they are in fact a married couple.

Cupid's Report

Studies have found that women can get just as aroused physically as men do when viewing pornography.

The most thrilling romantic journey begins in your mind. If you want to jump-start sexy thoughts, the way to do it is through mental positions, which are sexual fantasies. Thoughts act as a warm-up for the brain and are a way to get the whole body into the experience. Think of it this way: You warm up your body prior to exercising. Why not do the same for your mind before having sex?

In this section, you will find some sizzling fantasies to plant in your partner's mind. The focus is more on playful acting that starts when the two of you are apart. All you have to do is call your partner on the phone and read him or her the words from one of the following scripts. You don't have to tell your partner what you are doing; he or she will pick it up very quickly.

This way, the sexual tension will build up in both of your minds all day. If you're daring enough, you may even want to fully act out the scenes with dialogue and props, although it isn't necessary. Simple whispers of the fantasy will excite your partner.

When leaving messages, you'll want to make sure that someone other than your partner won't accidentally intercept your sexy messages. This could lead to embarrassment for both of you, especially if it happens in a professional setting. So, before leaving messages, make sure that your partner is the only one who has access to them.

Words of the Heart

"Love, as it exists in society, is nothing more than the exchange of two fantasies and the contact of two skins."

—Nicolas Chamfort, *Maximes et pensees*, 1796

Dr. Romance

If you are at a loss for fantasies to act out with your partner, just go to your local video rental store and look at the top rentals. Usually the most popular movies have great sex scenes in them that you and your partner can act out the next time you want to play.

Extramarital Activities

The Other Woman: "Are you alone? Can you talk? Is your wife nearby? I enjoyed sneaking away with you at the party last night. It's a miracle no one found out. I need to see you again. Can you meet me after work?"

The Call Girl: "Hi, this is Joe. Your services come very highly recommended. I'll be in town on the 25th and was wondering if you'd be able to schedule me for a two-hour block of time. I will pay you handsomely. This has to be kept just between you and me. Please schedule me in for a very private session at 7 P.M."

Men in Uniform

Pilot and Stewardess: "I know this is last-minute, but I'm flying to Paris and would like to know if you are available. The regular stewardess called in sick, and I have specially requested that you join the crew. Let's meet at the airport three hours before the flight. There's a new floatation device that you need to learn how to master."

Fireman and Victim: "I just wanted to thank you for putting out the fire last night. I learned my lesson not to rub things together. It's true what they say about friction starting sparks. I've never seen a fireman handle his hose quite like you did. I'd feel better if you came by today just to check things out. I think I smell smoke, but it may be just my imagination. You'll have to put your hose in some tight spots to see if anything is still burning."

Police Officer and Criminal: "Miss, I have a warrant out for your arrest, and I need to take you down to the station. Please come out with your hands up. When you get outside, lie face down on the ground with your arms and legs spread. Lie there until you feel me behind you. I'll tell you what to do next."

On the Job

Applicant and Interviewee: "Miss Salazar, this is Mr. Doug from the company you interviewed with last week. I've been asked to conduct the second round of interviews, and I must say, you are certainly the most impressive of the bunch.

Would you mind if we discuss the position over dinner? We can have a bottle of wine and get down to business. Quite frankly, I heard about your attributes, and I'd like to see them for myself. Make sure you remember to bring your application as well as your references. It may be a long evening, so do come prepared."

Co-workers: "Anne, this is Mark from Accounting. For three months now I've been working up the courage to ask you out. I think you are so sexy. Your smile lights up a room. I can't get you out of my mind. I won't tell you what I imagine each night when I go to bed. You may not know this, but I get to work early only so I can watch you walk past me and see your hips move from side to side. Let's have a drink after work."

Words of the Heart

"Alcohol is like love: the first kiss is magic, the second is intimate, the third is routine. After that, you just take the girl's clothes off."

—Raymond Chandler, *The Long Good-bye*, 1953

Around the House

Friendly Neighbors: "Hi Harry, this is Iris. You're not going to believe this, but I've locked myself out again. I'm on my cellular phone, and I was wondering if I could come over. I'm really embarrassed because I was just about to step into the shower, so all I have on is a towel."

Repairman and Housewife: "Thank you for coming out on such short notice. I don't know what's wrong with the shower, but the water won't shut off. I hooked up the shower massager, and things got a little out of control. Now I'm all wet! You look like you have experience with these things. If you need my help holding anything, I can be very accommodating."

Educational Matters

Professor and Student: "Professor, I stayed after class because I need to talk about my grade. I really need to pass the class, and it doesn't look like I'm going to. Maybe there is something I could do for you to earn bonus points? I see it when you look at me. I know you've noticed that I don't wear panties in class. I wanted you to notice. I've wanted you from the first day of class. I'll do anything you want just as long as I get a passing grade."

Parent and Teacher: "Mr. Clemens? This is Grace, Johnny's mom. I know that teacher appreciation week is coming up, and I wanted to show my appreciation for you. Please come over for dinner Friday night. I'm a great cook, and I'm sure you won't be able to resist what I'll be serving. Johnny will be in bed by 7 P.M., so how about if you come by about 8 P.M.? That way we won't be disturbed."

Dr. Romance

Do you remember how much fun dressing up was when you were a child? You were able to become the people who lived in your imagination. You could say things you'd never say as yourself and behave in ways you would never dare. As an adult, you can play dress-up with adult sexual themes and experience the same satisfaction you did as a child.

Medical Services

Doctor and Patient: "This is Dr. Jones. I had a moment to return your call. My nurse tells me that you won't be able to make it into the office for your appointment tomorrow. I do make house calls. Why don't I stop by your house on my way home from the office this evening? How is 7:30 P.M. for you? Be prepared, and I will do a thorough exam on you."

Hotel Settings

Two Guests: "Hi, my name is Jim. We bumped into each other in the lobby. I thought you were the most beautiful woman I've ever seen. I hope you aren't offended, but I pressured the hotel manager into telling me your room number. I was wondering if you would like to meet downstairs in the Jacuzzi. I hear its jets are to die for."

Bellboy and Guest: "Is this the front desk? This is Angelica in room 69. I need to have a strong bellboy come up to my room. I need some special services. I'll be in the shower, so tell him to just come on in."

There is no end to mischievous fantasies you can act out. Listed below are more characters to slip into, along with the come-on lines to use for each one:

Mechanic: Your car is ready. Would you like for me to bring it by your house?

Electrician: I hear your circuits are out of order.

Candy striper: It's time for your sponge bath, Mr. Smith.

Photographer: This shot requires some nudity. Are you comfortable with that?

Rock fan: I want your autograph where no one will see it but us!

Attorney: Yes, attorney-client privileges include sex.

Hitchhiker: I'll do anything for a ride.

Principal: I hear you've been a naughty little girl.

Real-estate agent: There's a room I just have to show you.

Paramedic: You need mouth-to-mouth in order to survive.

Flavorful Fantasies

Your taste in sexual activities reflects who you are. For example, a creative person is more likely to have creative expression in his sexual habits. A scientist will have a different sexual expression because his personality is different.

I'm now going to outline several types of sexual behaviors that are on the cusp of what society deems appropriate. They are behaviors that can enhance your sexual play when used in moderation. The following scenarios are mild enough for anyone to use. The only thing dangerous about them is the charge they send through your body. So go ahead and commit yourself to trying out at least one of the advanced bedroom behaviors with your partner the next time you see him or her. You don't have to go way out, just test the water with a cautious toe and see how it feels.

Words of the Heart

"Conscience is the inner voice that warns us somebody may be looking."

—H.L. Mencken, 1949

Sadism

Extreme sadists can be sexually satisfied only by inflicting pain on their partners. However, a little nibbling, scratching, and spanking never hurt anyone! Try giving your partner a nice swat on his or her behind the next time he or she does something you like. Don't forget to use one of the following expressions to make it convincing: "You need a good spanking," "I'm going to punish you for this," and "You've been very, very bad!"

Of course this won't be real punishment for your partner, and he or she will quickly try to please you by being "bad" again. Keep your paddle nearby because you have some lessons to instill!

Cupid's Report

The word *sadomasochism* comes from two men. The word *sadism* comes from the eighteenth-century French writer Marquis de Sade. His name came to stand for cruelty, vicious rough sex, and deriving pleasure from inflicting pain. He got this reputation after being jailed for notorious sexual acts. *Masochism* comes from Leopold von Sacher-Masoch, a nineteenth-century German writer who wrote novels about men who liked harsh, dominating women to humiliate and physically hurt them, preferably while wearing leather or fur.

Words of the Heart

"Nothing can intensify my passion more than the tyranny, cruelty, and especially the faithlessness of a beautiful woman."

—Leopold von Sacher-Masoch, *Venus in Furs*, 1870

Masochism

In order for a true masochist to find sexual satisfaction, he or she must experience physical pain that is inflicted by his or her partner. To dabble in masochistic behaviors without pain, try light bondage, blindfolding, and tickling until it hurts.

Voyeurism

A voyeur finds sexual satisfaction by watching other people take their clothes off and/or engage in sexual activity. Voyeurs usually bring themselves to orgasm while watching. It may surprise you, but many people have voyeuristic tendencies.

When was the last time a commercial got your full attention because it had sexy people in it? When was the last time you got excited watching lovers in a movie? When was the last time you lusted after the Victoria's Secret models? It can be pretty arousing to watch others.

Voyeurism with your partner can be fun. It can take the form of watching sexy videos together or watching each other. Just think about how erotic it would be to "catch" your partner taking a shower. You can be as creative as you want or as involved as your partner wants to take it.

Exhibitionism

An exhibitionist experiences sexual arousal when other people watch him or her perform various kinds of sexual behaviors. Amateur exhibitionists can have a lot of fun by taking the risk of doing "naughty" things in places where others might see them. The thrill of possibly being seen is what makes the experience exciting. This kind of excitement is what gives a couple the courage to take a blanket to the beach at night, sneak into a bathroom at a restaurant, and play with each other under the table.

Fetishism

For some, an object that has a strong sexual association attached to it is needed for arousal. This object is the *fetish*. The two most common fetishes are shoes and feet. For some people, these areas arouse them sexually if for no other reason than because of personal preference.

For most people, fetishes are already a part of their sexual repertoire. Certain objects or body parts add to their sexual arousal. They aren't necessary for stimulation, but they add to the moment. A fetish in this sense can be a hairstyle, lingerie, stockings, shoes, or even a collection of *Playboy* magazines. So go ahead and try a new prop and see if you find it arousing. It never hurts to try.

The Least You Need to Know

➤ If you haven't already told your partner what your sexual fantasies are, it's time to do it. Sharing will bring you closer together and will enhance your sex life.

➤ Just because your partner talks about a sexual thought or image, does not mean he or she wants to act it out. Many times fantasies are just as satisfying when they are explored verbally.

➤ If both people are excited by the fantasy, then why not go for it? Experimentation can be fun!

➤ Be thankful to live in a day and age that recognizes sexual fantasies in both sexes. With this kind of freedom of thought, who knows where your thoughts will take you?

Chapter 8

Romantic Sex

In This Chapter

➤ Making every kiss count

➤ Adding adventure to your sex life

➤ Taking tips from the *Kama Sutra*

Climbing into bed, April cuddles next to Mario and begins seductively stroking him. He's turned on his side away from her and not responding to her requests for making love. He's tired and wants to catch up on his sleep. April, on the other hand, is feeling frisky and wants to play!

So what do you do if your honey doesn't seem to be as sweet to the idea of making love as you are? This chapter will teach you how to get anyone in the mood. I'll start out with a discussion of kissing, because that's how most sex begins! Then I'll move on to discovering the sexual acts that your partner finds the most pleasing. Finally, I'll highlight some lessons from the *Kama Sutra*.

I'm Dying for a Kiss

Kissing has been around for a very long time. Some anthropologists believe that kissing originated from the act of a mother transferring food from her mouth to her child's. It's believed that erotic kissing first took place in India around 1500 B.C.E. when evidence was found in cave paintings and other artifacts.

Cupid's Report

The lips are erogenous zones that are highly sensitive to sexual stimulation. During a kiss, the lips swell, grow more sensitive, and become infused with color.

Everyone remembers his or her first kiss. It probably made your body feel as though a bolt of lightning had shot right through it. In adulthood, kissing can be just as electrifying. Have you ever watched new lovers? Their kisses are passionate, and they steal kisses at the least likely times and places.

As sad as it is, sometimes kissing just loses its spark. This most often happens because kissing has become predictable and routine. Let's say you've been involved with the same partner for five years. You give small pecks to each other to say good-bye or hello, and only once or twice a week, you let your passionate kisses out of the bag as you make love. This is boring! This is predictable! If this is what kissing has become for you, then you need to put a halt to it.

If you want to wow your partner, you have to put some fire in your kisses. Trying these tips will lead to happy kissing:

➤ Make eye contact and move in close. Very slowly plant one on your partner.

➤ Reward your partner with praise about his or her kissing style. It's a sure way to get him or her to keep up the good work!

➤ When your partner is expecting a small kiss, surprise him or her with a long kiss.

➤ Sneak up behind your partner and kiss the back of his or her neck.

➤ Don't save all your kissing for the bedroom.

➤ Initiate kisses in new places.

Send Your Partner to Kissing School

Not all people are talented kissers. Kissing should be as easy as breathing, but for some, it takes practice. If your partner isn't coming through with the kind of kiss you desire, then you will just have to teach him or her.

The first step is to demonstrate through your kisses how you want your partner to kiss. Sometimes, this is all it takes to get the other person to catch on. If simply demonstrating the type of kiss you want isn't working, you will have to use words.

Believe me, I know how uncomfortable a kissing lesson can be. However, if you love your partner, this lesson will be a gift you give the two of you. Expect it to be a little awkward, but once your partner catches on, it will all be worth it. Do the steps in the following sections, and before you know it, your partner's mouth will make you lose control.

Orientation

Make sure to give kissing lessons when you have hours to practice. Prepare your partner by saying, "I'm going to teach you how to kiss me the way I like to be kissed." You need to say this carefully. If you say it jokingly, your partner's feelings may be hurt. Say it in a soft, serious tone that communicates your caring.

No matter how you say it, your partner's feelings may still be hurt. Let your partner know that in the long run he or she will appreciate the help because he or she will know that you're truly satisfied. You will also want to reassure your partner how much you love them and love being with him or her.

Words of the Heart

"Give me a kiss, add to that kiss a score; Then to that twenty, add a hundred more; A thousand to that hundred; so kiss on, treble that million, and when that is done, let's kiss afresh, as when we first begun."

—Robert Herrick (1591–1674)

Hard and Pinched Kissing

Shelly liked Kevin a lot, but she hated to kiss him because his lips were always so tight. To her, his lips felt unresponsive instead of willing and filled with desire. She knew he wanted her, but his kissing certainly didn't reflect that.

For the partner whose lips are too hard or pinched, say, "I want you to soften your lips and put them on mine." You may have to have your partner do lip stretching exercises first by opening his mouth as wide as he can, then closing it, and repeating until his mouth is less tense. When your partner's lips are loose, kiss your partner very lightly. You'll have to practice this step a number of times.

Dr. Romance

Did you know that scientists have discovered that the human brain is equipped to help us find our partner's mouth in the dark? Studies can never be replicated enough, so put this one to the test with your partner and see whether you come up with the same results that the scientists did.

Forceful Kissing

Sam's kisses made Sarah feel like she was doing battle. Each time he kissed her, he was very rough. He'd put his hand behind her head and press her mouth to his forcefully. During the first three weeks of dating, she assumed that he was just being very passionate with her, but she quickly realized that was his style of kissing. For Sarah, kissing like that on a regular basis felt more like war than passion. She needed soft kisses with a gentle touch, too.

Words of the Heart

"A thousand kisses to your neck, your breasts, and lower down, much lower, that little black for-est I love so well."

—Napoleon to Josephine in 1796

Cupid's Report

Some people swear by the power of spices to cure sexual problems. Supposedly, all you have to do is add just a dash of these sexy spices to your food, and miracles will happen. I'll let you be the judge. For impotence, try garlic or cardamom. Cardamom also can prevent premature ejacula-tion. Cloves, pepper, vanilla, and ginger are supposed to increase sex drive. Have a small penis? Try sprinkling it with pepper. Saffron helps to handle low sensitivity.

If you have a partner whose kisses are too forceful, stop him when he's kissing you that way and say, "Sometimes I'd like you to kiss me gently, too." To demonstrate the type of gentleness you would like, first kiss your partner softly on his cheeks and neck. Slowly work your way to his mouth and kiss him gently. As soon as your partner responds with power-ful kisses, pull away and repeat the preceding phrase. Keep repeating this process until your partner kisses you the way you want.

Turning a Kiss into Something More

So you've completed kissing school, and your partner can't keep his or her passionate lips off you. Now it's time to make your kisses the most romantic they can be. In order to do this, you need the proper location and ambiance.

Undoubtedly, you can find these elements in your home, but romantic kissing can sometimes be even more thrilling outside your own four walls. You'll want to find a place that encourages uninterrupted affection.

In the evening, you will be able to find many places that offer privacy as well as ambiance to make the perfect kissing place. Here are just a few to keep in mind when looking for just the right spot:

➤ Most large hotels have inviting lounges with comfortable seating that attract plenty of romance-seeking couples.

➤ Restaurants that cater to adults usually have intimate tables for two.

➤ Cruises, carriage rides, or other modes of ro-mantic transportation set the stage for kissing.

➤ Any dark corner you can sneak away to when in public invites kissing.

➤ Star gazing on a boardwalk is a good time for a kiss.

➤ A dark dance floor while slow dancing is a good place for a kiss.

During the day, the following places may provide privacy and ambiance for kissing:

➤ The beach or any pool of water

➤ Nature walks

➤ Botanical gardens

➤ Parks

Don't be limited by your environment when it comes to kissing. If you feel in the mood for a kiss, just do it. Everyone seems to envy couples who openly demonstrate their love. Go ahead, be one of the couples who is admired. You'll enjoy every second of it.

Words of the Heart

"If you fake your pleasure, take care he doesn't see through you. Lead him on with your writhing and the look in your eyes. Demonstrate your delights with moans and heavy breathing."

—Ovid

The Main Attraction

When two people are in a sexual relationship, they bring two different backgrounds with them to the bedroom. Sometimes the two people are very sexually compatible, and other times, things don't go as nicely as each would hope.

The following tables are for you and your partner to fill in. These tables will help you assess what turns you on and what turns on your partner. (It will also let you know what each of you has been hiding under the sheets!) The important part of this table is the second section, which focuses on the sexual acts you would like to try with each other. This table will be the key that unlocks many romantic adventures with your partner.

Sexual Desires I Have Acted On

Mine	Partner's
1.	1.
2.	2.
3.	3.
4.	4.

Sexual Desires I Would Like to Act On

Mine	Partner's
1.	1.
2.	2.
3.	3.
4.	4.

Jessica had a fantasy about making love in a fountain, but she had not acted on it. One night she told her partner about her fantasy, and he became excited. He wanted to try it. They had one problem, though. They needed to find a fountain that they could use without getting arrested. They set a goal to find the perfect fountain and kept their eyes open for it. Finally, they found it in a pretty private park that people rarely used. Late one evening, with towels in hand, they climbed in the cool water under the summer night's sky and lived out her fantasy together.

Now that you and your partner have listed the acts that you would like to try, it's time to make a plan of action and follow through on your desires. Fill in the following information:

1. Date to try out sexual act: _____

2. Items you will need for act: _____

3. If there is anything holding you back, list it here:

   _____

4. How to resolve the issue holding you back: _____

You are now ready to fulfill your sexual desires with your partner because you have set a date, decided what you will need, and have worked out any possible problems that might prevent you from doing it.

Learn from the *Kama Sutra*

Remember what it was like when you were a virgin? You had all kinds of ideas about what sex would be like. As a romantic, sometimes it's best to erase what you already know and open your mind to a new perspective on sex.

This section will expose you to the Tantric way of looking at the act of making love. The Tantra not only gives advice on how to have sex, but it also confronts and deals with taboo subjects that arise in sexual matters. Think of this chapter as the risqué *Cliffs Notes* of the Tantra.

An Affair to Remember

Leander and Hero were two lovers from mythology who were divided by the sea. They met at a festival of Adonis, and they fell in love that afternoon. She told him of her home across the sea and persuaded him to swim to her that evening. He agreed as long as she would hold up a lamp to guide his way. Throughout the summer he swam the sea to her home, where they made love. By dawn, he swam back across the sea to his home. When winter came, the sea grew stormy, making it very difficult for him to swim across. On one particular evening, Hero stood on the shore with her lamp as Leander swam the rough sea. At one point, the wind blew strong and the flame went out, making it impossible for Leander to find his way to Hero. She stayed awake all night waiting for him. When the morning light came, she found Leander's body lying at the foundation of her tower. From the cliff, she plunged into the waves to her death.

Permission to Do It

Can you imagine a church that not only encourages its congregation to have sex, but also teaches them how to do it? It may be hard to fathom, but there is one. It's called the Church of the Tantra, and it dates back to 800 C.E. The belief system is still practiced today in some parts of the world.

Before you get too excited about going to your new church next Sunday, I should tell you that you won't find this church on the corner in your neighborhood. It's primarily practiced in Eastern cultures. Nevertheless, you will learn enough about the techniques here to practice them religiously at home!

As unusual as it may sound, the Church of the Tantra combines spirituality with sexuality. There is no shame or guilt in desiring sex. As a matter of fact, this church has an entire book of sexual techniques called the *Kama Sutra*.

Words of the Heart

This Tantric advice is geared for men with small penises, but anyone can use it: "Vadavaka (The Mare's Trick): Like a mare, gripping a stallion, your lover traps and milks your penis with her vagina, which can only be perfected with long practice. When she uses it, a woman should cease to kiss her lover and simply hold the lock."

Positions, Positions, Positions

The following list is a sample of instructions for various sexual positions from the *Kama Sutra*. This book makes *The Joy of Sex* look like a kindergarten book. If you have a partner who is willing, give any of the following positions a try the next time you play around:

➤ **Lying down:** "Full of desire, saying sweet words, approach her with your body stiff as a pole and drive straight forward to pierce her lotus and join your limbs." This position is called *Madandhvaja* (The Flag of Cupid).

➤ **Sitting position:** "She sits with raised thighs, her feet placed either side of your waist; penis enters vagina; you rain hard blows upon her body." This position is called *Kshudgaga* (Striking).

➤ **Rear entry:** "If the lady, eager for love, goes on all fours, humping her back like a doe, and you enjoy her from behind, rutting as though you'd lost all human nature." This position is called *Hirana* (The Deer).

➤ **Standing position:** "When she leans against a wall, planting her feet as widely apart as possible, and you enter the cave between her thighs, eager for lovemaking." This position is called *Sammukha* (Face to Face).

Taboos in the Bedroom

Sex isn't always free of problems or complications. During the course of a relationship, it is normal for a couple to experience any of a wide range of unexpected sexual issues: performance anxiety, impotence, venereal disease, inability to orgasm (male and female), pre-ejaculation, and lack of sexual interest are just a few.

A common reaction to sexual problems is to ignore them and hope they will go away. But ignoring the problem rarely cures it. The Tantra not only acknowledges problems, but is prepared to offer solutions as they surface.

For instance, Viagra may be the current cure for impotence, but the Tantra had ways to get a man back in working condition whether his condition was from exhaustion or inability. Here are just a couple of them:

➤ "The artificial phallus should be shaped to your natural proportions. It will be more arousing for the lady if the outside is studded."

➤ "If, during lovemaking, the erection cannot be sustained because the man is old or simply exhausted, he should use delicate oral techniques."

Sex Talk

One reason many people don't deal with a sexual issue until they have to is because they are uncomfortable with the subject of sex. The best way to get over being uncomfortable is to address the issue straight on. As a warm-up exercise, read the following list of sexually related words. After each word, see if you can come up with five other words to describe the same word. For instance, other expressions for the word *sex* are making love, screwing, getting laid, and so on. Now it's your turn:

Breasts:_____

Penis:_____

Vagina:_____

Buttocks:_____

Masturbation:_____

Oral sex:_____

Anal sex:_____

This exercise is a good way to begin to break the ice to help you become more comfortable talking about sex with your partner. This exercise can also be a lot of fun to do with your partner. At first you may be a little awkward or embarrassed, but before you know it, you'll be laughing and coming up with all sorts of terms.

You can make an art out of making love just like the *Kama Sutra* does. And what's more romantic than indulging yourself that way with someone you love? It's all about feeling safe enough to be intimate and making the time to do so. If there's one thing you learn from Tantric practices, it's that sex is not an after-thought at the end of your day. Make lovemaking a spiritual connection you share with your partner.

Cupid's Report

The most well-known aphrodisiac is the Spanish fly. The Spanish fly is an emerald-green blister beetle that is found in southern Europe. When used for a sexual stimulant, the bug is dried and crushed into a powder. This powder is toxic to those who take too much.

The Least You Need to Know

➤ Kissing is what you make of it. If you aren't happy with the way your partner kisses, teach your partner how you'd like to be kissed. It will be a gift you'll both share.

➤ Is there a sex act that you would like to try out with your partner but you haven't yet? If so, make a plan, set a date, and quench your desires.

➤ The *Kama Sutra* is a good place to start if you and your partner want to get creative during lovemaking.

➤ Do you talk about sex with your partner? If not, maybe breaking the ice by talking about the names you have for the different body parts will free you up to talk about more serious matters.

Part 3

Becoming a Modern-Day Romeo and Juliet

If technique is what you lack, this section is for you. Knowing how to show your partner you love her is crucial to a relationship. You will be introduced to various ways to woo, some familiar, some new. In all, you will be presented with the most simple, pragmatic ways to use them that you never thought possible. What's great is that all of the tools work for everyone, regardless of skill level or personality.

Chapter 9

Expressing Love Verbally

In This Chapter

➤ Picking the perfect pet name

➤ Declaring your love

➤ Raising a glass to your love

➤ Leaving romantic phone messages

If you pay attention to songs on the radio, you'll notice something interesting. Many of them have lyrics that mention regrets about words that should have been spoken. The situation almost always refers to romantic relationships. The themes usually fall into categories like these:

➤ "Why can't I tell you I love you?"

➤ "You used to say I love you."

➤ "I'm a little too late."

➤ "The words seem to come so easily to you."

➤ "It all depends on what you say right now."

➤ "If only I had known that then."

➤ "She already knows it. Why do I need to tell her?"

Is there anyone alive who doesn't love to hear, "I love you" from their partner? Despite that, many people either forget to express their feelings or feel that the words

Dr. Romance

When you think back through your relationship, which words of love do you remember? What about those particular words made them stand out from the others?

Cupid's Report

There actually was a man by the name of Cyrano de Bergerac, but he had very little in common with the hero of the Rostand play. He was born in Paris and was later educated by a priest in the village of Bergerac College de Beauvais. He acquired fame as a duelist and bohemian before enlisting in the army at the age of 20. He was severely wounded twice and eventually gave up his military career. At that point, he studied under the philosopher and mathematician Pierre Gassendi. Greatly influenced by Gassendi, he finally settled on a writing career.

are just too difficult for them to say. Certainly, your partner may know that you love him or her, but your partner needs to hear the words.

Speaking the words of love is easy when the words are already provided for you. That's the beauty of a book like this—you don't have to do any of the work. All you have to do is find the words you think your partner would like to hear and say them. In this chapter, you will learn how to take advantage of everyday situations that provide easy opportunities for saying heartfelt words to your partner, from the first "I love you" to the vows on your wedding day.

Say It Like Cyrano

No one spoke the words of love more romantically than Cyrano de Bergerac in the play by the same name by Edmond Rostand (1897). The story of Cyrano is one that every romantic person can learn from, because it shows that what truly makes a person fall in love with you is not the way you look, but what you communicate to your partner. Cyrano's story is one similar to that of The Beauty and The Beast. In each of these stories, the partner falls in love with an inner beauty.

The play is set in seventeenth century France and focuses on a love triangle between Cyrano, his friend Christian, and the woman they both love, Roxanne. Cyrano, a swordsman and poet, believes he is too ugly to ever win the love of the beautiful Roxanne. He describes the size of his nose as a "protuberance that precedes me by a quarter of an hour." So instead of trying to win her love, he loves her from afar.

Christian was very handsome, but he was awkward with both words and women. Cyrano, who had a gift for words, agreed to help him court Roxanne. Nightly, Christian stood beneath her window reciting the most beautiful words of love. Of course, the words belonged to Cyrano, who hid in a nearby bush and whispered them to Christian.

What made Cyrano's words so beautiful is that he put his mind and soul into the messages. He chose words that described how he felt about Roxanne. You can do the same by borrowing the words in this chapter and saying them to your Roxanne. She'll respond in the same way Roxanne did, by falling deeply and passionately in love with you.

Honey, Darling, Sweetie Pie

Nothing is more endearing than the first time your partner calls you by a pet name. One thing is sure—it signifies that your partner is comfortable with you. When you hear the name, it makes you feel special because it sets you apart from the others in his or her life. It's amazing what a little phrase of fondness can do.

Anyone can call you by your first name, but only a special person can make up his or her own name for you. Even friends and family can't use pet names on you. Sure, they can call you something other than your name, but it's not the same as when your partner says it.

An Affair to Remember

Ossie Davis and Ruby Dee, nicknamed Mr. and Mrs. Broadway, have been together for five decades. They met in New York in 1945 at the New Amsterdam Theater while appearing in the play *Jeb*. It was anything but love at first sight. Prior to their meeting, Ruby saw a publicity photo of Ossie and commented, "The casting people must have hired him because he looks like a country bumpkin—innocent, good-natured, and not too intelligent." Her perspective of Ossie changed dramatically one day when, out of the blue, she was struck by a bolt of attraction for him. The attraction was mutual. On and off stage they played a couple who were in love. Over fifty years later, they are still going strong in love.

Even the Famous Use Pet Names

Pet names know no boundaries. Whether rich or poor, famous or unknown, tall or short, pet names are used by all sorts of people. Here are some of the pet names that the rich and famous have called their partners:

➤ "Bunny" is what Theodore Roosevelt, Jr. called his wife Eleanor Butler Alexander Roosevelt in 1943.

➤ "Sweetheart" is what Zelda Sayre called her husband, F. Scott Fitzgerald in 1919.

➤ "Darling" came from the lips of Winston Churchill to his wife Clemintine Hozier in 1935.

➤ "Beloved" was the pet name Sophia Peabody called her husband Nathaniel Hawthorne in 1839.

➤ "Dear" was the way Anton Chekhov addressed his wife Olga Knippeer in 1902.

➤ "Darling" is what Robert Peary called his wife Josephine Diebitsch in 1908.

➤ "Dearest Girl" was the affectionate name John Keats called Fanny Brawne in 1819.

➤ "Soul" was what Leos Janacek called Kamila Stosslova in 1927.

Words of the Heart

"For beauty being the best of all we know, sums up the unsearchable and secret aims of nature."

—Robert Bridges, *The Growth of Love*, 1876

Pet Names Can Be Awkward

Using pet names is a difficult thing for some people. For some, it almost feels like they are making a commitment by using anything other than their partner's first name. For others, they just feel too reserved to use an affectionate term. If this describes you, don't feel like you are the only one, because others are uncomfortable with this form of intimacy as well. For some, using a pet name flows easily, and for others, it takes a little practice.

It's always easier to practice over the phone if you are the slightest bit uncomfortable. All you have to do is answer the phone, and when you hear your partner's voice, without hesitation, say, "Hi there, handsome/ beautiful!" Then take a deep breath and know that the next time will be easier. You can bet your partner, on the other end, will be smiling from ear to ear. She'll feel so special just because you called her something special. It works every time; test it out for yourself.

What's in a Name?

Some pet names are easier to use than others. The easiest terms are the ones that sound more like compliments. The following table has a few pet name ideas to help you get started:

Categories of Pet Names

Sweets	Other Foods	Pedestal	Basic
Cupcake	Pumpkin	Princess	Sweetheart
Sweet cakes	Sweet pea	Prince	Handsome

Sweets	Other Foods	Pedestal	Basic
Sugar	Sugar plum	Angel	Beautiful
Honey	Peach	Knight	Baby
Cookie	Hot Tamale	Goddess	Darling

I Just Called to Say I Love You

Saying "I love you" is the most beautiful gift you can give to your partner. These words are the most treasured a person can hear. You can say it a million times, and your partner will still want to hear it again, and again, and again. Relationships offer plenty of built-in opportunities to express your love through momentous occasions that you will read about in this section: declaring your love for the first time, proposing marriage, and exchanging your wedding vows.

Dr. Romance

Saying "I love you" is like watering your plants. You need to do it daily. If you don't, your relationship may wither away and die.

The First Time

Does anyone know when the perfect time is to say "I love you" for the first time? It's hard to say if it should be said after a week, month, or year after knowing your partner. Logic doesn't seem to be a part of it. Instead, this is one decision that is usually dominated by pure emotion.

You will know when the time is right. Like a baby that's ready to be born, there's no holding it back. If you are at that point in your relationship and feel unsure about doing it, just use these tips to help guide you:

➤ If there is a strong affection or warm attachment (not just sexual), love is not far behind.

➤ Choose a quiet moment so your partner can hear you.

➤ Be sober when you say it.

➤ Say it as you are either holding your partner's hands or stroking his or her face.

➤ Look your partner straight in the eye and say it.

➤ Once you have discovered someone who makes you feel special enough to think it, don't let someone else say it before you do.

➤ Mean it when you say it.

Words of the Heart

"He proposed seven times: once in a hackney-coach, once in a boat, once in a pew, once on a donkey at Tunbridge Wells, and the rest on his knees."

—Charles Dickens, 1857

Cupid's Report

Proposing marriage to someone isn't always the easiest thing to prepare for, unless you have some help. Will You Marry Me? Proposal Planners is a unique company that does all the work for you. When you are ready to propose, all you have to do is call this company, and it organizes the night for you. You have nothing to worry about except asking the big question. You can find this company at www.2propose.com.

➤ Don't waste any time once you realize how you feel.

➤ Be sincere.

➤ Say it in a foreign language first if you don't want her to understand you. This way you will be able to test it out and see how you feel.

I Want to Spend the Rest of My Life with You

Because a wedding proposal is a story that will be told and retold, it needs to be done in a way to create a storybook tale of the event. Basically, something that you will be proud to tell people the rest of your lives. Here are some guidelines to help you propose with style:

➤ Choose a meaningful date that is easy to remember, such as Valentine's Day.

➤ Choose a place that has personal meaning, such as the first place you went on a date.

➤ Incorporate details that personalize the history of your relationship.

➤ Plan the proposal for a day that your partner won't be too rushed or stressed to enjoy the moment.

➤ Select a private place, unless you don't mind others watching.

Wedding Vows

The wedding vow is the most well-known demonstration of verbal love. A vow is a line of words that are a solemn promise or assertion someone makes that binds him or her to an act, service, or condition. In the case of a wedding, it's a declaration of love.

Because religion plays a significant role in many people's lives, some of the more traditional vows were created by individual churches. Each vow has a slightly different way of phrasing the dedication words to make them fit each belief system better. The following are some of the more common religious vows:

➤ **Roman Catholic:** "I, Stephanie, take you, Craig, to be my husband. I promise to be true to you in good times and bad, in sickness and in health. I will love you and honor you all the days of my life."

➤ **Muslim:** "I pledge in honesty and with sincerity to be for you an obedient and faithful wife." "I pledge, in honesty and sincerity to be for you a faithful and helpful husband."

➤ **Jewish:** The groom says, "Behold thou art consecrated unto me by this ring according to the law of Moses and Israel." The bride remains silent, as is customary, and they are married.

➤ **Carpatho Russian Orthodox:** "I, Craig, take you, Stephanie, as my wedded wife and I promise you love, honor, and respect: to be faithful to you and not to forsake you until death do us part, so help me God, one in the Holy Trinity and all the Saints."

Words of the Heart

Here is an old English (1700s) groom's toast: "Love, be true to her; Life, be dear to her; Health, stay close to her; Joy, draw near to her; Fortune, find what you can do for her, Search your treasure-house through for her, Follow her footsteps the wide world over, And keep her always your lover!"

➤ **Traditional Hindu Mantra Baha'i Faith:** "I am the word, and you are the melody. I am the melody, and you are the word."

➤ **Baha'i Faith:** "We will all verily abide by the will of God."

➤ **Protestant:** "I, Stephanie, choose you, Craig, to be my husband, my friend, my love, the father of our children. I will be yours in plenty and in want, in sickness and in health, in failure and in triumph. I will cherish you and respect you, comfort and encourage you, and together we shall live freed and bound by our love."

➤ **United Church:** "Stephanie, I take you to be my wife, to laugh with you in joy, to grieve with you in sorrow, to grow with you in love, serving mankind in peace and hope, as long as we both shall live."

Personalizing Vows

Many couples choose to continue with tradition and repeat the vow just as others in love have done for thousands of years. However, a contemporary trend has been for couples to write their own vows.

Cupid's Report

When the Japanese marry, the vows they exchange are nonverbal. The couple participates in a ritualized ceremony of sipping three times from each of three cups of sake at a Shinto shrine during the service.

Words of the Heart

"I give you my hand!

I give you my love, more precious than money,

I give you myself before preaching or low;

Will you give me yourself? Will you come travel with me?

Shall we stick by each other as long as we live?"

—Walt Whitman

Because the heart of the wedding ceremony is the exchange of vows, creating your own can be a wonderful opportunity to share aloud just why you have chosen your mate. This declaration of intent is specifically what the ritual is about anyway. To help you begin to formulate your ideas about what you will eventually write as your wedding vow, use the following tips. They will guide you to the most beautiful, loving words designed for your wedding day:

1. You don't have to completely rewrite the traditional vows; you can simply replace certain words, phrases, or sentences to fit your thoughts.

2. Ask the officiator about ideas he may have, guidance he might offer, or what's acceptable in a vow.

3. The library offers many books on how to write personalized wedding vows. Read as many as you can so that you get a good feeling about how to write yours.

4. Collect phrases that you like.

5. Attend weddings and make notes about the words you liked in others' vows.

6. Sit down with your partner and write your vows together. Even if you don't share what you are writing, the collaborative effort will be bonding.

7. Begin early before the crunch of the wedding consumes you and you no longer have time to write something meaningful.

Saying traditional vows is nerve-wracking enough, but the thought of reciting personal vows can be absolutely terrifying for some people. The fear of forgetting something causes some people to choose not to write personal vows at all.

You don't have to let this fear come between you and what you want to say to your partner in a vow. It's common to have the person performing the ceremony to read the vow and have you repeat it after him. Most wedding ceremonies are performed this way, so you won't have to worry about fully memorizing your lines.

A Toast to Your Love

Toasting a drink to your partner is a great way to renew your commitment to each other. The nice thing about toasting is that you have drinks fairly often, making it a good way to express your love frequently.

When toasting your partner, just say the first thing that comes to your mind. Don't burden this moment with searching for the right words to say. Just cover the basics:

➤ Why you love your partner ("To the most supportive person I know")

➤ Why your partner is significant to you ("To the smartest, funniest person I've ever known")

➤ How your partner brought meaning to your life ("Here's to the person who changed my life for the better")

➤ The hopes you have for the future ("Here's to the many adventures we still have in front of us")

By doing this, both of you will fall into a routine of expressing your love a new way every time the two of you hold a glass in your hand.

"I Love You" in Other Languages

What's more romantic than saying "I love you" in a foreign tongue? Doesn't it just seem so mysteriously seductive? You can add that magic to your words with the help of the following phrases. Don't worry yourself over pronunciation. Most likely if you sound like you know how to say it, your lover will buy it. Remember, there are no sweeter words than "I love you."

Abkhazian: *Sa-u-gu-ap-x-ueit'*
Albanian: *Te dashuroje*
Apache: *Shi ingolth-a*
Bangba: *Nobato owe*
Blackfoot: *Nitsikakumimm*
Bulgarian: *Obicom te*
Canienga: *Konoronkwa'*
Carib: *Ki-sano:ma-ya*
Cherokee: *Kykeyu*
Chibcha: *Hycha mue tyzisuca*
Cornish: *Da garaf*
Cree: *Kisakihitin*
Dutch: *Ik houd van jou*
Eskimo: *Nagligivagit*
French: *Je t'aime*
Fipa: *Nene na-ku-kunda*
Georgian: *Me mi-q'var-kar-sen*

Gypsy: *Mandi komova toot*
Hausa: *Ina sanki*
Hawaiian: *Ke aloha nei au ia'oe*
Icelandic: *Eg elska pig*
Ipurina: *Nu-tarata-i*
Jivaro: *yayaxmaxmwe*
Kaggaba: *Nas ma narhluni*
Lingala: *Nalingi yo*
Mandarin: *Wo ai ni*
Nayoro: *Ku'ani 'e' ani ci'eramasu'an*
Nubian: *Ai dol-is ik-ka*
Oriya: *Mu tumaku valapai*
Pahto: *Sto sera mina*
Quechua: *Kuyaikim*
Rumanian: *Eu te inbesc*
Saka: *A tham briyaa*
Spanish: *Te amo*
Tangut: *Nga na ndu-vie*
Ubykh: *Si-gi w-a-qe-n*
Vietnamese: *Anh yeu em*
Witoto: *Odueruiteke*
Yuki: *Li miit huc*
Zulu: *Ngi ya thandela wena*

These phrases also make wonderful additions to love notes (and you don't have to worry about your pronunciation in that case).

You Have a Message

Phone messages are a fun way to communicate your love through words. All you have to do is call your partner when you know he isn't home. If you're at a loss for what to say, use one of the short messages I suggest here. Go ahead and try one out on your partner. You may be surprised by the response you get!

1. "I didn't think about you once today. Twice, three, six times maybe, but not once."

2. "Hi, I just called the hotline, and they said you are on duty tonight. My romantic side needs first aid; what is your prescription? Please return this call ASAP."

3. "I always wondered where the missing part of my heart was until I found you."

4. "I never quite understood how time could stand still until I met you."

5. "You're you, and I'm me, but I like "we" better. I can hardly wait to see you."

6. "I was walking in the garden a few minutes ago and smelled an incredible flower and thought about you. It's beautiful to see our love blossom."

7. "Hi! This is the person who's crazy about you. Please be ready for a warm hug when I see you tonight."

8. "No one has ever touched my heart the way you have. Please keep touching it."

Each day is another opportunity to express your ever-evolving feelings of love. With all of life's ups and downs, you will be able to express your feelings a million different ways if you go with what you're feeling at any given moment. The important part is letting the one you love know that you care.

The Least You Need to Know

➤ If you feel like saying, "I love you," just say it. These words are always welcomed.

➤ If you don't want to follow tradition, choosing to write your own wedding vows is a great way to go.

➤ Each time you share a drink with your partner, whether tea, soda, or wine, take advantage of the opportunity to make a toast to each other.

➤ Leaving a phone message for your partner can be a creative way to express your feelings.

Romantic Readings

During their first week of dating, David asked Sharon if anyone had ever read her a bedtime story. She thought about it for a minute and gave him a puzzled look. Before she could answer, he jumped right in and said, "Well, that's too long. What time do you go to bed? I'd like to read one of my favorite stories to you tonight." That night he read her a delightful three-minute story. She loved it so much that now, even 15 years later, he still reads her bedtime stories almost every night.

Reading aloud is a unique, intimate, and romantic experience to share with your partner. You can do it to entertain your partner, educate her, or even to express your feelings through the words in a book. Overall, reading is a loving gesture that shows your partner you care and are eager to share something that you think he or she will find interesting.

Most people consider reading to be a solo activity. But in this chapter, you will learn how to make it an enjoyable couple's activity by reading out loud to each other. You'll learn how to find the perfect material to read to your partner based on what he or she is interested in. You'll also discover the best time to read depending on the type of material. By the end of this chapter, you'll discover a uniquely romantic way to grow closer to each other.

Will You Read Me a Story?

What was your favorite story to have read to you as a child? Did you enjoy Dr. Seuss, Winnie the Pooh, the Berenstain Bears? Whatever it was, I bet there are warm memories tied to it. These memories aren't only a result of the story's content; they are important because the time was special. Storytime was an intimate time when you sat close to the one you loved, enjoying a story.

Words of the Heart

"Like freight cars of a train, words carry things. They are a delivery system that picks up something from one place and delivers them to another. They carry more than thoughts and feelings; they also carry all of the other freight that those thoughts and feelings have picked up along the way."

—Jesse Dillinger, Ph.D., from *Reasonably Thin*, 1998

Reading transforms a person whether someone reads to you or you read to yourself. It relaxes the mind and puts a new energy in a person as their eyes or ears take in the words. Unfortunately, as youth fades away and adulthood settles in, the act of shared reading seems to lose its appeal. This doesn't have to be. All you have to do is recapture the warm memories you had as a child and bring that magic back to life with your partner.

What Shelf Do I Look On?

What does your partner like to read? If you're not sure, just take a look at the pile of books your partner has in the corner or glance at his or her bookshelf. If you still don't have a clue, ask! If you don't know what your partner reads, you are missing a real opportunity to grow closer to him or her.

Growth with your partner begins through reading, but not just any reading. If you are going to read to your partner, it needs to be something that will catch his or her ear; otherwise, your partner won't hear a word you're reading. Before I teach you how to read to your partner, first take inventory of what is interesting to him or her. Use the following chart to circle all the areas your partner likes. Remember, these are the things that interest your partner, not you.

Categories of Books

Art	Architecture	Biographies
Business	Computers	Cooking
Culture	Electronics	Entertainment
Family	Fiction and Literature	Gay and Lesbian
History	Home and Garden	Horror
Humor	Kids	Medical
Mind and Spirit	Mystery	Nonfiction
Poetry	Photography	Reference

Romance	Relationships	Science
Science Fiction	Small Business	Software
Sports	Teens	Thrillers
Travel	Weddings	Wellness

By now, you should be shaping a list of topics that your partner likes. Make a list of at least five. For instance, Pat's wife Rosemary knows that he likes to read about business, electronics, computers, sports, and science fiction. Now, Rosemary has no interest in any of these subjects, so what is she going to do? How is she to develop a list of material to read to him if she hates the subjects he likes? Well, just like Rosemary, you need to take your list to the library and look through each subject area until you find a few books that look interesting to share with your partner. Bring your books home and start searching for your first material to try out on your partner.

A Book in the Hand and a Partner for the Courting

Romantic storytelling came into vogue about the time that the troubadours began to compose songs of love and yearning. As time passed, the invention of the printing press produced mass quantities of books, making them available to just about everyone. With this change, many people became literate and took up reading as a form of entertainment.

Couples also began to use reading in their courting. Both men and women took turns reading their favorite passages or poems aloud. Through books, lovers found the words they couldn't say on their own. Lovers would spend hours searching the texts for just the right words for their partner and an equal amount of time reading it to them. Books were given as gifts with special words highlighted and dedications written to make them more special. Lovers had discovered a way to tell each other their thoughts, feelings, hopes, and dreams through printed words.

Dr. Romance

Lord Byron is a great source of romantic poetry you can read to your partner. Listed here are a few short quotes that will put a lump in your partner's throat:

"Where the virgins are soft as the roses they twine, and all, save the spirit of man, is divine?"

"Maid of Athens, where we part, Give, oh give me back my heart! Or, since that has left my breast, Keep it now, and take the rest!"

"His madness was not of the head, but heart!"

"Oh! Too convincing—dangerously dear—In woman's eye the unanswerable tear!"

"Be warm, but pure: be amorous, but chaste."

An Affair to Remember

Shakespeare's *Romeo and Juliet* was set in Italy in the late 1500s. One night Romeo sneaked into a party held by Juliet's father—Romeo's father's archenemy. The moment he laid eyes on Juliet, he fell madly in love with her. They secretly married. Afterwards, her father told her she was to marry another man. Devastated by this news, she devised a scheme to stop her father's wedding plans. On the day of the wedding, Juliet drank a potion that made her appear dead. Her plan was to be put in a burial vault and taken out by Romeo. Romeo got word of Juliet's death and believed it to be true. With no purpose to live, he decided he would drink poison and end his life. He went to Juliet's vault, drank the poison, and lay next to her to die. By the time Juliet woke up, Romeo was dead beside her. The heartbroken Juliet took Romeo's dagger and killed herself so she could rest in peace beside her husband.

Words of the Heart

"When love is real love, when people's souls go out to their beloved, when they lose their hearts to them, when they act in the unselfish way in which these exquisite Old English phrases denote, a miracle is produced."

—Ernest Dimnet, from *France Herself Again*, 1916

Reading Builds Good Communication Skills

Why not pick up reading as a new aspect of your courting? It will make life more interesting than automobiles, electricity, and a big bonus at the end of the fiscal year. Reading is a form of communication training that naturally develops effective listening and communication skills. When you know how to communicate effectively, your relationship will stand a better chance of being a happy one.

If you think about what reading to your partner teaches you, it's worth more than anything you can do for your relationship. It teaches each partner how to take turns listening, and then speaking, and then giving feedback about what you've heard. This is a wonderful way of communicating. Reading to your partner will not only make you feel closer, but it will strengthen your relationship as well.

Encouraging Your Partner to Read to You

People have different comfort levels with reading out loud, so you need to be sensitive to this. The best way to get your partner to read to you is to first let him or her know it's what you would like. Second, encourage him or her to do it.

If your partner is uncomfortable reading or you suspect that he or she is, follow these tips to make reading to you more desirable for your partner:

➤ Don't read over your partner's shoulder.

➤ Cuddle up next to your partner as he or she reads, but don't follow along as your partner reads.

➤ Don't correct your partner's mispronunciations of words.

➤ Listen without interrupting.

➤ Praise your partner afterwards for reading to you. (For example, say, "You made me feel so special by reading that to me.")

➤ Compliment your partner's voice and reading ability. ("You have such a great voice, I could listen to it every night." "You should read to me more often; you're so good at it.")

➤ Close your eyes as your partner reads to you.

➤ Give your undivided attention to your partner.

When encouraging your partner to read, make his or her attempt as rewarding as possible. Sometimes people are uncomfortable reading out loud because of bad experiences in the past. By following the preceding tips, you will show your partner that reading to you is a positive experience.

Daybreak and Nightfall

Love that endures must be nurtured, built up through infusions of thoughtful words and actions. Reading to each other or providing reading material for your partner satisfies both of these requirements. It's a loving act that you can do at any time.

In this section, I've broken reading times into two periods: morning and night. These times are when most couples have time for each other.

Dr. Romance

All relationships go through easy times and difficult times. These ups and downs are just part of a being a couple. Reading to your partner when times are tough is a great way to add positive interaction between the two of you. If you have a specific problem, a good idea is to read from books about that subject matter. For instance, if Dirk and Cassie are having a problem maintaining romance after the birth of a first child, nightly readings on the subject will help the transition period to be smoother.

Morning Coffee Inspiration

You can be the catalyst that gives your partner sunshine on his or her rainy days. All you have to do is provide the appropriate reading material. When reading to your partner in the morning, keep it short. Read one paragraph up to one page, but no more. If you keep it brief, you'll keep your partner's interest.

I've listed five types of morning reading. One of these types is bound to give your partner what he or she needs to start the day off on a positive note:

1. Inspirational
2. Spiritual
3. Foretelling
4. Meditations
5. Comic relief

Inspirational

Inspirational readings teach you how to take charge of your own life through empowering messages. Because most people work every day, this is a wonderful area of reading to share with your partner. Everyday work situations can get a person down, but with a little inspiration from you, the workday will seem a little brighter.

Remember Rosemary and Pat? She decided to begin reading business material to her husband, even though she didn't have much interest in it. An interesting thing happened to Rosemary. Her perception of what business reading was changed. She came to look forward to doing it every morning. Pat, too, found that he looked forward to his daily dose of encouragement.

Here are three excellent inspirational books to start with:

➤ In *How to Win Friends & Influence People,* Dale Carnegie teaches you how to go after the job you want, improve the job you have, or make any situation work for you. Carnegie does this by teaching you commonsense principles of courteous human interactions and how to make people like you, win people over to your way of thinking, and change people without causing resentment.

➤ In *The Sky's the Limit,* Dr. Wayne Dyer teaches new ways to enhance your life by implementing strategies for liking yourself more, turning an everyday job you hate into a play break, and using many other methods to help you have career success.

➤ *Think and Grow Rich* by Napoleon Hill contains what a person needs to know about money-making secrets. The simple techniques are based on what men of great wealth and achievement have done to get there. It not only explains what to do, but how to do it.

Spiritual

If inspirational reading isn't your partner's bag, you might try something in the spiritual department. Renewing your partner's spirit in the morning will give him or her the extra strength to get through even the toughest days.

If you're a religious person, a good place to start is your religion's teachings. For example, in the Christian church, the Bible would be the source for a morning reading to your partner. For Islamic religions, it would be the Koran. Confine what you read to a paragraph or two. Just remember to read something encouraging from whichever source you read from.

If you're Christian, a good place to read from is the Psalms. These are short, uplifting songs. A sample Psalm is: "Through heaviness and pangs full sore, abide with us all night, The lord to joy shall us restore before the day be light ...." (Psalms 30:6)

Foretelling

Daily horoscopes are always fun to read. These days, horoscopes come in every subject, from love horoscopes all the way to mother-in-law horoscopes! If your partner is worried about something, choose the corresponding daily horoscope and read it to him or her. You can bet it will tell him that his troubles will soon be over.

Here is how the signs match up in terms of romance:

Sign	Best Partner	Other Compatible Signs
Aries	Libra	Leo, Sagittarius
Taurus	Scorpio	Capricorn, Virgo
Gemini	Sagittarius	Aquarius, Libra
Cancer	Capricorn	Pisces, Scorpio
Leo	Aquarius	Aries, Sagittarius
Virgo	Pisces	Capricorn, Taurus
Libra	Aries	Aquarius, Gemini
Scorpio	Taurus	Pisces, Cancer

Sign	Best Partner	Other Compatible Signs
Sagittarius	Gemini	Aries, Leo
Capricorn	Gemini	Aries, Leo
Aquarius	Leo	Aries, Sagittarius
Pisces	Virgo	Cancer, Scorpio

Meditations

Meditations are short, positive, encouraging messages. They come in a variety of subjects and are usually one or two paragraphs in length. When choosing a meditation subject to read to your partner, pick one that is an area that he or she struggles with: addictions, patience, anger, parenting, identity, and so on.

Comic Relief

Everyone enjoys a good laugh. Laughter lessens tensions and lifts your spirit even when you are at your lowest. There are lots of humor books out there to keep your partner laughing every day of the year. If your partner likes cartoons, you might start reading his favorite one to him. You might even go to the library and check out a collection of cartoons or humor books. He'll love you for it.

Silky Night Caresses

The end of the day is another good time to read to your partner. Bedtime is typically the time of day when people have extra moments to devote to themselves and their partner.

Whereas morning readings should be upbeat and filled with inspiration, evening readings should reach a deeper level. Reading at this time should be used as a time to grow closer intimately. In other words, leave educational material or relationship repair material for another time. The evening readings I recommend are those that deal with three areas: erotica; romantic poetry; and mind, body, and soul heartfelt short stories.

Erotica

Nothing takes your mind off the day's worries like stories of sexual fantasy. I guarantee you your partner will look forward to his bedtime story each night. Before you know it, your book along with your clothes will be thrown from the bed.

These bedtime stories will definitely keep your partner awake:

- ➤ *My Secret Garden* by Nancy Friday
- ➤ *Men in Love* by Nancy Friday
- ➤ *Women on Top* by Nancy Friday
- ➤ *Gates of Paradise* by Alberto Manguel
- ➤ *Passionate Hearts: The Poetry of Sexual Love* edited by Wendy Maltz
- ➤ *Forbidden Journeys: Fairy Tales & Fantasies by Victorian Women Writers* edited by Nina Auerbach
- ➤ *Pleasures: Erotica for Women by Women* edited by Lonnie Barbach
- ➤ *Beauty's Revenge* by Anne Rice
- ➤ *101 Nights of Great Sex* by Laura Corn
- ➤ *Yellow Silk: Erotic Arts and Letters* edited by Lily Pond and Richard Russo

Romantic Poetry

For some, poetry is an acquired taste, but for others, it's a real passion. Don't try to force poetry on your partner if your partner says he or she doesn't like it. You're better off reading something your partner likes. However, the idea that all men don't like poetry is just a myth.

An Affair to Remember

The story of Ester and King Ahasuerus is the biblical version of *Cinderella*. The king's first marriage ended one day when he called for his wife and she refused to come. He believed this kind of behavior would give the women of the kingdom permission to treat their husbands in the same disrespectful manner, so he divorced her. A new queen was needed to sit on the throne with him. So, just like in *Cinderella*, a notice went out announcing that the king wanted all the fair young ladies of the land to come to his castle. However, in this story, the ladies were asked to live there for two years so he could find just the right wife. During that time, they were pampered with the finest of everything. Eventually, the time came for the king to choose his new queen. All the beautiful women paraded in front of him, and he was undecided until Ester appeared. His breath was taken away when he saw her, and she became his new queen.

Because most people have heard of Shakespeare, I'll begin with him. Sure, he's better known for his plays than anything else, but listed here are three quotes from sonnets (short poems) that you can read to your partner:

➤ From Sonnet 17: "If I could write the beauty of your eyes and in fresh numbers number all your graces, the age to come would say, 'This poet lies; such heavenly touches ne'er touch'd earthly faces.'"

➤ From Sonnet 20: "A woman's face, with Nature's own hand painted, Haste thou, the master mistress of my passion."

➤ From Sonnet 154: "Love's fire heats water, water cools not love."

If you want classic love poetry to read to your partner, one of the best poets is Ovid. He was one of the first poets to bring unbridled passion and desire public:

> … *Love's climax never should be rushed, I say, but worked up softly, lingering all the way. The parts a woman loves to have caressed. Once found, caress, though modesty protest. You'll see her eyes lit up with trembling gleams, as sunlight glitters in pellucid streams; then plaintive tones and loving murmurs rise. And playful words and softly sounding sighs …*

Words of the Heart

"Mysterious is the fusion of two loving spirits: each takes the best from the other, but only to give it back again enriched with love."

—Romain Rolland

Mind, Body, and Soul Stories

Go into any bookstore, and you will see the booming mind, body, and soul section that is filled with heartfelt stories. This is the kind of book like *Chicken Soup for the Soul* or *Chocolate for a Woman's Soul*. These stories tell of triumph, morals, and significant events that change the course of someone's life. The stories keep you guessing all the way through as you wonder how people can survive the things they do. Reading these stories to your partner will give your partner a sense of thankfulness for all he or she has. Because you will be the one reading the story to your partner, he or she will include you on the list of what he or she is thankful for.

This chapter exposed you to a new way to bring closeness to your relationships by reading to your partner. Romance, as you've discovered, doesn't have to be about flowers, candy, and gifts; it's about being close and sharing. The gift of reading is one of the best gifts of all because it's given to the inside of your partner and can be treasured as long as he or she has memories.

The Least You Need to Know

➤ What you read to your partner isn't as important as the act of including it in your time together.

➤ Tailor your reading to what your partner's interests are and what he or she is experiencing in daily life.

➤ The best times of day to read to your partner are morning and bedtime.

Chapter 11

Writing a Love Letter

In This Chapter

➤ The history of love letters

➤ A love letter formula

➤ Poetry and quotations

When was the last time you received a love letter? Can you remember how exhilarated you felt when you opened it? You probably reread the letter a dozen times before you put it away for safe keeping in a special place.

If love letters make such an impact on a person, why don't more people write them? For one thing, most people don't know how to do it. (There is an art to it, you know.) By the time you finish reading this chapter, though, you'll find that writing a love letter is as easy as batting your eyes.

In this chapter, I'm going to teach you how to focus on the feeling you want to communicate to your partner. Once you've done that, it's just a matter of borrowing romantic sentiments right out of the pages to come or using them to inspire your own romantic sentiments. There's nothing more romantic than a love letter, so get ready to woo!

Words of the Heart

"For as long as I can remember, I have longed for a shared bond of intimacy and companionship with a truly significant other. To hold a genuine closeness made of trust, respect, admiration, and desire. To labour love's rich meanings and open hearts together. To share life with a special partner who takes a lifetime to know. A very unique person, yet the reflection of my soul. A partner who sees the world as a very big sandbox where we can play together."

—F. Potts, from a love letter

Dr. Romance

When writing a love letter, you don't have to write only about your undying love. Love letters can also be used to tell secrets, address concerns, express jealousy, and communicate anything that you need to say to your partner. Regardless of the type of letter, always end on a positive note so that your partner is left with a good feeling.

Passion on Paper

Although there hasn't been a comparison study, I would venture to guess that more people win the lottery these days than receive love letters. Scratching a card or picking a few numbers is much easier than writing your feelings on paper.

Putting feelings into words can be a difficult thing. Why do you think Hallmark does such great business? But when it comes to greeting cards, where is the real intimacy? The words may be beautiful, but everyone knows they're mass-produced. That takes the specialness out of them. What's missing is the labor of love.

Love Letters Predate Stamps

Love letters took centuries to evolve. Ancient Egyptian hieroglyphics told of love, and anthropologists discovered anonymous love poems on papyri and vases that dated from around 1300 B.C.E. What's interesting about these early love messages is that the emotional themes in them are the same as the love letters of today: passion, jealousy, secrecy, longing, and so on.

No Need to Reinvent the Wheel

I have included a few quotes from some famous love letters throughout history in this section for two reasons. First, I think these examples do a good job of exhibiting the flow of emotions that someone in love can create. Second, these quotes should give you some handy turns of phrase to include in your own love letters. A thoughtful, romantic citation is sure to bowl over your lover.

Let these writers be your example of how to write eloquently with passionate desire:

➤ Napoleon to Josephine (1797): "I hope to hold you in my arms before long, when I shall lavish upon you a million kisses, burning as the equatorial sun."

➤ Mozart to his wife Constanze (1790): "An astonishing number of kisses are flying about—The deuce!—I see a whole crowd of them! Ha! Ha! … I have just caught three—They are delicious!"

An Affair to Remember

The year was 1846. Robert Browning, 34, was a struggling Victorian poet who made his first contact with Elizabeth Barrett in the form of a letter. Elizabeth, 40, was an accomplished poet by this time, and Robert's correspondence was in response to her latest book of poems. This letter led to over 600 correspondences within a two-year period. A cherished friendship between the two emerged along with a deep love for one another. Elizabeth's life was not an easy one: She was physically disabled from a back injury and lived under her father's care. Her father grew fearful that he would lose his daughter as he watched her love for Browning grow deeper. The two lovers eloped, and Elizabeth informed her father of her marriage in a letter. Her father responded by choosing never to speak or write to Elizabeth again; he died 11 years later. Over the next 15 years, Robert and Elizabeth lived a lovely life together enjoying each other to the fullest. It came to an end only on the day she died. Robert held her close in his arms until her final breath.

➤ Ovid to his wife (43 B.C.E.–17 C.E.): "I am lying here worn out, among the remotest tribes and regions ... And ... you, my wife ... occupy more than your equal share in my heart. My voice names you only; no night, no day comes to me without you ... your name is ever on my wandering lips ... Tears sometimes have the weight of words."

➤ Pietro Bembo to Lucrezia Borgia (1503): "Eight days have passed since I parted from F.F., and already it is as though I had been eight years away from her, although I can avow that not one hour has passed without her memory, which has become such a close companion to my thoughts that now more than ever it is the food and sustenance of my soul."

➤ Sophia Peabody to her husband Nathaniel Hawthorne (1839): "What a year this has been to us! My definition of Beauty is, that it is love, and therefore includes both truth and good. But those only who love as we do can feel the significance of force of this."

➤ Winston Churchill to his wife Clementine (1935): "What it has been to me to live all these years in your heart and companionship no phrases can convey. Time passes swiftly, but is it not joyous to see how great and growing is the treasure we have gathered together, amid the storms and stresses of so many eventful and to millions tragic and terrible years?"

Words of the Heart

"Shall I compare thee to a summer's day?

Thou art more lovely and more temperate:

Rough winds do shake the darling buds of May,

And Summer's lease hath all too short a date.

Sometime too hot the eye of heaven shines,

And often is his gold complexion dimm'd;

And every fair from fair sometime declines,

By chance or nature's changing course untrimm'd'

But thy eternal summer shall not fade

Nor lose possession of that fair thou ow'st,

Nor shall death brag thou wand'rest in his shade

When in eternal lines to time thou grow'st.

So long as men can breathe or eyes can see,

So long lives this, and this gives life to thee."

—William Shakespeare, Sonnet 17

➤ Napoleon to Josephine (1797): "Every moment takes me further from you my adorable one, and at every moment, I find less strength to be parted from you. You are the constant object of my thoughts, and my imagination exhausts itself in wondering what you are doing."

➤ George Bernard Shaw to Ellen Terry (1897): "Yes, as you guess, Ellen, I am having a bad attack of you at present. I am restless; and a man's restlessness always means a woman; and my restlessness means Ellen."

➤ Ludwig van Beethoven to unknown (1811): "Even when I am in bed my thoughts rush to you, my eternally beloved, now and then joyfully, then again sadly … To face life I must live altogether with you or never see you. Yes, I am resolved to be a wanderer abroad until I can fly to your arms and say that I have found my true home with you and enfolded in your arms can let my soul be wafted to the realm of blessed spirits."

The Elements of a Love Letter

There are three elements to the perfect love letter:

1. Addressing your partner
2. Stating your feelings
3. The final word

Addressing Your Partner

The easiest part of a letter is the opening. That's probably because it's the part that gets the least amount of attention. Your partner is likely to rush right past it in order to get to the good parts. However, how you address the letter shouldn't be taken too lightly, because it sets the tone. For instance, a letter that begins with "My dearest love" is certainly more appealing than "To whom it may concern."

As you learned in Chapter 9, "Expressing Love Verbally," people love pet names—why not use one in the opening part of your love letter? If you're a stranger to pet names, this is a great way to try it out. You might find that writing a pet name is a lot easier than saying it, and it will make a big impact on your partner.

You might be tempted to skip the opening and start off instead with the body of the letter. Don't do it! Launching straight into the letter itself takes away from the overall warmness of the letter. Take the extra second to address your partner with a loving phrase.

If you get stuck trying to come up with an opening to your letter, try one of these:

Best Beloved

Dear

Dearest

My Dearest

Dearest and Best

Hello Love

Sweets

My Sweetest of Masters

To My Well-Beloved

To My Love

Dear Soul Mate

My Beloved

Mine Own

My Own Dearest

Ever Dearest

My Dear One

My Very Dear

Dearest of All

Cupid's Report

Grace Kelly made her way into the Prince of Monaco's heart through letters. After a brief photo shoot with Prince Rainier, she sent him a thank-you note. Smitten, Prince Rainier took advantage of the opportunity to begin a correspondence. After six months of writing letters, they fell in love. Grace eventually became the Princess of Monaco.

Most Beloved

My Darling

My Dear Love

My Dear, My Own

My Love

My Most Dearest

Soul Mate

Sweetheart

Sweet Person

There is one exception to the address rule. You can skip the salutation when you are out to achieve a dramatic or mysterious effect. This kind of letter has no opening and no ending. For most letters, however, a good opening will give your partner a special feeling right away.

Short and Sweet

A love letter doesn't have to be long. It can be any length you choose, from one sentence to 20 pages long. Length phobia is one reason people decide not to send love letters. Don't fall prey to this. You can communicate the same message by using many words or a select few. The fewer the words, the more powerful the message is. (Abraham Lincoln knew the value of brevity—just look at the *Gettysburg Address!*)

Love-Struck Themes

All great love letters have a theme. This section presents a few categories of themes for you to choose from. After you've chosen your theme, incorporate one of the accompanying quotes into your letter.

I can't get you off my mind.

This theme works well at times of intensity and at times of separation. These quotes suggest this emotional state:

➤ "I am always conscious of my nearness to you, your presence never leaves me."
—Johann Wolfgang Von Goethe

➤ "I wanted to sleep so I could be with you again in my dreams, but my day-dreams kept me up."
—Ellen Nelle

➤ "I will tend to these feelings with care, like orchids. To make sure that they stay as beautiful from the beginning and grow deep and rooted and soulful, protected from the elements and nourished with friendship and candor."
—Anonymous

Words of the Heart

"Whenever I'm caught between two evils, I take the one I've never tried."

—Mae West, *Klondike Annie*, 1936

I miss you.

When you're in love, you miss the object of your affections when separated. This feeling is part of the magic that holds couples together. So if you miss your partner and you feel like you are going to wither away and die, view it as a blessing, because it is. Here are some "missing you" quotes to help you put your feelings into words:

➤ "Away from you the world is a desert. You have taken more than my soul … "
—Napoleon to Josephine

➤ "… Facts that keep our lips from kissing, though our souls are one … I feel your fingers in my hair, and your cheek brushing mine, but mingles in some exquisite ecstasy with yours. I feel incomplete without you."
—Oscar Wilde to Constance

➤ "This bud of love, by summer's ripening breath, May prove a beauteous flower when next we meet."
—Shakespeare

The passion is unstoppable.

Passion and love are synonymous. What good is one without the other? A passionate statement will make your partner desire you more. Here are some quotes to help you tell your partner in words what your heart feels:

Dr. Romance

When composing your love letter, make sure you use pen and nice paper (no Post-it notes or scratch paper). Watch for misspellings and try to write as neatly as you can.

➤ "The most powerful symptom of love is a tenderness which becomes at times almost insupportable."
—Victor Hugo

➤ "I generally avoid temptation unless I can't resist it."
—Mae West

➤ "How can love make us strong, when it makes me so weak?"
—Anonymous

Words of the Heart

"There is no more to say: only believe

That onto you my whole heart gives

one cry, And writing, writes down more than

you receive; Sending you kisses through my

fingertips—Lady, O read my letter with your

lips!"

—Cyrano de Bergerac

I cherish you.

Who else in your life stands by you like your mate? Not many. So let your partner know just how much he or she is cherished. To help you communicate how you feel about your partner, use one of these quotes:

➤ "How is it that I have deserved so much love, so much affection? In body and soul, ever your slave."
—Prince Albert to Queen Victoria

➤ "I will stand by you, not for duty, not for pity, not for honour, but for love ... no matter whether the wine is bitter or sweet, we shall share it together and find happiness ... "
—Edith Bolling to Woodrow Wilson

➤ "I am powerless under your spell."
—Anonymous

➤ "You drive me nuts, you make me laugh, I could cry for you at the drop of a hat, you taste like peaches and cream, and I die a thousand little deaths every time I see the love in your eyes."
—Anonymous

Regardless of the feelings you have for your partner, always remember to write them down every once in a while in a love letter. Love letters are cherished because they preserve your feelings. Sometimes they are the only voice left to hold close to your heart after a relationship has passed. Life can be very unpredictable, so pass along something that your partner can keep forever.

The Final Word

Ending a letter can sometimes be more of a struggle than creating the body of the letter. Call it curiosity, but the last word or phrase is typically the first place the eyes go to when someone reads a love letter.

Here is a list of how a few historical figures ended their love letters:

➤ Zelda Sayre to F. Scott Fitzgerald (1919): "All my heart—I love you"

➤ Johann von Goethe to Charlotte von Stein (1784): "Adieu, you whom I love a thousand times"

➤ Theodore Roosevelt Jr. to his wife, Bunny (1943): "Much, much love"

➤ Lord Randolph Churchill to Jennie Jerome (1873): "Yours devotedly and lovingly"

➤ Leos Janacek to Kamila Stosslova (1927): "Keep well"

➤ John Keats to Fanny Brawne (1819): "Yours forever"

➤ John Constable to Marie Bicknell (1816): "Most faithful yours"

➤ Winston Churchill to Clementine (1935): "Your loving husband"

If you like traditional endings, there are plenty to choose from. Keep in mind that simplicity does not mean you are sacrificing significance. Just relax and go with your first impulse. Look at the following list and see which word or phrase jumps out at you:

Affectionately

All my heart and soul

Be mine

Desperately in love

I eagerly await

I hold you in my thoughts

I love you

I miss you

Longing for you

Love

Lovingly

Tenderly

Until then

Your own

Your soul mate

Yours

Yours for eternity

Yours truly

Cupid's Report

If you are Internet-savvy, you can send your partner an online love letter. All you have to do is go on the Internet and type in Love@aol.com. There you will find an icon labeled Love-Letter Generator that will take you step by step through creating a love letter especially written for your partner. After you finish, the letter is automatically sent to your partner's e-mail address.

Poetry (For Those Who Dare)

A poem is an enchanting way to tell your partner you love him or her. It's a way to express your words with a musical flair that can be very romantic. You can add poetry to a letter or send it alone as the message itself. See Appendix B, "Love Poetry," for famous poetry to quote in your love letters. The rule of thumb for using poetry is simple: If your partner likes poetry, send poetry. If your partner has no interest in it, don't send it.

The Least You Need to Know

➤ You don't need to have a reason for writing a specific love letter. The best occasion is simply because you feel like telling your partner how deeply you feel.

➤ Quotations are a good thing to include in your love letters, helping you to convey feelings you may otherwise have difficulty expressing.

➤ Love letters can be as complicated or as simple as you make them.

➤ When writing a letter, give as much attention to how you address your partner and how you end your letter as you do to the body of the letter.

That's Entertainment

He followed the guard to the carriage, and at the door of the compartment he stopped to make room for a lady who was getting out ... he felt he must glance at her once more. As she passed close by him, there was something peculiarly caressing and soft. As he looked round, she too turned her head. Her shining gray eyes, that looked dark from the thick lashes, rested with friendly attention on his face, as though she were recognizing him ... deliberately she shrouded the light in her eyes, but it shone against her will in the faintly perceptible smile.

This scene is from the movie *Anna Karenina* (1935), in which Greta Garbo plays the heroine in Tolstoy's tragic love story. This scene, like many others on film, moves our souls with desire and passion. You know—the same emotions you feel in your relationship with your partner—or would like to feel.

In the area of love, there are two creative mediums that can have a powerful effect on your relationship. These are music and film. This chapter will explore each of these mediums. You'll learn how entertainment can stimulate your sense of romance as well as how to use each medium to heighten the connection you have with your partner.

Music: A Course in Love

"I love you; you love me; we're a happy family …." Do you remember that song from childhood? You may even recognize it as the popular song Barney sings. Through music we explore and learn about myths, ideals, and the parameters of love.

With each year, our understanding of what we hear and feel in music deepens, especially as we begin to experience love. We hear thoughts similar to ours being sung on the radio. We listen with curiosity and hope of happy endings or perhaps guidance to help us. We learn that music intensifies our feelings, triggers emotions, and binds memories forever to songs that are associated with our love lives. We learn that music is our friend and our teacher. Because of this, music has attained a central importance in the world of romance and romantic relationships.

Musical Inspiration

Music makes an evening extra romantic. It just has a way of making people want to be close to their partners. That's what happened when roommates Norma, Barbara, and Brenda had their boyfriends over for dinner. The evening went well, but the highlight was after dessert when the music was turned on. Norma's boyfriend looked at her and said, "Would you like to dance?" She giggled from embarrassment and said, "Only if everyone else does." So they did. Barbara turned up the soft music and turned down the lights, and everyone paired off, swaying to the romantic music for the rest of the evening. The night just wouldn't have been the same without music.

Music can inspire or influence romance in so many ways. It's hard for music not to inspire; it stirs the emotions when singers sing about love's emotional extremes. When you hear a song that says, "I'm in the mood for love simply because you're near me," it's hard to resist having an emotional reaction to what you hear. Music facilitates romance between you and your partner by moving both the intellect and emotions.

An Affair to Remember

Mozart, the great composer, had a devoted love affair with his wife Constanze. They met while Mozart was staying with his mother. Near her lived the Webber family with four daughters. Initially, Mozart fell in love with Constanze's sister, Aloysia. That relationship lasted for one year until her feelings for him cooled. As time went on, Mozart began to long for a wife, and he turned to Constanze. Their relationship developed into one of deep affection and understanding. He needed her as much as she needed him. Their life together was filled with constant adversity. Both Mozart and Constanze suffered ill health and grieved the loss of four out of six of their children. There were constant financial struggles and frequent separations as Mozart traveled to faraway places to earn money. During times of separation, Mozart and Constanze stayed close by writing love letters to each other. Eventually, after many years of great struggles, Mozart's health began to deteriorate. The night he died, his wife worried that he was overworking himself while trying to complete a commissioned score. He never completed the piece. One hour prior to his death, his devotion remained with Constanze. He asked his sister-in-law to take care of his wife after his death.

Using Music to Draw Out Romance

Now that you know how music can naturally foster romance, the following tips will help you to use music in your own relationship to increase romance between you and your partner:

➤ If you are out and about doing something with your partner and you hear your partner say, "Wow, I love that song," don't just let the moment pass. Find out what the song is and buy it. Add it to your romantic collection.

➤ If you attend a Broadway show or a romantic film that moves you emotionally, buy the soundtrack. This way, you'll be able to bring back the intense emotions you experienced again and again with your partner.

➤ Jump at the chance to dance together when music moves you.

➤ Going to concerts—especially by singers well known for romantic ballads—can put you in the middle of emotional moments that are bigger than life.

Cupid's Report

Try these romantic CDs: *Breathless* by Kenny G; *Love Deluxe* by Sade; *What Matters Most* by Tom Postilio; *Falling Into You* by Celine Dion; *Saxuality* by Candy Dulfer; *Love Songs* by David Sanborn; *Because You Loved Me* by Johnny Mathis; and *We Are in Love* by Harry Connick Jr.

What Love Songs Do for Us

Couples have been using music in courtship for a very long time. Have you ever wondered why? Although the answer varies from person to person, there are some common reasons:

➤ It has a way of speaking the words that couples feel for each other or assists people in saying what they are too uncomfortable to say on their own.

➤ It gets you in the mood for love.

➤ It keeps the idea of romance alive.

➤ It encourages people to express love in graceful ways.

➤ It can help draw souls together as though they were one.

➤ It idealizes what we don't have, but would like to.

➤ It is hypnotic and seductive.

➤ It revives romantic memories.

➤ It has the power to transform and enrich your life.

➤ It draws out hidden emotions.

➤ It makes you sing with joy, sorrow, or longing.

➤ It gives you strength.

➤ It softens your heart, making it easier for someone's love to enter your world.

➤ It stokes hot fantasies.

➤ It causes the body to either relax or become excited.

➤ It changes your mood.

➤ It intensifies your experience of feelings of love.

➤ It causes yearning for love.

➤ It heightens the senses.

➤ It allows you to share in various moods with your partner.

Words of the Heart

"There is music here that softer falls than petals from blown roses on the grass."

—Alfred Lord Tennyson

Love songs help to break down a person's defenses and open them up to love. If music can calm the savage beast, imagine what it will do to a partner who loves you. This is why it's important to make music a part of your relationship.

Let Me Serenade You

The act of serenading the one you love has been around for as long as there has been music. The Cheyenne, for instance, used serenading during their courtship period to win over a woman's heart. The man would hide in the woods until his love passed by. When she did, he'd serenade her with a special love flute, hoping his love songs would open her heart to him.

If you are considering serenading your partner or encouraging your partner to sing to you, but are afraid to try, remember the following:

➤ It doesn't matter whether you have a bad voice—your lover will be bowled over by the effort and the expression of emotion your serenade conveys.

➤ A serenade is an act of complete selflessness, done strictly for the pleasure of your partner.

➤ There can be tremendous bonuses in terms of how special it makes your partner feel about you.

➤ If your partner sings to you, make sure you praise him for it, compliment his voice, and never laugh at him.

➤ Serenading doesn't have to be done outside the window; you can serenade your partner while doing the dishes or making the bed.

➤ You don't need to compose your own lyrics and music; just sing your favorite love songs.

➤ You don't have to sing at the top of your lungs; try whispering a song in the ear of the one you love.

Setting the Mood

Music entertains us and can help set the mood for romance. In case you don't have time to research romantic songs, refer to this list the next time you feel like serenading your love or simply want songs to serenade the two of you:

"All I Ask of You" from *The Phantom of the Opera* by Rice and Webber
"All My Life" by K-ci & Jojo
"As Long As You Love Me" by The Backstreet Boys
"Crazy for You" by Madonna
"Endless Love" by Lionel Richie and Diana Ross
"Everything I Do (I Do It for You)" by Bryan Adams

"Fallin' in Love" by Hamilton, Joe Frank, and Reynolds

"Have You Ever Really Loved a Woman?" by Bryan Adams

"I Won't Believe My Eyes" by Tom Postilio

"Knocks Me Off My Feet" by Stevie Wonder

"Lady in Red" by Chris deBurg

"Love Is a Gift" by Olivia Newton-John

"My Heart Will Go On" by Celine Dion

"One More Night" by Phil Collins

"Sweet Love" by Anita Baker

"The Body That Loves You" by Janet Jackson

"The First Time Ever I Saw Your Face" by Roberta Flack

"The Roof" by Mariah Carey

"Truly, Madly, Deeply" by Savage Garden

Movies as Romantic Inspiration

In the movie *Somewhere in Time*, Christopher Reeve plays a man who falls in love with a woman (Jane Seymour) in a portrait. He becomes entranced by the look in her eyes and the enchanting smile on her face. However, it would seem impossible for a relationship to develop because she lived in another era. Somehow, he wills himself back in time. Just as luck would have it, she's engaged to be married; however, she falls in love with him at first sight. Ironically, this takes place as he's walking past her as she's having her portrait painted. That, of course, was the look captured in the portrait he fell in love with initially. In his room at the end of the day, he is pulled back to the present when he pulls modern coins from his pocket. There is a happy ending, but it takes his dying an actual death from a broken heart to be reunited with his love.

Cupid's Report

An estimated 22 million people go to the movies once a week.

Watching a romantic movie gets a person's heart pounding. And don't believe anyone who says that only women become emotional during movies—it isn't true. Men have the same range of emotions that women have; it's just that they have been trained to hide them better. That is, they can hide them until they sit down to watch a romantic love story with their partner.

An Affair to Remember

Screen legend Greta Garbo was a figure of loveliness. Actor John Gilbert had dark, Valentino-like looks with expressive eyes. Garbo and Gilbert were first paired in the movie *Flesh and the Devil*. During their first love scene together, the chemistry was so strong between the two of them that the director admitted that he was embarrassed to call "Cut." Instead, he and his six-man crew quietly left the studio, so they could finish the scene in privacy. The couple fell passionately in love. Gilbert desperately wanted to marry Garbo, but she chickened out three times. Gilbert took to heavy drinking to help him cope. Finally, she ended their love affair after starring in their last movie together. Eventually, Garbo left Hollywood at the age of 36 because she was tired of it. She never married. Gilbert ended up marrying four times and met a drunken death at the age of 39.

Just What the Doctor Ordered

Watching romantic movies with your partner is good for your relationship. In case you aren't sure why, just read the following reasons. They are sure to make you want to run out and rent one tonight:

1. They give you a chance to cuddle.

2. They take your mind off of current problems that may be causing stress in your relationship.

3. They make you appreciate your partner more.

4. They make you thankful for the situation you and your partner are in.

5. They serve as role models of how to resolve similar problems you may be facing in your relationship.

6. They open the lines of communication to talk about relationship issues.

7. They allow a couple to be transported vicariously to another time and place by identifying with the couple on the screen.

8. They spark your creative imagination by giving you new ways to romance each other.

9. They enable you to communicate messages to your partner through body language during the film—for example, by squeezing your partner's hand when the actors say what you want your partner to hear.

Make It a Blockbuster Night

One of the most fun ways to be romantic with your partner is by watching a video at home alone together. This list of romantic movies will help you get started:

➤ *Anna Karenina* (1935) stars Greta Garbo in a story about an adulterous love affair in nineteenth-century Russia.

➤ In *Casablanca* (1945), Humphrey Bogart and Ingrid Bergman play star-crossed lovers during World War II in Morocco.

➤ In *The African Queen* (1951), Humphrey Bogart and Katharine Hepburn find unlikely love while trying to escape the Germans in a boat on the river.

➤ *Dr. Zhivago* (1965) stars Omar Sharif and Julie Christie as lovers who are separated during the Russian Revolution.

➤ *10* (1979) stars Bo Derek, Dudley Moore, and Julie Andrews in a comical love triangle.

➤ *The Woman in Red* (1984) is a light-hearted love comedy about obsession starring Kelly LeBrock, Gilda Radner, Gene Wilder, and Charles Grodin.

➤ *The Bodyguard* (1992) stars Kevin Costner and Whitney Houston in a love affair between two unlikely people.

Dr. Romance

Before you start popping the popcorn and pouring the sodas, send your partner two movie tickets in the mail. Along with the movie tickets, send a simple invitation to come to your house for dinner and a movie. The ticket will say which movie you'll be showing in your theater that night.

Romantic Categories

Nearly all movies treat love in some respect, but romantic movies are those that focus exclusively on love. In these movies, the themes can cover a broad range of subjects, from virginal love, love after marriage, love in the hereafter, and everything in between. Movies offer a wide range of exposure to the issues that arise in everyday relationships, and they do so within three different romantic categories: light-hearted love, dramatic love, and sexual love.

The three categories have a dual purpose for couples who watch them. First of all, they allow you to view various movie topics at a level you find comfortable. Second, sometimes watching a movie together can be for reasons other than pure viewing pleasure. Sometimes you will want to share subject matter with your partner.

The following is an outline of the three categories. The next time you want to watch a movie with your partner, let this guide help direct which kind of movie category would best meet your relationship needs.

Light-hearted love films (for example, *You've Got Mail* or *Pretty Woman*) help you to do the following:

➤ Take the seriousness of life away for a little while

➤ Make you laugh and soften up

➤ Cause you to laugh at your own situation by laughing at actors onscreen

➤ Discharge some stress

➤ Experience a happy ending

Dramatic love films (for example, *When a Man Loves a Woman* or *Stepmom*) help you do the following:

➤ Take a serious look at a serious relationship issue

➤ Let yourself cry in a safe environment or experience a cathartic release with your partner

➤ Show your partner what your issue is

➤ Provide a reality check on your own relationship

➤ Reassess how important or unimportant much of what we worry about really is

Sexual love films (for example, *9 ½ Weeks* or *Eyes Wide Shut*) help you do the following:

➤ Learn (or teach your partner) new techniques

➤ Have exposure to alternative lifestyles you fantasize about

➤ Try out something visually before experimenting with it physically

➤ Provide an erotic thrill or satisfy voyeuristic curiosity

➤ Set the mood for passion

➤ Give yourself permission to be frisky or erotic

➤ Stretch the boundaries of your sexual repertoire

Cupid's Report

In the book *Kisses*, editor Lena Taboi compiled a list of some of the women who had the privilege of pressing their lips to the mouth of Clark Gable in passionate kisses during his movie career: Mary Astor, Carroll Baker, Constance Bennett, Claudette Colbert, Joan Crawford, Marion Davies, Doris Day, Yvonne de Carlo, Madge Evans, Greta Garbo, Ava Gardner, Greer Garson, Jean Harlow, Helen Hayes, Susan Hayward, Grace Kelly, Deborah Kerr, Hedy Lamarr, Vivien Leigh, Carole Lombard, Sophia Loren, Myrna Loy, Jeanette Macdonald, Marilyn Monroe, Eleanor Parker, Marie Prevost, Jane Russell, Norma Shearer, Alexis Smith, Barbara Stanwyck, Gene Tierney, Lana Turner, Fay Wray, and Loretta Young.

Taking Love Cues from Movies

Hollywood specializes in dramatizing love, so consider the tips it gives you. How often does the average couple experience what couples do in the movies? Not very often, but if you take lessons from the lovers onscreen, you can learn to enhance your relationships by duplicating some of what you see.

For example, you may not be able to afford to fill your partner's home with 100 bouquets of long-stem roses as shown in the movie *Bed of Roses*, but you can cover your bed with rose petals for a similar effect. Likewise, you may not have a chance to do the *Ghost* experience and make love covered with sculpting clay. However, you can reenact the tub scene that you saw in *The English Patient* or *Bull Durham*.

The point is that you have an opportunity to learn a few new things from what you see in the movies, so why not try them out on your partner? It could be a breathlessly romantic experience for the two of you!

The Least You Need to Know

➤ Music and film are great ways to broaden your experience of romance with your partner.

➤ Let music draw out the passion in your romance by setting the tone for the mood you want to experience with your partner.

➤ Serenading your partner takes a lot of guts, but the rewards will be bountiful.

➤ Watching romantic movies heightens your emotional awareness.

Chapter 13

A Taste of Love

In This Chapter

➤ Desirable dining

➤ Sexy snacks

➤ Passionate picnics

Barbara and Wes were quite the spectacle when they went out to eat. They'd been dating only a few weeks, and their passion was evident in how they dined. They didn't just eat their food, they seductively fed each other.

Not only this, but they did so using their hands and suggestive gestures. It was a little embarrassing for others to watch, but at the same time, people couldn't help but admire the chemistry they had and their passion for each other. And the food provided the means of expression.

Romance would not be the same without food. Have you ever watched a couple in love eat dinner in a restaurant? It's hard to tell what they think is more delicious—the meal or each other!

Eating gives us an opportunity to be close to our partners. It's a time to sit near them, a time to share in conversation, and a time to enjoy not only the meal but the pleasure of each other. In this chapter, I'll teach you how to make your meals passionately romantic. You'll see that what you eat isn't necessarily the main ingredient to your meals. The craving that you have for your partner and the presentation of the meal

Words of the Heart

"There is something to me very softening in the presence of a woman, some strange influence, even if one is not in love with them ...."

—George Gordon Byron, 1814

Cupid's Report

In ancient civilizations, various fruits and vegetables were believed to promote fertility. Interestingly, they were believed to hold this value merely because of the phallic-shaped outsides or inside markings that resembled genitalia such as bananas, cucumbers, or the insides of a strawberry and figs.

are what make it tasty. You will learn how to impress your partner by "just whipping up something," cooking dinner at home, serving breakfast in bed, or preparing a lavish picnic on the grass. All the tips are just ahead, so keep reading.

The Food Quiz

You can tell a lot about a couple by watching them eat a meal. For people who are very close, a meal is an occasion to connect. Take the following quiz to find out how you and your partner fare:

1. When you are out to dinner with your partner, you

   a. Share food by feeding your partner with your fork.

   b. Feed your partner with your fingers.

   c. Let your partner dip his fork in your food and take a bite.

   d. Don't share food with your partner.

2. If a little sauce is on your partner's mouth during dinner, you

   a. Wipe off your partner's face with your napkin.

   b. Tell your partner he has sauce on his mouth and lick his face seductively.

   c. Verbally tease your partner that you will use your tongue to lick off the sauce, but don't actually do it.

   d. Don't say a word because you know he'll eventually wipe it off.

3. After dinner, when it's time for dessert, do you

   a. Share one dessert using two forks, possibly feeding your partner a bite off your fork.

   b. Use one fork to feed each other.

   c. Maybe have just a bite of your partner's dessert but order a cappuccino and enjoy his company and more conversation.

   d. Skip dessert and head home because you're out of things to say to each other or you have things to do at home.

Scoring this test is very simple. All you have to do is count up how many a's, b's, c's, and d's you have. The category with the most like letters is the one that your relationship falls into.

Mostly A's: New Love

If most of your answers fell into this category, there's a good chance that your relationship is still in the early stages of blossoming love. It's like a new flower: fresh, beautiful, untainted. Meals are a reason to spend time together, a chance to be physically and conversationally close to each other. Early romance is a time when you are on your best behavior and a little uncertain of the commitment. Eating a meal together offers the chance to demonstrate your affection for your partner. Although each partner sticks to his own plate for the most part, you might share one or two furtive tastes and hold hands through the meal or share a light kiss or two.

Mostly B's: Lustful Love

This category is what poets write about and artists paint. It's the passionate core of love. You move into this stage when you begin to feel confident that your romantic feelings are mutual. This is the time when you want to devour every aspect of your partner: his words, his touch, his soul, his mind, everything. This is when you experience an inability to concentrate, sleep, or eat. It's when you feel that you can't be away from each other for more than a minute. Eating takes on a sensuousness as you hand-feed your partner, lick his fingers, and quell one appetite while stimulating another.

Mostly C's: Comfortable Love

This category is the ideal category, so be happy if you are here. You and your partner have a close, strong bond to each other. The two of you are still playful with each other; it isn't as blatantly sexual as before, but there is an unmistakable intimacy between you.

Dr. Romance

Each person grows up experiencing different associations with food. Do you know your partner's background? Does she know yours? Look at your relationship and see if your different food backgrounds have affected your relationship at all. Usually this becomes a topic of discussion during holidays. If you don't know, now is the best time to find out. You can make it your next dinner conversation topic.

Mostly D's: Red Alert Love

If your quiz score landed you in this category, then you should be concerned. The closeness you once felt for your partner just isn't there anymore. During meals, you don't touch each other, you don't share food, and the conversation has died down. Dining together is no longer a bonding experience, but a time to fill your stomach. In the process, you are neglecting to feed your love. You might try more of the behaviors specified in the C choices to reignite the passion you once felt.

Don't lose hope if you didn't score as high as you would like to. This is not a pass-fail exam, but more of a practice test for your real-life relationship. And guess what? You've lucked out, because this chapter contains the study material to help you pass the test with your partner!

Tickling Your Heart with Food

As the old saying goes, "Laughter is brightest where food is best." The trick to having bright laughter and good food is to share a meal with your partner. Sharing a meal does not mean rushing through each bite with the focus on the food. If you do this, you miss the main course: your partner. Eating and making love are not entirely dissimilar, especially if you view your partner as a delicious delicacy to kiss, lick, and nibble.

It's time to get into the kitchen. For those of you who don't know your way around the kitchen, don't fret. I'm here to help you work around whatever cooking deficit you might have.

A meal can be anything you want it to be. It can be a midnight snack, a four-course dinner, or strawberries dipped in champagne. More than a meal, it's an indulgence in your senses you'll want to share with your partner.

Words of the Heart

"Time was away and somewhere else, there were two glasses and two chairs and two people with one pulse."

—Louis MacNeice, 1941

Whip Up a Little Something

A lot of people snack more often than they eat a full meal, so snacks are a good place to start sharing food with your partner. No, I'm not referring to popcorn or pretzels, but sensuous, romantic bites to devour with your lover. Anyone can prepare these no-fail romantic snacks:

➤ **Fresh strawberries or a bowl of mixed berries.** Make sure to include a bowl of whipped cream for dipping. For a sweeter dip, try a bowl of melted chocolate. For this, all you do is melt chocolate chips in the microwave for 30 seconds, stir, and dip.

➤ **Crackers, cheese, grapes, and wine.** For this snack, browse the cracker isle and find a tasty-looking cracker. Make sure the cracker is large enough to hold cheese. For a cheese, go to the deli section and look for a kind of sliced cheese that you like. Always ask the deli worker for a sample if you are not sure of your choice.

➤ **A plate of assorted cookies, fruit slices, and chocolates.** The easiest way to collect these items is in the bakery of your grocery store. To make the plate look irresistible, choose a variety of items with different colors and textures. Pick out around eight items, and you'll be set.

➤ **Steamed vegetables with melted butter for dipping.** To prepare this snack, pick a variety of vegetables. For a good array, try using asparagus (green), carrots (orange), baby corn from a can (yellow), bell peppers (yellow, orange, red, green), and any kind of sturdy vegetable. To prepare the vegetables, wash them and slice them into thick strips. Steam them for 10 minutes, and then serve them with melted butter or margarine.

➤ **Bite-size sandwiches on seed-covered rolls.** On a platter, place a variety of sliced meats and cheeses and wheat, rye, and sourdough rolls. Don't forget the bowls of condiments.

Get Some Snaction

To snack romantically, you need to make the snack special. Use these tips to set the stage:

1. The presentation of food is very important. Put snacks in glass bowls or pretty containers to make them look inviting.

2. Snacks that are dipped into sauces or creams have a little extra passion power. Place sauces in small dishes on the side of the snack.

3. When snacking the romantic way, make sure you have plenty of time on your hands.

4. Use cloth napkins to add an element of extravagance.

5. Dim the lights and play soft music to set the mood. The message conveyed will be that you are going to be eating for a while, so you need to get comfortable.

6. Wear comfortable but sexy clothing that you don't mind dripping things on. Items that can be unbuttoned or unzipped work best.

7. Don't be afraid to sample your snacks on areas other than the mouth and fingers. Necks and wrists make a good place to begin.

8. Feeding each other is always more fun than feeding yourself.

9. A kiss between bites will make the snack *really* tasty!

Put a Little Spice into It

Centuries ago, spices were commonly used to express certain sentiments, just as flowers are today. When a man wanted to communicate something to his partner, he let the spices do it for him. The following list provides the meanings of the more common spices. So the next time your partner invites you over for dinner, don't bring the traditional bouquet of flowers; bring spices instead. And make sure your partner understands what you are saying.

Spice	Message
Allspice	Compassion
Basil (common)	Hatred
Basil (sweet)	Good wishes
Bay leaf	Consistency (I'll never change)
Cloves	Dignity
Coriander	Concealed merit
Dill	Good spirits
Fennel	Strength
Nutmeg	Expected
Parsley	Festivity, useful knowledge
Rosemary	Memories
Saffron	Don't abuse our relationship
Sage (garden)	Esteem
Sage	Domestic virtue
Tarragon	Unselfishness
Thyme	Activity; thriftiness

Do It Together

Have you ever cooked a dinner with your partner? If you have, you know just how fun it can be. The trick to making it a success is a good bottle of wine, seductive music, and sharing in the preparations. In fact, your time together in the kitchen can be the highlight of dinner!

Putting together a dinner at home can seem overwhelming if you're not a regular in the kitchen. You have nothing to worry about. I have just the solution with an Italian meal anyone can fix:

> Lasagna with meat sauce
> Tossed green salad
> Garlic bread

This meal is easy to prepare, and there will be a lot left over for late-night snacking. All you have to do is boil your lasagna noodles until they are cooked (about 20 minutes) and then alternate layers of noodles, meat sauce (jar sauce works fine), and mozzarella cheese until you reach the top of the pan. Sprinkle the top with parmesan cheese, and then bake it for 45 minutes at 350 degrees. Toss your salad, heat up your bread, and your romantic dinner is ready!

Words of the Heart

"Youth, beauty, graceful action seldom fail; but common interest always will prevail."

—John Dryden, 1672

Breakfast in Bed

Breakfast has a different feel than dinner—the birds singing, the sun shining, the smell of hot coffee coming your way. This is a lazy time to lounge around together and laugh and giggle while nibbling on something light.

I don't recommend spending a lot of time cooking for breakfast in bed (after all, the idea is to get back under the covers with your honey as soon as possible). If you do a little shopping ahead of time, you should be able to put together a breakfast of muffins, fruit, orange juice, and coffee in no time.

Don't forget the special touches that make a meal extra special. What candles do for a dinner table is what a single flower does for breakfast: it adds romance to the meal.

Do You Want to Go on a Picnic, Boo Boo?

What better way to feed your love than to share a meal on a picnic blanket? It's the most natural combination: food, romance, and the great outdoors.

When preparing for a picnic, consider the location and the food. Location is possibly more important than food because it sets the stage for the meal. When you are thinking about places to picnic, make privacy a priority. Consider scouting out your spot beforehand to avoid winding up picnicking alongside a Little League game.

Here are a few location suggestions:

➤ Under a grove of trees

➤ On a cliff along the shore

➤ On the grass next to a lake

➤ Along a river front

➤ At the beach

➤ Under the stars at midnight

➤ In a boat in the middle of a lake

➤ At the top of a mountain

➤ In a field of wildflowers

➤ Next to a waterfall

➤ In the wine country next to a vineyard

➤ Under a shady tree in the country

➤ At a park next to a stream

➤ Overlooking city lights

How to Prepare

You have a few choices in terms of how to prepare. One option is to have your meal put together by a gourmet grocery store. (Just make sure that you talk with them about what you would like.) A lot of stores will even go so far as to provide the picnic basket. This is the ideal way to go because the store does everything for you, including picking out the wine in some cases.

If you make a picnic meal yourself, however, you add a warm home-cooking touch to the picnic. Some suggestions for what to bring are turkey sandwiches on focaccia bread, pasta salad, sliced fruit, and cookies.

Making Your Picnic Extra Special

When you get to your location, take special care in setting up your picnic spot. You want it to be as romantic and comfortable as possible.

Words of the Heart

"An empty stomach is not a good political adviser."

—Albert Einstein, 1931

Here are some tips for setting up:

1. Spread out the largest and thickest blanket you can find. The color isn't important at all, because this will only be the background.

2. On the top of the blanket, spread out a crisp, white tablecloth. It's important to make it white so that the variety of food is highlighted against the starkness of the white.

3. Bring the finest silverware and dishes you have. Remember, this is not a casual meal; it's a special treat for you and your partner.

Dr. Romance

Surprising your partner with a little lasciviousness during a meal is a great way to recharge romance between the two of you.

4. When arranging the food, make sure you have plenty of baskets lined with white napkins to hold assortments of fruit and breads.

5. If you are having wine or champagne, bring an ice bucket and ice for chilling before the meal.

6. Bring a couple of small pillows to rest your heads on and a throw blanket in case it gets a little chilly.

7. Bring along a cassette player and romantic music if you prefer man-made music to the music of nature.

8. Bring a vase and pick some wildflowers for the centerpiece.

Making a picnic grand takes a little more planning than just picking up fast food and bringing it along. Keep in mind that a real picnic is not just a meal, it's an opportunity for romance. So go ahead and pack all you need to—you'll enjoy every second of it!

One Last Bite

Eating a meal can be an unforgettable experience. Sometimes this feeling is due to the kind of food we are eating. Other times, it's because the company is so enjoyable. Either way, food and love are undeniably sensual delights. Nothing makes the mouth water like pleasing food or a luscious partner.

Sharing a meal with the one you love makes you complete. It promotes an exquisite feeling of mutual warmth and generosity. Any time of day is good for sharing delectable foods with the one you love; it's just a matter of doing it.

The Least You Need to Know

➤ The day you stop feasting on your partner is the day your emotions begin to get hungry.

➤ Bring back the fun to your relationship by enjoying a meal together. Sit close, look at each other, and alternate bites of food with kisses. It will be so delicious that you'll want the same thing for dinner the next night.

➤ Eating with your partner can be a sensuous experience, especially if you eat or serve the food in a sexually suggestive way.

➤ Transform any meal with music, candles, and the best tableware you have. Don't just save your best for special occasions; use it to just celebrate being together.

Seducing Your Senses

Long, long ago, when a knight took a maiden to dinner, he usually wore his suit of armor. Although he looked nice, it prevented him from feeling his maiden's gentle caresses, hearing her soft voice, seeing her beauty, tasting her lips, and inhaling the fragrance of her delicate skin. This happened date after date until finally, one day, the maiden learned how to seduce the suit of armor right off of the knight. She did it by intensely focusing on his senses, one at a time, until she was able to penetrate his protective armor.

Do you ever feel numb enough to your senses that you relate to the knight in armor? Maybe you are wearing a metaphorical suit of armor when you're with your partner. Sure, you may need to keep your armor on in your everyday world, but you shouldn't be wearing it with your partner. The quickest way to remove your protective layer or your partner's is to seduce the senses: sight, touch, smell, sound, and taste. Pleasing your partner's five senses is also the secret to great romance.

Dr. Romance

Spend a night concentrating on each of your lover's senses. Five senses may seem like a lot, but most of the senses don't require much effort to please. For example, while eating dinner (taste), burn a scented candle (sight and smell), play music (sound), and pat or stroke your partner's arm (touch). Give it a shot and see just how pleasing your evening is for the two of you.

The ability to both give and receive love is the most important aspect of a relationship. This chapter will show you five new aspects of giving through each of the senses. You are going to learn how to satisfy each one of them at a level you never thought possible and leave your partner wanting more. When you fill your partner's senses, you fill his soul.

A Vision of Romance

The sense of sight is a key player in keeping your romance alive. As humans, we prefer to look at things that look good. This includes you; if you look good, your partner is more likely to keep his or her eyes on you. Because visuals are so very important to romance, I spend the majority of this chapter teaching you how to appeal to your partner's sense of sight.

Because looking good is important, you need to work with what you have as a way to attract your partner's attention. You don't need to go on a crash diet or undergo plastic surgery to reshape your body. You just need to learn how to maximize your potential through your appearance.

Mirrors Don't Lie

Take a good look at yourself in the mirror. Look critically, as though you were a stranger. Notice all the details that make you who you are. What physical features do you like? You'll want to build on them to make your overall package look the best it can look.

Once you know your strengths, you need to examine yourself for areas that need improvement. Many people get so used to the way they look that they don't see the minor fix-ups that could be done. I'm not suggesting you call a plastic surgeon, but it might not hurt to call your hairdresser.

Appearance is an interesting thing, because it's the *sum* of the parts that make you attractive, not the individual parts. What this means is that your partner will view you as more appealing if you focus on your overall package rather than just on your best feature.

An Affair to Remember

The great love affair between Cleopatra and Mark Antony took place around 30 B.C.E. against the backdrop of the Roman Empire. Cleopatra was described as beautiful and bewitching to all who met her. Julius Caesar was so entranced with her that he made her the queen of Egypt. Three years after Caesar's assassination, the Roman Empire came under control of Mark Antony, who was described as flamboyant, generous, and a courageous general. Cleopatra kept a close eye on Antony and accompanied him everywhere he went. In time, she bore him a set of twins, one of each sex. His love for her began to distract him from his work in the military. At one point, Antony accused Cleopatra of betraying him with the enemy camp, Octavian. In anger, she fled to a secret hideaway and sent word of her own death. It is said that when he was told of the news, he cried out, "I shall soon be with you!" and fell on his sword to die. Cleopatra had him brought to her as he lingered in death. She held him on her bed and cradled him in her arms. Wanting to be buried in the same tomb as Antony, she killed herself with the bite of a poisonous snake.

To show you what I mean, let's take a look at 45-year-old Bill. He knew that he had such nice-looking green eyes that, at one point in his life, he centered his wardrobe around them. One day, however, it dawned on him that he hadn't bought new clothes in nearly 10 years. As he stood in front of his mirror, he noticed that not only did his clothing lack vibrancy, but so did his overall appearance. At that point, he realized that he needed some updating. His wife was going to be out of town for a week, and he wanted to surprise her when she returned, so he got to work.

That week he went to the dentist and had his teeth whitened, had his hair cut and colored, got a manicure and pedicure, and bought updated clothes, a nice watch, and modern eye-glasses. He looked like a new person! Not only

Cupid's Report

"Intimacy must be created and re-created. It's not an accomplishment that sits like a trophy on your mantle. It's a feeling, an experience, that is only alive in the moment, in the now."
—Gregory Godek, from *Romantic Questions*

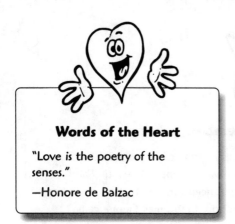

Words of the Heart

"Love is the poetry of the senses."

—Honore de Balzac

that, but he also felt better than he had ever felt, and it showed. Bill's wife didn't recognize him when he picked her up at the airport a week later. As a matter of fact, she couldn't take her hands off of him. Bill said it was the best investment that he could have ever made in his relationship. The changes Bill made were minor. What was major, however, was how much more attractive he looked.

The Big Three

There are three main areas that people let slip in their appearance: teeth, hair, and clothing. As people age, teeth gradually discolor from food, drink, and tobacco (if you smoke). The change is so gradual that it goes unnoticed. However, like it or not, your smile probably isn't as bright as it once was, and that makes you less attractive.

Hair is another area that tends to get neglected. Scissors and hair color were invented for a reason, you know! Whether you are a man or a woman, it's easy to get stuck wearing one hairstyle that you think looks good on you. If you don't watch it, you'll end up looking outdated. If you look like an extra on *The Mary Tyler Moore Show*, change the channel already!

The last area of appearance that people forget about is the way they dress. Too often I hear people complaining that their partners just don't seem to care about how they look anymore. It's so easy to get into a rut and wear the same clothes year after year. Sure, this may be comfortable, but it becomes visually boring. This is one reason why updating your wardrobe is important—it adds variety. So the next time you are shopping, pick out new colors and styles to give you that extra visual spark when your partner sees you.

Throw Out Those Granny Panties

I don't know a man alive who would consider granny panties (big, white, cotton underwear) sexy. Trust me on this: If you wear them around your partner, then you are not pleasing his sense of sight. I know granny underwear is comfortable, but there is such a thing as sexy *and* comfortable.

Walking into a lingerie store can be a bit overwhelming, especially if you don't know much about lingerie. Here are a few definitions to help you on your initial foray into the world of undergarments:

Body stocking   A full body suit made of stretch lace. (Usually comes with a cutaway crotch for obvious reasons.)

Chemise   A short gown with thin straps usually made of silk or satin.

Daywear   This is lingerie worn under day clothes: bras, panties, camisoles (a slip to go under blouses with thin straps, which looks like a tank top), and slips.

Nightgown   A floor-length chemise in various cuts and styles, usually made of silk or satin.

Romper   A short, one-piece body suit with flared legs. It almost looks like a chemise except that the bottom half is connected into a loose pair of shorts.

Sleepwear   This is lingerie to sleep in: pajamas, nightgowns, boxers, and night-shirts.

Teddy   A body suit cut high on the thighs in either a French cut or thong style.

Cupid's Report

A **demi bra** has lower than usual bra cups that expose more of the breasts, giving the illusion of a larger bust line.

Words of the Heart

"All love is sweet, given or returned. Common as light is love, and its familiar voice wearies not ever."

—Percy Bysshe Shelley

If you're a man buying for a woman, keep in mind that most women dislike one or more of their body parts. You need to pay attention to this when you select an item for her. If she complains about her fat thighs, for example, don't buy her something that shows them off.

If you have no idea what size to buy, sneak a peak at the labels on her clothes. If you forget and you are at the store, look for a lady with a similar size and point her out to the salesperson. Salespeople have a keen sense of size and will be able to pick something that fits your partner well.

Use the following table when buying lingerie, whether for yourself or your partner. To use the chart, all you have to do is know which part of your body you like the least. This shouldn't be hard to do; most women have a least one area they aren't happy with. This will guide you in finding what looks best on you. To use the table, all you have to do is locate the body flaw on the left-hand side of the table. Next to it will be the type of lingerie that looks best on a person with that figure flaw. The last column shows the type of lingerie that looks the least flattering on each figure flaw.

Characteristic	Lingerie to buy	Lingerie to avoid
Fat stomach	Romper or chemise	Long, straight gown
Flat-chested	Gown with matching robe	Demi Bra, teddy, camisole
Big butt	Short chemise	Items that cling; stretch lace
Large breasts	Bras	Padded items or items with little or no support
Too thin	Long gowns	Flannel gowns
Too tall	Long gowns	Bright colors or prints, body stockings
Overweight	Chemise with robe	Prints and cotton

Words of the Heart

"Women are angels, wooing: Things won are done; joy's soul lies in the doing."

—William Shakespeare, *Troilus and Cressida*

Boxers or Briefs?

Women may not be as visually oriented as men, but they do use their sense of sight when they look at their partners. In other words, what men wear under their clothes is important, too.

Until recent years, designers didn't think much about men's underwear. Nowadays, most stores carry a large assortment of it, so men don't have to stick with one kind of underwear. Men shouldn't always wear white underwear, for example, because this gets boring for a woman to look at. You don't necessarily have to change the type of underwear you wear, just add a little variety to the color. Your partner will thank you for it.

The following table outlines the main types of men's underwear. This chart will tell you or your partner what kind of underwear looks best on you based on your body type.

Underwear type	Suited for	Not good for	Underwear message
Briefs	Average	Skinny	I'm practical
		Overweight	I'm conservative
Bikini	Well-built	Overweight	I'm sexy
	Average	Skinny	I feel good
Thong	Well-built	All others	I like sex
			I'm not the boy next door

Underwear type	Suited for	Not good for	Underwear message
Boxers (white)	All	None	I'm conservative
Boxers (colored)	Most	Overweight	I'm playful I'm creative

A Needed Touch

Physical touch is not only romantic, it also makes you feel valuable, protected, and loved. How many ways can you think of to touch your partner? There are many, but in this section you will read about two main types that are very romantic: dancing and massaging.

Research has shown that people need to be touched. Here is a list of nonsexual ways to touch your partner:

➤ Rest your head on his shoulder

➤ Put your arm around her

➤ Touch his arm when talking

➤ Caress his cheek when you're talking

➤ Sweep her off her feet and carry her to bed

➤ Bathe his feet, shampoo his hair, or fully bathe him

➤ Brush her hair away from her face

➤ Hold her hand to help her get out of the car

➤ Pat his shoulder when you walk past him

➤ Hold hands when you walk

➤ Bump or lean into each other

➤ Play footsies under the table

Desire on the Dance Floor

George Bernard Shaw described dancing as "a perpendicular expression of a horizontal desire." This is precisely what Iris discovered with Harry. When Harry danced, he showed passion. This was out of step with his usual personality away from the dance floor. Iris also loved to dance, so she enrolled the two of them in weekly ballroom dance lessons and enjoyed her passionate Harry every tango, salsa, and fox trot step of the way.

For many, dancing is considered the best foreplay there is. After hours of close contact, rubbing, and gyrating with their partner, they're warmed up and ready to be touched in a whole new way. The nice thing about slow dancing is that everyone can do it, regardless of age, weight, or height.

Cupid's Report

The waltz was the first dance that allowed a man to put his arms around a woman in public. This was considered very racy for the time, not to mention sinful to the church.

Words of the Heart

Every plant provides one **essential oil.** Essential oils are oils that are naturally produced in a plant. Like sap from a tree, it's just a part of the plant. Different kinds of oils are produced in the various parts of the plant. For instance, the leaf of a plant will contain a separate oil from the flower of the plant. Essential oils are known to have relaxation as well as medicinal purposes when used.

A more energetic couple might consider swing dancing, which has made a comeback in recent years. For those of you who aren't familiar with this style of dance, it's fast-paced and requires continual close contact with your partner. It's very romantic!

Dancing of all sorts is a form of romantic expression, whether it's through physical touching or arousing your partner with seductive movements. Because of this, dancing is a great way to add romance to your relationship. All it takes to dance is a partner who wants to move his or her body next to yours while romantic music plays in the background.

Romance at Your Fingertips

Not much is more pleasurable than a massage. Sometimes, a loving pair of hands and a little lotion is all it takes to make you feel like you have it all.

You don't have to receive formal training to please your partner in the massage department. Here is a list of massage reminders for the next time you go to work on the one you love:

➤ Vary the position of your hands to create different feelings on your partner's body. Your hands have lots of massaging tools: fingers, knuckles, palms, the sides of hands, and thumbs. All of these create different sensations when used on your partner's body.

➤ Use either body oil or lotion.

➤ Don't assume you know where your partner wants to be rubbed. A lot of people make the mistake of massaging only the areas that they like to have massaged. Ask your partner where he or she likes it the most.

➤ Different bodies hold stress and tension in different spots, so let your hands roam to lots of areas.

➤ Don't forget the feet.

➤ Touching gently can be incredibly erotic and relaxing. Not all massaging has to be rough.

Fragrances and Temporary Insanity

The sense of smell has a powerful impact on romance. The effect is so strong that research has proven that our sense of smell gives us the ability to choose partners who are genetically compatible. So nature's way of keeping the human race going is based to some degree on the way someone smells to us. All that happens is that we are attracted to some people's smells and turned off by others. Appealing to the sense of smell doesn't stop here. Scents can also be used to heighten arousal and emotions in your partner.

For centuries, lovers have used fragrances to increase their sense of intimacy. Any time you concentrate on one of the senses, by the way, it heightens the responsiveness of the other senses. The most common use of fragrances in romance is through aromatherapy. This fancy word describes the way certain smells affect you. These effects range from stress reduction to sexual enhancement. Depending on the effect you are after, you can be your own witch doctor!

Stephany, for example, enjoyed creating a relaxing environment at home for her and Brett. Typically she'd get home an hour before he did, which gave her the time to set up a romantic nest for helping the two of them begin their weekends right away. By the time Brett arrived home, the house had a relaxing smell of vanilla, apple, lemon, or some other tension relaxer that burned in a decanter. They would both notice that within an hour they were feeling more relaxed, all because of putting a certain aroma in the air.

You can use essential oils in a few different ways: massaged into the skin, inhaled through the air (through candles and incense), added to the bath, dabbed on your pillow, or heated in a *diffuser*. The essential oils are potent, and just a few drops are needed per use. The standard recipe for using oil is the following:

➤ Two or three drops in the bath

➤ Three or four drops in the diffuser

➤ One or two drops mixed with a base oil for massaging

➤ Two or three drops on a wet washcloth that's thrown into the dryer

Cupid's Report

A **diffuser** is a small bowl with a candle beneath it. The essential oil is placed in the diffuser and the candle is lit, releasing the aroma of the oil.

Words of the Heart

"Scents are surer than sights and sounds to make your heart strings crack."

—Rudyard Kipling

To make your first aromatic experience simple, use just one oil. The following list of the basic essential oils describes what each is thought to address. This list is a good place to start. If you need more information, you can look in the reference books listed in Appendix A.

Essential Oils for Romance

Oil	Smell	Used for
Benzoin	Vanilla	Combats loneliness and anxiety, relaxes, invigorates
Bergaot	Lemon	Lifts spirits, gets rid of anxiety, acts as an antidepressant
Cardamom	Ginger	Enhances sex
Chamomile	Apple	Calms, relieves muscle pain, relieves stress symptoms
Clary sage	Nutty	Relaxes, reduces stress, relieves tension, gives euphoric feeling, enhances sex
Eucalyptus	Floral	Relieves stress, depression, and mental exhaustion
Frankincense	Balsamic	Calms, relieves stress, relaxes
Geranium	Rose	Acts as an antidepressant
Jasmine	Floral	Enhances sex, relieves tension and anxiety
Lemon	Lemon	Helps to manage stress, relieves anxiety, tension, and mental fatigue
Melissa	Lemon	Reduces anxiety and depression
Peppermint	Mint	Relieves stress, depression, and tension
Rose	Rose	Stimulates sexual feelings for women
Ylang-ylang	Floral	Eases anxiety, enhances sex

Experimenting with your sense of smell and the use of essential oils is a nose-awakening way to spice up your love life. Most oils encourage relaxation, which is the most seductive prelude to romance.

What Romance Sounds Like

As explained in Chapter 12, "That's Entertainment," music sets the mood for romance. It's a part of almost every romantic scenario. However, sometimes the absence of sound can be romantic, too.

Take a second and listen to the environment that you're in right now. What sounds do you hear? I'll bet something is clinging, clanking, or ringing. If you always paid attention to the sounds around you, the sounds would be far too annoying to tolerate.

Noises distract from romance whether we're aware of it or not. Barbara, for example, was the type of woman who always wanted things to be right for her home-cooked dinners with Vernon, her boyfriend. This included having just the right music playing in the background. As luck would have it, one night her stereo wouldn't work. As she listened, she heard all sorts of noises that she didn't like: the buzzing sound from the living room light, the clicking on the clock, the washer and dryer, and the television in the next room. To get rid of the noises, she turned things off. What a transformation! She got creative and opened the window to let the sound of rain be the music. The dinner ended up being the most romantic the two of them had ever had in her home.

When you are in a quiet place, you feel relaxed and refreshed. This is because constant noise is tiring. When you are tired, your senses are dulled, which adds a dull edge to romance as well.

Getting rid of noise is the best thing you can do to heighten romance. Some noises disappear with the push of a button or click of a remote. Other noises, like the dishwasher, can be rescheduled for times when romance is not on the agenda. When your environment is quiet, you can tune into the nuances of your partner's sounds. You will be amazed by what you hear when you have nothing to listen to but your partner. Isn't this a better sound than hearing the spin cycle?

Cupid's Report

According to aromatherapy experts, you can create a seduction scene by using the following fragrant oils: cinnamon, clary sage, frankincense, jasmine, myrtle, rose, sandalwood, and ylang-ylang.

Words of the Heart

"One half of the world cannot understand the pleasures of the other."

—Jane Austen, *Emma*, 1816,

A Taste of the Erogenous Zones

The first thing that comes to mind when you think of tasting is food. But think of tasting in terms of tasting your partner. You can't get any more romantic than that!

When thinking over which parts of your partner you are going to taste, do it according to his or her erogenous zones. These zones can be stimulated easily. Think about your own body. Do you know which areas give you the chills when your partner

157

touches them? For some people, a kiss on the back of the neck is erogenous. For others, nibbling on the ears is arousing. Usually erogenous areas are the parts of our bodies that aren't used to being touched. When they are touched, watch out!

When you taste your partner, you can savor these areas the same way you would food: chewing, sucking, licking, nibbling, biting, and swallowing. Arousing your sense of taste will make the rest of your senses even more responsive.

The best way to discover what your partner's erogenous zones are is by tasting his or her body as though your partner were a buffet. Take a little taste here, a little taste there. Before you know it, you'll be stuffed with pleasure, but definitely ready for the main course!

As you can see, enhancing romance is easy when it's done through the senses, whether it's sight, sound, touch, taste, or smell. Focusing on one sense helps to intensify the others, making for one incredibly romantic experience!

The Least You Need to Know

➤ By paying attention your partner's five senses, you will be able to bring your romance to new levels of pleasure.

➤ You don't have to sacrifice sexiness for comfort. When choosing your underclothing or sleepwear, make sure it looks good with your body shape.

➤ Don't forget to touch your partner daily. You'd be surprised by how valuable it will make your partner feel.

➤ Fragrances promote a sense of intimacy between lovers. Bring your partner closer with alluring smells.

➤ You don't always need music to create romance. Sometimes just the natural sounds around you create just the right mood for loving.

➤ There is more to taste than food. Your partner can make a delicious appetizer as well!

OH BABY...

Chapter 15

Technology and Romance

In This Chapter

➤ Romantic e-mail

➤ Chat rooms and other online games

➤ A facsimile of romance

➤ Codes between pagers

John and Ellen make the most of their modern world by sending love notes to each other each day on their computers under the screen names of JR917 (John) and EF858 (Ellen). Each time they see their screen names they know that something exciting is about to be read. One day, for instance, JR917 sent a note to EF858 asking her to meet him for dinner. She wrote back, "Of course I'll meet you for dinner. It would take five strong men to keep me from you." He responded with, "Five strong men? I'm stronger than 10 strong men. Plus, I'll have my arms around you, and you won't be able to get away."

Even in their busy lives, John and Ellen have found a way to send quick, playful, and romantic notes to each other so that they feel close. An e-mail message can be a romantic surprise that leaves a lasting impression on your partner. E-mails from your partner are like little unexpected presents, and you are excited about opening them to see what's inside.

Dr. Romance

Take this quick quiz to find out how e-mail savvy you are. Can you name the following cartoon couple? Hint: Turn your head to the left to see their identities:

(_8^(|)=[Cartoon Husband
@@@@@:-)={ Cartoon Wife

If you guessed Homer and Marge Simpson, you're right.

Words of the Heart

"Diffidence and awkwardness are the two antidotes to love."

—William Hazlitt

Computers, fax machines, cellular phones, answering machines, pagers, and copy machines are just a few examples of business technology that can double as romantic tools. In this chapter, you'll learn how to take advantage of the technological times to romance the one you love. It's all a matter of rethinking the uses of the machines you have all around you. I'll teach you how to turn an ordinary e-mail into an unforgettable love letter, give virtual affection, send faxes in a secret love language that only you and your partner can decipher, and a whole lot more.

A Name Only You Will Know

With people being so busy, the last thing you want to do is call at the wrong time. But then again, who says you have to call at all? E-mail gives you the advantage of sending your messages when you feel the need. Within seconds, you can send your partner a love note. E-mail also lets your partner read the message when he or she has a minute. It makes giving so easy.

Instant Romance in an Instant World

Technology has ushered in a new age of communicating with your partner. You can instantly communicate what you are feeling just by clicking the Send button with your mouse.

Instant communication allows you to say what you need to say and not have to wait for just the right moment. It's the easiest way to get something off your chest, whether it's to say, "I miss you so much I can't stand it," or "You left your earrings here. I'll bring them to you tonight."

Spice It Up with Font, Size, and Color

E-mail can be boring to look at unless you know how to bring it to life with a few tricks. Fonts and formatting are two ways of jazzing up your letters.

Some fonts are more romantic than others. When writing a romantic letter, you will want to stay away from plain fonts such as Courier, because they don't have a romantic flair. The font, as well as the message, will convey romance if you choose a style that has more shine. Here is a list of common romantic fonts to use when writing romantic e-mails:

➤ Book Antiqua

➤ Bookman Old Style

➤ Calisto MT

➤ Century Gothic

➤ Comic Sands MS

➤ Copperplate Gothic

➤ Lucida Handwriting

➤ Lucida Console

➤ Lucida Sans

➤ Matisse ITC

➤ Mistral

➤ News Gothic Mt

➤ Tempus Sans ITC

➤ Westminster

To make your words more dramatic (and readable), write your letters in a larger size, such as 14 or 16 points. You can also use formatting to help emphasize certain parts of your message or make the overall message stand out. Click the formatting option and play around with all of the options available.

The following are a few examples of how to add pizzazz to your letters:

I Love You

I Love You

You can get as creative as you would like. For instance, you can express your words in a variety of print colors. You can also add animation to a word or words by making some words flash or sparkle. You'll be amazed at what you can do once you start playing around with the features behind each icon. The only drawback is that you and your sweetie have to be on compatible systems in order for your creative e-mails to go through. If you're not, the messages that are sent will look as plain as the text in all the other e-mails.

Say It with a Smiley

E-mail doesn't have the benefits of body language, but it does have a unique way to communicate your happiness: Mr. Smiley. If you are unfamiliar with Mr. Smiley, he's the little smiley face, ☺, we all knew and loved in the '70s. In e-mail, Mr. Smiley is sideways as he displays a range of emotions using common keyboard keys:

:-|	Bored
:'(	Crying
:-@	Cursing
:*	Kiss
:-*	Kiss
:D	Laughing
:-D	Laughing
:X	Lips sealed
:-X	Lips sealed
:-(	Sad
:(	Sad
:-()	Shouting
{{:-!	Worried
:)	Smile
:]	Smile
:^)	Smile
:-)	Smile
:-]	Smile
:->	Smile
:-O	Surprised
:-o	Surprised
:-P	Tongue out
:P	Tongue out
:-[	Vampire
;)	Wink
;-)	Wink

Giving with the Touch of a Key

If you hate to shop, but love to surprise your sweetie with gifts from the heart, then the computer is just the thing for you. Regardless of what you want to give her, you are certain to find it online.

To find a present to send to your partner, go to an Internet search engine and type the name of the item that you're interested in. You can order presents that can even be sent the next day. Online shopping eliminates having to search a mall or waiting in lines, and you can even comparison shop!

Virtual Gifts

Giving virtual gifts makes shopping easy. You don't have to worry about getting the right size, having enough money, or even wrapping it. Go online and type in www.virtualpresents.com. At this Web address, you will find an online virtual gift store. The store has every gift your partner could ever fantasize about: vacation packages, furniture, jewelry, everyday items, cars, planes, apparel, pets, flowers, tools, odds and ends, cards, and even food.

There is no cost for shopping in the virtual gift store, so you can pick out and send as many gifts to your partner as you would like. To send a gift, all you do is pick out a present, write a loving note, and then click Send.

The present will be sent to your partner's e-mail address in seconds. Instructions will tell her how to retrieve her gift. Just think—you can make her feel like a virtual queen by sending her virtual jewels. She'll love you all the more for thinking of her.

Greetings, Cyberlover

Have you ever forgotten to send your partner a card to celebrate his or her birthday or some other occasion? At the last minute it dawns on you that it slipped your mind. By that point it's too late. You're out of time, so you can't stop and pick one up. As you well know, this is not the best way to begin a celebration.

Dr. Romance

Try this e-mail come-on line: "Here's a @—>— (rose) for my rose. How would you like to have a Q>—| (martini) with me tonight?"

Words of the Heart

"Woman begins by resisting a man's advances and ends by blocking his retreat."

—Oscar Wilde

This predicament is a thing of the past with the invention of the virtual card shop. All you have to do is go online, pick out a card, and send it to her. You can even pick one out way ahead of time and click the Send Later button. The best online site to go to is www.startingpage.com/html/greeting_cards.htm. This site gives 50+ free greeting card sites to explore.

Some of the online card shops even offer a service that takes away the stress of remembering when to send cards. For a nominal fee, they will keep track of all the occasions in your life that require cards. All you do is provide them with the names and dates for each occasion, and they do the remembering for you.

Instant Virtual Affection

Who ever said that you had to be with your partner to be affectionate with him or her? Nowadays you can receive or send loving gestures over your computer for eye-opening virtual affection. You can send whatever your partner needs. Does your partner need a kiss goodnight? A hug for a job well done? No problem—you can give your partner what she or he needs in the way of virtual hugs and kisses through your computer. It's great for when you can't be there. Just think how special your partner will feel when he receives a little cyber love and affection.

> **Cupid's Report**
>
> America Online has a site, www.Love@AOL.com, that allows you to send either a kiss, hug, or rose to the one you love.

Play with Your Partner Online

Games and chat rooms are perfect for times when you and the one you love either can't be together or would rather stay in. For the times you are apart, the two of you can arrange a time to both be online. This way you can play online together. Only the two of you will recognize each other's screen names when they show up in the same place.

At other times, if the two of you decide to stay in, you can have a lot of fun by playing games or going to chat lines and talking to others. As you can see, your computer time can double as couple time when you discover playful ways to interact in cyberspace.

Cyber Classes

You and your partner can learn online together in scheduled community chat rooms that offer classes. However, classes are only offered to AOL subscribers. So, if AOL is your system, taking a class together could be a lot of fun. A "class" is a lecture or seminar on a particular subject. The enrollment is limited so that some order is maintained, because classes are interactive with one host, or teacher, who facilitates the class.

> **Dr. Romance**
>
> Many newer computers have card maker programs already installed on the hard drive. This kind of program makes greeting cards in a matter of minutes. All you have to do is select the type of card that fits the occasion, type in the person's name, and print.

To find a class, all you have to do is click Keyword and type in: chat rooms. Most classes are one hour long and filled with fun, love-related topics. If you are interested in participating, you have to arrive early and be quick to get in when the clock strikes the appointed time. Some class subjects are more popular and fill up quickly, so be prepared.

Class subjects change regularly, but there are always plenty with the theme of love. Here is a sample of some of the classes offered:

➤ Lyrical Love: A Game That Tests Your Knowledge of Love Song Lyrics

➤ Lovelines: Members Help Write a Wacky Love Story Line by Line

➤ Gender Battle: Men Vs. Women. See Which Knows More About the Other.

➤ Hollywood Bed Buddies: Famous Lovers (real and fictional) Trivia

➤ Strip Trivia! Sexual Trivia Where Players Get "Virtually" Naked.

It doesn't take an imaginative mind to see the possibilities that await you and your partner if you play together online.

The Thrill of the Chat

Entering a chat room is easy. All you have to do is go online and click the chatroom icon on your screen. That will take you to the main chat area. The chat room you go into will depend on the game you want to play with your partner. Depending on who you are, your initial chat room adventures can range from boring to highly arousing.

After the novelty of chat rooms wears off, they can become ho-hum unless you bring your own excitement to them. One of the easiest ways to do that is to meet your mate in a room where you can live out some of your fantasies.

Chat rooms have a way of bringing out the beast in all of us. They offer a way of acting out hidden fantasies behind the protection of the computer screen. Even if you think you know your partner, you will be surprised by how uninhibited he is when he's in a chat room talking to a "stranger."

There are a few games that you can play with your partner in a chat room. Because there are no limits other than the rules the two of you set, you can make it as innocent or as daring as you want. The following sections describe a few games you might like to try.

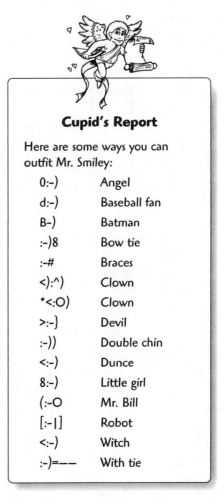

Cupid's Report

Here are some ways you can outfit Mr. Smiley:

0:-)	Angel
d:-)	Baseball fan
B-)	Batman
:-)8	Bow tie
:-#	Braces
<):^)	Clown
*<:O)	Clown
>:-}	Devil
:-))	Double chin
<:-)	Dunce
8:-)	Little girl
(:-O	Mr. Bill
[:-|]	Robot
<:-)	Witch
:-)=---	With tie

Words of the Heart

I like my body when it is with your

Body. It is so quite new a thing.

Muscles better and nerves more.

I like your body. I like what it does,

I like its hows. I like to feel the spine

Of your body and its bones, and the trembling

Firm-smoothness and which I will

Again and again and again

Kiss, I like kissing this and that of you,

I like slowly stroking the shocking fuzz

Of your electric fur, and what-is-it comes

Over parting flesh ... and eyes big love-brumbs,

And possibly I like the thrill

Of under me you so quiet new

—e. e. Cummings

Meet Me for a Private Chat

For this game, you and your partner will go into your own private room to play with each other. All you have to do is click the Private Chat button when you are on the main chat screen. Type in a name for your room—for example, "Sexy Blue Eyes"—and then click Go Chat. That will put you in a private room.

You can invite your love interest aside in one of two ways. If you have compatible Internet service providers, then you can send him an instant message. Otherwise, you can send him an e-mail to let him know you are online. Just tell him the name of your private room so he can find you. You can also schedule a meeting time and meet there. Remember that your room is private and no one can enter it but the two of you, for as long as you like. Enjoy your stay!

Please Place Your Order

This game is the cybersex version of wearing a costume and acting out a role. In this game, one player is the customer, and the other is the professional. To add a little mystery to this game, you can create new screen names. It adds a touch of newness to your partner, which makes him or her seem a little like a stranger (and all the more exciting).

"Group" Sex

Some couples have a bold spirit about them and like the idea of having a cyber ménage à trois by inviting others into their sexual conversation. The way you do this is by choosing the appropriate chat room or by creating your own public room. This game is different than the other three because it can be played in one of two ways. The first is by playing it with each of you meeting up in a chat room. The other way to play is by using one computer that both of you share.

The Last Word on Romantic Technology

Because technology is so ubiquitous these days, it's available either free or at a nominal fee at public libraries and copy stores. Technology is a romantic tool to try out even if you don't own your own computer, fax, or any other device of modern times.

Fax Appeal

The fax machine is a fun way to add romance to your workday. Because fax printouts are not private, you'll want to keep your letters free of content that may embarrass your significant other. Some subjects go over better at work than others, so steer clear of blatant sexuality and stick with humor, quotes, poetry, invitations to dinner or drinks, and light love messages, such as "I miss you."

You can take this a little further by developing your own secret language that won't make sense to anyone but your honey. For example, "Can you meet me at Nordstrom's at 8?" could be code for "I'll be waiting in the bath when you get home." No one would ever guess that a shopping trip invitation could trigger such excitement!

Love Between Pagers

A vibrating beeper can cause big excitement if it displays a love message from your partner. Forget typing in a return number. Depending on the type of pager your lover has, you may be able to write messages using your telephone keypad.

If you have an older model, you and your partner will just have to create your own codes for deciphering. Some couples get pretty creative and send simple but powerful messages to their partners, such as XXX (Kiss), OOO (Hugs), or 911 ("I want you now"). The point is to be creative and take advantage of the technology to send love messages to your partner when he or she least expects one.

Cupid's Report

The Internet offers many online greeting card stores, but the most popular one is American Greetings. To get there, go to www.americangreetings.com. The first card you send is free, and the cards after that are half the price of the cards you buy from a card shop. Other card shops offer an unlimited amount of free cards. To find them, go to an Internet search engine and type in *cards*. That will take you to more card shops than you know what to do with.

Words of the Heart

Where true love burns desire is Love's pure flame;

It is the reflex of our earthy frame,

That takes its meaning from the nobler part,

And but translates the language of the heart.

—Samuel Taylor Coleridge

The Least You Need to Know

➤ With the help of your computer, being romantic is the easiest it has ever been. Take full advantage of the romantic tools available to you.

➤ Making your e-mail love letters snazzy is not only fun, it's also simple.

➤ If you haven't given in to technology, now is the time to do it.

➤ Developing a romantic coding system with your partner can make receiving a page an exciting experience.

Part 4

Going for the Gusto

We all dream about the tales we see in movies, watch on TV, and read about in novels. It's romance at its peak. In this section, you'll experience this lifestyle firsthand. The means are out there—all you have to do is jump on board and go! However, this ride is not for just any couple. This is only for those who can afford to travel to the places their hearts yearn to be, give the gifts only a few can afford, and live the jet-set life that is reserved for a lucky few.

This section ends with a chapter for everyone, regardless of your budget. It introduces a life of realistic extravagance that you can share with your partner. It will show you how a little savings can add up to big fun during the time you devote to the one you love.

Chapter 16

Extravagant Travel

In This Chapter

➤ Love is in the air

➤ The train that could

➤ Ports of call that call your name

You're heading to your closet thinking you need to pack for a weekend getaway when you suddenly hear your partner say, "The jet leaves at noon, make sure you pack enough to go around the world!" Of course, you think he's joking—until he shows you the itinerary! Traveling with the one you love is one of the most romantic things you can do together. Heightened romance is guaranteed when you go to exotic lands that open your mind to completely new experiences. How can you concentrate on the office when you are lying on the beach in Bora Bora?

In this chapter, you'll discover the most extravagant travel adventures available for you and your partner to experience. Each place is guaranteed to bring an air of love and romance to your souls.

Where Do You Begin?

The world has seven continents to play on and explore with your partner. Deciding where your adventure will take place is a huge decision, unless you have someone to help you along. Although you can go to your local travel agent to get help, there are two exclusive nationwide travel companies that specialize in extravagant travel:

Cupid's Report

Do you remember the Brooke Shields movie, *The Blue Lagoon*? That movie was filmed on Turtle Island in the South Pacific. As a matter of fact, Colombia Pictures surveyed a thousand possible sites before deciding to film the entire movie on this exquisite island. Turtle Island is the perfect location for intimacy. A maximum of 14 couples is allowed on the island at a time, which keeps it quaint. Each day of your stay you can choose from a variety of activities: scuba diving, snorkeling, wind surfing, relaxing in a hammock, deep-sea fishing, horseback riding, excursions to neighboring islands, or any number of things to enjoy with the one you love. You can expect to pay approximately $800 per person per day for a minimum of seven days. This price includes all meals and activities. All you have to do is contact a travel agent for details.

Abercombie & Kent International (www.abercombiekent.com) and Travcoa (www.travcoa.com). You can't go wrong with either of them.

These companies are expensive because they tailor trips for couples with impeccable tastes (and the money to act on these tastes) and leave the lovey-dovey couple with nothing to worry about except each other. These companies don't ignore the adventure of getting to your dream destination, either. Hot air balloons, jets, helicopters, barges, yachts, and trains are all available.

Seduction in the Air

Traveling by air is the only way to gain entrance into one of the most exclusive clubs known: The Mile-High Club. To be a member of this club, you have to have had sex during a flight. If you haven't joined the ranks of other wild lovers, consider signing up today! It's definitely a tight squeeze, but the thrill can bring you to new heights.

Travel by air is the most common means couples use to get to their destinations. What most people don't realize is that flying can be much more than boarding a boring old 747. Other flight experiences are less common, more expensive, and much more exciting than the traditional flight. Each is an incredible way to see your sites romantically.

Hot Air Balloons

If you and your partner are not afraid of heights, then hot air balloon travel might be ideal for you. Just think of how close you will feel to your partner as he or she holds you tight in a small basket while you take in the sights, sounds, and smells of a foreign land.

Hot air balloon travel is not just something that happens in romantic movies. Imagine flying over the countryside in France by day and sleeping in castles by night. This is only one of the many tour packages you will find when you look into hot air ballooning. A great way to test this type of travel is to look for local balloon rides.

Jetting into the Sunset

How many times have you spent a long flight sitting next to someone who drove you crazy? It happens to everyone, and it can make your hours in the sky miserable. When you fly by chartered jet, this doesn't happen! Instead, your time in the air is comfortable, and you are surrounded by far fewer people, which makes flying more enjoyable. Some people want even more space, so they charter a jet just for themselves. Travel by private jet is unique because it offers so much freedom in terms of where you go and when.

One of the most romantic aspects of plane travel is the anticipation of starting an exciting adventure once you land. Your romance can begin once you board the plane. The time in the air is time to sit close, touch, smooch, and plan all the romantic things you are going to do together.

Use these tips to spice up your air time:

➤ Cuddle under a blanket and play footsie or kiss.

➤ Have drinks together.

➤ Take turns massaging each other's hands with lotion.

➤ Surprise your partner with a small gift.

➤ Cuddle and share your fantasies.

➤ Plan the first place you will make love when you get off the plane.

➤ Sing a romantic song in your partner's ear.

Helicopters

Helicopters can take you to remote places that can't be reached by any other means. Helicopter trips are usually a day long at the most, but they can offer some of the most unbelievable experiences. If you call up your local travel agent, you'll find all kinds of flight companies that offer this kind of travel. Some places offer set tours; others let you decide where you want to go. The fees for this vary greatly, so make sure you compare prices and services before you make your decision.

Words of the Heart

"Let us be very strange and well bred: Let us be as strange as if we had been married a great while; and as well bred as if we were not married at all."

—William Congreve, from *The Way of the World* (1700), IV.i

Cupid's Report

If you are looking for a great city or island to visit in Europe, look into the following: Amsterdam, Athens, Barcelona, Berlin, Brussels, Budapest, Capri, Copenhagen, Corsica, Crete, Dublin, Edinburgh, Florence, Geneva, Ibiza, Istanbul, Lisbon, London, Luxembourg, Madrid, Mallorca, Milan, Monte Carlo, Munich, Mykonos, Naples, Nice, Oslo, Paris, Prague, Rhodes, Rome, Santorini, Sardinia, Seville, Sicily, Stockholm, St. Petersburg, Venice, Vienna, and Zurich.

Words of the Heart

"Your partner's idea of intimacy may be vastly different from yours. Try it his way, and keep an open mind. Honor his idea of closeness as you wish him to honor yours."

—Toni Sciarra Poynter, from *From This Day Forward*, 1995

Cupid's Report

Looking for some great U.S. cities to visit? Try the following: Boston, Charleston, S.C., Chicago, Dallas, Denver, Hilton Head, Houston, Key West, Los Angeles, Miami, Martha's Vineyard, Nantucket, Nashville, New Orleans, New York City, Orlando, Palm Beach, Portland, San Diego, San Francisco, Santa Fe, Savannah, Seattle, St. Louis, and Washington, D.C.

Use these ideas to brainstorm about places to take your partner:

➤ If fishing is a hobby, why not take a helicopter to a remote lake or river?

➤ Why not picnic on a remote mountaintop?

➤ See a glacier up close in the warmth of your helicopter.

Helicopters can take you almost anywhere you want to go. Whether you want to see the city lights after dinner, visit your friends to inform them of your engagement, or just go for a stroll in a secluded spot, all you have to do is jump aboard a private helicopter, and you'll get there in a flash.

A Hotel on Wheels

The love affair with train travel prevails all over the world. When traveling with your partner, you will want to take advantage of the romantic benefits to this slower mode of travel. Consider these romantic tips when traveling on a train:

➤ Sleeping compartments are generally pretty small. If you want to be more comfortable, upgrade from a private cabin to a stateroom to have more room when you sneak away for a rest.

➤ The romantic aspect to train travel is in the slow pace of the transportation itself. The adventure is in the journey, not in arriving at the destination. Sit back, relax, and enjoy all the sites along the way. Each one can be an adventure in and of itself.

➤ Take a few minutes to sneak away from your partner to plan a surprise for him or her later. Write out a quick love note and give it to the steward with instructions to deliver it to your partner during dinner.

➤ Sleep with your window open. The unfamiliar sounds will fill your sleeping quarters with exotic music.

➤ Pretend to be a honeymooning couple on your first trip together. Tell the story and stick to it with all the new people you meet.

➤ Keep drinking to a minimum to lessen any chance of motion sickness.

➤ Get off the train at each stop and explore the town, meet the people, and add to your adventure.

Words of the Heart

"Tunneling through the night, the trains pass in a splendor of power, with a sound like thunder shaking the orchards, waking the young from a dream, scattering like glass the old men's sleep; laying a black trail over the still bloom of the orchards. The trains go north with guns."

—Judith Wright, 1946

American Train Travel

The most indulgent kind of rail travel is to charter a private train. This is the ideal way to travel for a couple who wants to see the beauty of the United States from the best view, which is off the beaten path. This kind of luxurious travel is custom designed: If you want to stop in the backwoods of Missouri to visit your Grandma Brown, just write that into your itinerary. There are few limits because railroad lines go just about everywhere.

A chartered train is not the only indulgence in train travel. There are public trains that are very luxurious and expensive. As a matter of fact, they seem more like vacationing in a five-star hotel on wheels.

The Express returns you to the romantic days of deluxe rail travel aboard a beautiful train of vintage rail cars from the streamliner era. Passengers are pampered and served gourmet meals on dining tables set with china, silver, crystal, and linen in a club-like atmosphere. This luxury train travels through some of the most stunning landscapes in North America. Part of what's romantic about this trip is listening to expert lecturers talking about the areas you travel through: the Rockies, Yellowstone, the Northwest, and Glacier National Park.

The Goldleaf Train Service travels a romantic path in the majestic Pacific Northwest and Canada. You see it all from your seat inside the cozy, opulent, full-domed rail cars. You will marvel at scenery that is so magnificent it takes your breath away. You'll journey beside a raging river; spot deer, moose, and bears; and peer up at world-famous mountains. Imagine the atmosphere this scenery will add to each gourmet meal the two of you share. The romance will be steamy.

Foreign Train Travel

Luxury train travel is available all over the world. Foreign train travel is known for having a romantic flair to it for many reasons. Completely immersing yourself in new cultures, customs, languages, sites, foods, and lifestyles is exciting. Romance is an adventure, and adding an experience like foreign train travel only intensifies it.

The most famous train to travel aboard is the luxurious Orient Express. Actually, there are two Orient Expresses. One is the elegant Venice Simplon-Orient Express that takes you through Europe. The other is the Eastern & Oriental Express that travels between Singapore and Bangkok.

Both Orient Expresses are lavishly decorated in the 1930s colonial style. The train consists of 13 sleeping cars, two restaurant cars, a bar car, an observation/lounge car, and a saloon car. You will also find a boutique, entertainers, and an on-board astrologer to predict your romantic future if you wish. You'll watch as the countryside unfolds out your window. How can you not be swept off your feet when in the middle of an adventure that takes you through the heart of Asia or Europe in such a unique way?

The Great South Pacific train is the ideal centerpiece of a romantic trip to Australia. This train takes you to Brisbane, Cairnes, and Sydney in the finest style aboard a train detailed in Australian railway heritage.

The Al Andalus Express, a 1920s Belle Epoque–style train, rolls smoothly across southern Spain, making stops at the Cordoba, Madrid, Granada, Ronda, Marabella, and Jerez. This train has two romantic aspects to it that many others don't. First of all, it gives you the opportunity to stop and dine in local restaurants along the route so that you and your partner can experience the foreign land first-hand. Second, it provides live music for after-dinner dancing in the parlor car. How romantic is that?

The Royal Scotsman sets the mood for romance with sites of Scotland's unspoiled vistas of secluded glens, pristine lochs, craggy mountains, and magnificent moors. Romance abounds during visits to castles and gardens and when meeting Scottish locals.

If you'd love to go to Africa and see the sites, the Blue Train could meet your needs. This luxurious train is known for its unsurpassed accommodations and gourmet cuisine, which soothe the body and soul. In the comfort and luxury of a five-star hotel, you journey into a timeless world of grace, elegance, and romance en route to Cape Town, Pretoria, Eastern Transvall, and Victoria Falls.

The Love Boat

When Cleopatra set her sights on Mark Antony, she set sail up the Nile on a guided barge with purple sails. Antony was helpless from the start: What man would be able to refuse the allure of a beautiful, charming woman in front of a backdrop of gentle, rocking waves?

If the great warrior Mark Antony could be conquered by a seductive boat environment, then your partner certainly can. Traveling by boat is one of the most romantic ways to go. It's set up for romance: strolling on deck in the moonlight, dressing up for candlelit gourmet dinners, slow dancing each night, taking adventurous excursions to different ports of call, and being thoroughly pampered.

For lovebirds who like a slow pace, water travel is just what the doctor ordered. You have a variety of vessels to choose from. They range from the intimate barges that meander the canals and rivers to the ocean liners that cut across the sea. There is a ship waiting for every kind of traveler.

Dr. Romance

If your partner loves an adventure, why not treat him or her to a haunted house tour? *Hans Holzer's Travel Guide to Haunted Houses: A Practical Guide to Places Haunted by Ghosts, Poltergeists, and Spirits* is a great book that tells you where the haunted houses are in North America and Europe. One of the emotions that heightens sexuality is fear, so a trip like this could add to your sexual relationship!

Cruising by Barge

Water travel by barges is most popular in Europe. Barges were originally designed for carrying cargo deep into the heart of countries in shallow waterways where other boats couldn't go. Nowadays, barges are also used for luxury travel and are designed more like a beautiful small hotel with a large open deck for lounging.

One of the biggest appeals of a barge is that you get to see a lot of different sites. Barges travel through narrow canals that a cruise ship could never go, all the while floating past world-famous sites and beautiful countrysides. Each day the barge docks, and passengers take off on whatever activity they choose: sightseeing, shopping, going to museums, or doing whatever their interest is.

Cupid's Report

When looking into travel by boat, look into the following cruise lines: Best Large Cruise Lines, Best Small Cruise Lines, Carnival Cruise Line, Celebrity Cruises, Costa Cruise Lines, Crystal Cruises, Holland Cruise Lines, Princess Cruise Lines, Radisson, Renaissance Cruises, Royal Caribbean Cruise Lines, Seabourn Cruise Line, Seven Sea, Silversea Cruise, and Windstar Cruises.

The Cruise Ship Experience

Sometimes confinement is a bad thing. Being on a boat, however, tends to foster love. Whether a cruise ship is large or small, you'll be in an environment that encourages couplehood. Many of the organized activities are for couples, so it's a perfect place to have romantic fun.

Traveling by boat is an excellent way to keep romance alive. Because everything is done for you, all you have to do is relax and enjoy your lover's company. The ports of call are the spice of your trip, where the two of you can immerse yourselves in new cultures and new ways to have fun together.

The large cruise lines offer more in terms of entertainment, amenities, and crowds. If you are traveling alone and looking for love, this is a good option for you. If you want to avoid the family travelers (and their screaming children), then a smaller cruise line would probably be better suited to your needs.

Smaller cruise lines have a lot to offer. They pay particular attention to the small details of someone's trip, which can make all the difference. For instance, even the bathrooms are filled with marble and fully equipped, which gives you a definite sense of luxury. Also, a big perk is that they cater more to couples and their needs. They spoil you by waiting on you hand and foot so you'll choose them again the next time you want to sail with your partner.

The Least You Need to Know

➤ Traveling with your partner is the most exotic way to spend time together. Nothing is more intimate than exploring new places together.

➤ Visiting new sites, hearing unfamiliar sounds, experimenting with new tastes, and sharing novel experiences builds a bond between you and your partner.

➤ Even flying in an airplane can be romantic if you create the atmosphere for it.

➤ Every mode of travel offers a unique way to experience love. That's part of what makes each kind of travel romantic.

What a Little Extra Money Can Do

For two months, Dick and Reena have been looking forward to today. Money has been tight, but they managed to put away enough for a weekend stay at the local five-star hotel. They've walked the hotel grounds a hundred times and always said, "Someday we'll have to stay here for a weekend." That someday is finally here, and they are both so excited to go. They are going to do everything to the hilt: one evening of great seats at the theater, another of fine dining and dancing, sleeping in late, sunbathing while sipping cocktails, and sitting in the Jacuzzi at midnight drinking champagne under the moon.

A guaranteed way to reignite your romance is to add a touch of extravagance to your everyday relationship. There is nothing like lavishness to make love exciting.

In the last chapter, you read about how to make your dating relationship romantic by taking exotic vacations together. This chapter will show you how to achieve the same feeling of being spoiled on romantic dates without blowing the rent money.

This may surprise you, but extravagance doesn't have to be expensive (if it's done in moderation!). Regardless of your income, there are ways to go all out and not stress over doing so. All it takes is desire and a plan to make it happen. This chapter gives

Words of the Heart

"Adventure must be held in delicate fingers. It should be handled, not embraced. It should be sipped, not swallowed at a gulp."

—Ashley Dukes, 1924

Dr. Romance

If you are going to be visiting a city other than your own, call the visitors' bureau for that area and do some research in advance about romantic restaurants, romantic hotels, and romantic things to do when you visit.

you that plan. After reading this chapter, you will discover how to stretch your dollar and make extravagant dates possible for you and your partner.

Making Extravagant Dates Possible

You can finance your dreams as long as you plan for them, regardless of the budget you are on. Just keep in mind that the more money you put away toward your dream date fund, the sooner you will have your adventure. For some, saving for a date may take months; for others, saving may take years. Either way, keep in mind that with every dollar you save, you are on your way to making your dream dates happen.

Realistic Extravagances

The term realistic extravagance may sound like an oxymoron, but it isn't. Most people don't have a lot of extra money to spend on lavish gifts, travel, and lifestyle to enhance their relationship on a regular basis. Many couples assume that they just have to accept the fact that they will never have these things.

I'm here to say that you can have extravagance in your romantic life. It's as easy as setting your sights on what you want and going for it. When you realize what you can have, you will be excited about the possible adventures you'll have with your partner.

The Excitement of Planning

If you feel like you and your partner have grown apart, the easiest way to grow close again is through an extravagant date lasting at least 16 hours. When you spend this much time with someone, you can't help but to catch up on all the changes in their lives.

Sometimes just the thought of the possible extravagant dates you can have with your partner is very romantic. Mutual planning bonds people because it's a shared experience in which both of you put your thoughts, money, and excitement into making the date come to life.

Simply discussing and deciding what the two of you will be doing on your date will add romance to your life long before the actual date arrives. You'll spend many excited hours discussing the romantic things you will do. Plus, just knowing that you have something exciting on your calendar will invigorate the connection between the two of you. Now that you know you can do it, part of the excitement is deciding on what the two of you will find romantic. The rest of this chapter helps you to discover what that will be.

Words of the Heart

"If you resolve to give up smoking, drinking, and loving, you don't actually live longer; it just seems longer."

—Clement Freud, *The Observer*, 1964

A Day's Adventure

When Dick and Reena first began to plan for their big weekend date at the local five-star hotel, they had some things to consider:

➤ What did they want to do?

➤ When could they do it?

➤ When was the best time?

➤ Would they need to take time off from work?

➤ Who would watch the kids?

➤ How much would they need to save for the date?

They calculated that it would take them two months to save for the weekend. They looked at their calendar, circled the date, and called to make reservations. Within no time, all the details were ironed out. They had a sitter for the children, and they bought tickets for the play they were going to. Now all they had to do was enjoy the anticipation for their extravagant date.

Making Your Plans

Dick and Reena knew ahead of time what they wanted to do on an extravagant date together. For some couples, it's not that easy. As you read through this chapter, take notes so that you can answer the following questions. Sometimes the hardest part of planning an unusual date is not the cost, but deciding what to do. These questions will help you:

1. What is exciting to your partner?

2. What sounds like fun to you?

3. If you have different ideas about what kind of an extravagant date you'd like to go on, what would a good compromise be so that both of you would be happy?

4. Are there any limitations or obstacles that would get in the way of following through on your date? If so, how can you resolve them?

Dr. Romance

Did you know that you can hire performers to do just about anything you can think of? If you love music, you can hire a private violinist to play for you while you have dinner at home or at a restaurant. All you have to do is tell the musician what time you need him and where to play. If it's at a restaurant, you need to okay it with the manager first.

Adventurous Dining

Having an intimate dinner with your partner is nice, but dinner oozes with romance when it takes place in an unusual place with lots of ambiance. The following dinner suggestions provide built-in entertainment for your extravagant date.

Meals on Rail

Almost all major cities have dinner train rides with incredible gourmet cuisine. Experiencing dinner in a dining car is also a splendid way to enjoy your partner. It brings you back to an era long gone, where you dress up and board a dining car destined to pass great scenery. During this one-of-a-kind dining experience, you won't be rushed through dinner in order to free your table for another customer. Instead, you're expected to enjoy a leisurely meal until your train comes to a halt three hours later. What a way to enjoy dinner!

Dinner Cruises

Dinner on a boat is one of the most romantic dining experiences you can share with your partner. Boats have a way of rocking the tension right out of you so that you can enjoy your partner even more. An after-dinner walk on deck is also a must.

Adventurous Dating

Romance is where you make it, and the biggest part of being romantic is sharing in an activity that you both enjoy—whether it's taking in a sporting event or visiting the local amusement park. If you know your partner is happy, you will be happy.

Amusement Parks

Do you and your partner love to ride roller coasters? If you do, why not build your date time around visiting a theme park for the pure thrill of it? Why only fantasize about Disneyland or Sea World? Why not plan to go play in one for the day by making it your next extravagant date?

Many times you can find an amusement park within driving distance, and it doesn't necessarily have to be a big name park for you to have fun. Amusement parks have their own kind of romance: holding your partner close on frightening rides, holding hands, winning stuffed animals for your partner in the arcade, and sharing cotton candy.

Words of the Heart

"Daisy, Daisy, give me your answer, do!

I'm half crazy, all for the love of you!

It won't be a stylish marriage,

I can't afford a carriage,

But you'll look sweet upon the seat

Of a bicycle made for two!"

—Harry Dacre, "Daisy Bell" song, 1928

Sporting Events

Are you and your partner into sports or exercising? Splurging on an athletic pursuit is one of the easiest extravagant dates to plan for. Your date will depend on the type of event you are interested in. For instance, if you like golf and want to play a round with your partner, you can find enticing courses all over the world. Pick one, pack, and make a weekend out of it. Or, if you love baseball, visiting different ball parks throughout the country can be a bonding experience between you and your partner.

To make it extra special, you can get great tickets, say box seats, to an upcoming sports event. To make it really romantic, have a great meal either before or after the event. Don't forget the champagne!

Sightseeing

You don't have to be a tourist to go sightseeing. If you live in a city that attracts a lot of tourists, chances are that you haven't seen many of the sights yourself. If you haven't, you can plan a day of going from place to place as though you are from out of town. Leave your house early in the morning the way a tourist would. Plan your meals at the tourist places and take lots of pictures. You might even want to check into a hotel at the end of the day, which can be very romantic! At the end of your day, you will be so exhausted you won't feel like doing anything except relaxing in the hotel Jacuzzi. After you're revived, play tourist again and put on your dancing shoes and head out to the hot spots.

Fun and Entertainment

The best kinds of dates are the fun kind, where you laugh and really enjoy your partner. Some people find this kind of fun at a water park. For others, attending a charity dinner where your favorite stars will be is a lot of fun. Whatever is fun for you and your partner, make plans to schedule a special date so that you can experience the intensity an all-day adventure can bring you.

Here is a list of ideas that are guaranteed to bring you a fun-filled date together:

➤ Hot air balloon rides

➤ Glass-bottom boat rides

➤ Visits to natural hot springs

➤ Gondola rides

➤ Pampering at a day spa

Dr. Romance

For a very special date with your partner, hire a group of actors to perform your partner's favorite play in a private or public setting. All you have to do is tell them the play you want performed, the number of actors, and the length of time for the production. You'll be amazed at what life they will bring to your evening's event.

Distinguished Tastes

If you love to shop, taste wine, or attend cultural events, you can make a wonderfully romantic and extravagant date out of any of the following ideas.

The Store Opens at 9 A.M.

Good shopping used to be limited to big cities, but nowadays, you can find good shopping opportunities in almost every area of the country. Think about what your area is known for. Is it antiques? Art? Designer clothing?

Just think about how much fun you and your partner will have spending a whole day looking for treasures to take home. Shopping can also be very romantic if you remember to do at least some of the following things:

➤ Kiss and hug on the escalator

➤ Share a little passion in an elevator

➤ Share a dressing room with your partner

➤ Model lingerie for your partner

➤ Walk arm in arm

➤ Hold hands

Shopping together isn't all about purchasing items, it's about spending time together talking and sharing things. Even if you can't afford to buy anything, you can still make a day out of window shopping and having lunch in a nice restaurant.

Tasting the Grapes

Almost all areas of the country have vineyards, so if you love the taste of wine, going to a local vineyard could be a lot of fun and very romantic. You might want to do a little research to see which wineries are within driving distance and then contact them to see what kinds of events they have in the upcoming months.

Wine tastings have become a popular event over the years, so most vineyards have tasting rooms for you to try out their products first hand. Many wineries even have special occasions such as jazz concerts or black tie events in the vineyards.

Because you will be tasting the wine with your partner, you can do all sorts of things to make the occasion more romantic:

➤ Make a special toast to each other before you sample each wine.

➤ Bring a blanket and a picnic basket with cheese, crackers, and grapes to go with one of the vineyard's bottles of wine. Pick out a beautiful spot and enjoy a romantic meal together.

➤ If you start to get tipsy, give in to your lack of inhibition and kiss your partner each time the thought goes through your mind.

➤ Sneak off into the vineyards and take a walk hand in hand.

➤ Interlock arms and sip from each other's glass as you look into each other's eyes.

Words of the Heart

"I entertained on a cruising trip that was so much fun that I had to sink my yacht to make my guests go home."

—F. Scott Fitzgerald, 1945

Dr. Romance

Create a list of your favorite songs and hire singers to serenade the two of you as you romance your partner.

Cultural Events

Cultural events include museums, films, jazz festivals, plays, operas, ballets, and anything that involves sharing an emotional expression in art form. The local newspaper is a good place to find out what events are happening in your area.

If you and your partner enjoy the arts, keep in mind that you don't have to stay indoors to have a great time. Each year, for instance, many cities across the country hold outdoor Shakespearean festivals where you can watch actors in full costume perform some of Shakespeare's best-known plays.

Words of the Heart

"Women never look so well as when one comes in wet and dirty from hunting."

—R. S. Surtees, 1853

Fantasy Rentals

The beauty of renting is that if you can't afford to own it, you can still experience it for one night. You'd be surprised at all the things you can rent. One fun item to rent is a limousine, but you don't have to stop there—all kinds of fancy cars can be rented to make an evening extra special. If you think something could make a date more romantic, chances are, it can be rented.

Your Chariot Awaits

A lot of newly married couples rent limousines to take them from their wedding to the start of their honeymoon. Why save this luxury for the wedding? Think about it—a time when you are feeling less stress is a better time to enjoy it fully. You'll feel like royalty if you go for the glamor and rent a limo and driver for your evening. Some places will even rent classic cars. Your limo can take you anywhere you want to go: Maybe you'd like to go out for a fancy dinner or to a secluded spot for a private picnic. Or maybe you'll find it most romantic to just cruise.

As you've read in this chapter, every once in a while it's a good idea to make an ordinary date extraordinary. Romance is an adventure, and the easiest way to mix in romance when it begins to run low is to have an extravagant date. It's guaranteed to work. How can it not when each partner feels a sense of excitement about the planned upcoming date? The only way to keep a relationship happy is to continue to refuel it with the energy of discovery.

The Least You Need to Know

➤ Regardless of your budget, making extravagant dates happen is easy if you believe it can be done.

➤ Extending the length of dates is a great way to get to know your partner again.

➤ Take the time to plan an extravagant date that both of you will enjoy doing. What you choose should be determined by mutual interest.

➤ Romance can be added to anything you do together. Don't forget to include it!

Chapter 18

Sweep Me off My Feet

In This Chapter

➤ Fabulous parties and luxurious spas

➤ Designer clothes and gorgeous jewelry

➤ Yachts, islands, and other ultraromantic gifts

How would you like to sweep your partner off his or her feet in extravagant style? This type of magical, romantic adventure would make you both feel like a prince and princess. You would go on a magic carpet ride to places most couples don't get to experience.

This kind of adventure doesn't require rubbing a genie's bottle, wishing on a star, or even breaking a leg—it takes money and lots of it! If you've ever wondered what life would be like for a couple on the envied side of the tracks, this chapter will expose this lifestyle for what it really is—heavenly!

If you don't have a silver spoon in your mouth, you will still be able to enjoy every savory bite vicariously. You may even feel inspired to take some of the ideas from this chapter and save them for a later indulgence. Splurging on a once-in-a-lifetime activity will definitely lead to many years of wonderful memories for the two of you. All things are possible; you just have to make them happen.

Getting Your Romantic Needs Met Luxuriously

The goals for a couple at the top of the financial pyramid are not any different from any other couple in terms of what you strive for. Everyone's objective is to maintain their relationship by providing the necessary romantic atmosphere to keep it going. The only difference is that a rich couple can afford a more expensive atmosphere!

Keep in mind that although money has the ability to create dreams, it doesn't necessarily make romance happen. In order to do that, you must remember to create it. So what are you waiting for? Start planning. You have lavish adventures to discover with your partner.

The Party Circuit at a Whole New Level

Upscale parties add a touch of fairy-tale magic to your relationship because they usually take place in elegant places. You'll find some parties in beautiful privately owned mansions, in exquisite hotels, and in exciting areas of town.

Parties add a sense of drama to your relationship, especially the formal kind or costume party. Getting all dressed up is very romantic because it allows you to look your best and feel great looking good together. For instance, John, who typically wears casual wear to work, gets to put on a tuxedo, and Ellen changes from business clothes into a sleek black dress for an evening out. This change in your appearance makes both of you feel good and want to have a fun time at the party.

Even if you can afford to party expensively, it doesn't mean that you know where the parties are. This list of ideas will help put you in the path of the most exclusive parties:

➤ Donating to charities is the best way to get on the list of great parties. Contact charities and ask about fundraising parties.

➤ Get on the mailing list for wineries in the better neighborhoods.

➤ Attend opening night events and the parties that follow them.

➤ Look into events associated with museums and art galleries.

➤ Performing arts centers and repertories are known for formal parties, so give them a call and see what they have going on.

➤ Read nationwide and local magazines that cater to a more exclusive readership. They always advertise events.

➤ Sports such as polo, sailing, and golf cater to a more affluent population, as do the parties associated with them.

After you've decided to go to a party, make the adventure as romantic as possible by following these tips:

➤ Slow dancing with your partner is a must.

➤ Hold hands while you walk with your partner.

➤ Take a walk outside (even if it's cold) and kiss passionately under the night sky.

➤ Wear perfume or cologne to smell irresistible.

➤ Arrive in a limousine and drink champagne.

Repairing the Damage in Style

The only way to stay in tiptop shape is to pamper yourself and let others spoil you, too. The best environment for this pampering is at a spa, where people focus on catering to your every need. But you can't go to just any spa. To completely rejuvenate yourself for another play session with your partner, only the most luxurious spa will do.

Going to a spa with your partner is a great way to unwind from your lives and get you back to a relaxed state of loving. This section describes the very best spas the world has to offer. Any of these spas would be a perfect place for you to unwind with your partner and plan your next excursion.

Dr. Romance

Here are some good reasons to go to an exquisite spa with your partner: to feel closer, to eliminate stress, to have fun, to be pampered, to relax, and to rejuvenate the mind and soul.

➤ **The Aspen Club in Aspen, Colorado.** The Aspen Club is primarily a day spa–athletic club in the downtown area of Aspen that caters to the high-society types from Hollywood, Texas, and New York. This spa will teach you about your body and how to stay fit. Its emphasis is on fitness and sports, good nutritional guidance, and weight loss. Although you can't stay at the club, there are exquisite hotels nearby.

➤ **Badrutt's Palace Hotel in the Acapulco Spa in St. Moritz, Switzerland.** You and your partner will begin to feel at peace the moment you see the majestic setting of this club. The panoramic view of St. Moritz, its lake, and the Alps is nothing but spectacular. The emphasis of this club is on sports, especially in ski season.

➤ **Hotel Ritz–Healthy Club Ritz in Paris, France.** Earnest Hemingway helped to make this spa famous when he wrote, "When I dream of the afterlife in heaven, the actions always take place at the Paris Ritz." This spa is located in one of the most beautiful cities of the world and decorated exquisitely with a regal emphasis. If you and your partner would like to experience pampering at its finest, then this is the spot for you.

The one thing all of these spas have in common is that they reunite your body and soul. They all do it with variations of the same recipe: good food, exercise, and relaxation. By the time you and your partner are all put back together, you're ready to go off again to new adventures on the diamond-lined trail of romantic love.

Extravagant Gifts

Money may not be able to buy happiness, but it certainly makes giving gifts a lot more exciting. Money gives you the opportunity to spoil your love partner with expensive gifts. If money were no problem, what sort of gifts would you buy for your partner to show how much you love him or her? In this section, you will discover the unbelievable gifts that are available if you have the money.

If you are going to surprise your partner with a gift, you'll want to buy something that he or she will love. Just because a present is expensive doesn't mean your partner will want it. When shopping for a gift, it's best to know what your partner would just die for.

Over the next week, pay close attention to what your partner talks about that might give you an idea of what to buy. For instance, Brett overheard his girlfriend on the phone talking about how much she used to love jumping on trampolines as a child and would love to do it again. Bingo! He's just discovered a present to buy for her. This is the fun part of gift giving: discovering what your partner really wants and giving it to him or her. Make a list of five things your partner would love:

1. _____
2. _____
3. _____
4. _____
5. _____

Clothing for Royalty

If your partner loves clothing, then nothing is better than a gift of designer apparel. If you want to truly impress your partner, the clothing must be the best of the best.

The characteristics that follow should give you a good idea of what the perfect apparel present should be:

➤ It's a one-of-a-kind item.

➤ It was designed by a top designer.

➤ It should be very expensive.

Words of the Heart

"If thou follow thy star, thou canst not fail of a glorious haven."

—Dante Alighieri

There, now you have the guidelines for giving the ultimate piece of clothing. But where do you find it? Exorbitantly tagged one-of-a-kind items can be found in most designer boutiques.

The Million-Dollar Bra

Designer clothing, of course, makes a very special gift, but what about the times when you want to really wow your partner with something so original she would feel like the most special woman in the world? Sometimes a clothing item comes along that seems too unbelievable to be real.

Victoria's Secret introduced its staggering one-million-dollar diamond and semi-precious stone-studded Miracle bra in its 1998 Christmas gift catalog. This bra was followed by the three-million-dollar Diamond Dream bra. Keeping in line with this tradition, it then released the most glamorous and romantic bra in the world: the five-million-dollar Dream Angels bra. It had more than 600 glittering precious gems sewn into it, making it the most breathtaking bra ever. A bra like this would no doubt make you game for a little strip poker!

The five-million-dollar bra.

So you see, if you want to buy special clothing for your partner, all you have to do is keep your eyes open for unique offers! If you don't find them, you can always use your own imagination and work with a designer to help create attire for your partner that is anything but tiring.

A Sparkle in Everyone's Eyes: Jewelry

Sometimes real-life stories seem more like fairy tales when money is involved. For instance, in a true-life fantasy come true, Oliver wanted to get his wife something special for their anniversary, so he decided to buy her a jewelry box and fill it with the finest jewels he could find. This was no ordinary jewelry box, however. It was a 4.5-foot safe that contained eight gold drawers filled with the most exquisite jewels. The cost of the safe alone was $75,000, so you can only imagine what he paid for the jewels inside.

Got a lot of money to spend? Here are some ideas for jewelry gifts from the Tiffany's catalog:

➤ Emerald-cut yellow and white diamond necklace: $1.25 million dollars

➤ Petal Mosaic diamond necklace: $135,000; matching bracelet: $53,000; matching earrings: $17,000

➤ Schlumberger aquamarine earrings: $39,750; four buds ring: $56,450

➤ Cultured Tahitian pearls and diamond necklace set in platinum: $85,000; matching bracelet: $51,000; matching earrings: $27,000

➤ Emerald and diamond necklace: $200,000; matching earrings: $345,000

Shopping for men's jewelry is much less complicated than shopping for women's jewelry. Men's jewelry gifts fall into basically three items: watches, cuff links, and pens. You can expect to pay less for men's jewelry than you would for the same caliber of women's jewelry, but it will still be very expensive if you buy the best. For example, Tiffany offers a ball-point pen for $2,300 and an 18K gold fountain pen for $3,000.

Charting the Waters

If your partner likes big toys, a customized yacht should do the trick. There are plenty of top-notch companies that will custom design an ideal look and layout for a boat for you and your honey to romance each other on.

The drawback to building your own yacht is that many times it takes more than two years to complete. If you are not interested in waiting, there is a surplus of previously owned yachts to choose from that are available immediately. You can find them in any shape and size to fit what you think your partner would like. Just think, you could buy one, and within no time, take your partner down to the harbor and show her a very big present just waiting for her.

Cupid's Report

If you want to check on either your or your partner's health, you can fly to downtown Norfolk for a one-day medical assessment.

The Sentara center at www.eecva.com offers the most sophisticated and comprehensive evaluation of your health. You'll receive a thorough review of your results by the end of the day. This way you will be able to detect any health abnormalities in time for life-saving early prevention. It's the best way to keep your love alive.

Words of the Heart

"Admire the process of partnership as it unfolds naturally between you, the result of your dedication and steadfast love."

—Toni Sciarra Poynter, from *From This Day Forward*

Dr. Romance

When giving a gift, do so because you want to give. Giving to get something in return only spoils the present.

An added bonus to giving your loved one a boat is that you can personalize it with the name. When choosing a name, make sure you stick with something meaningful. Think along the lines of nicknames or the place and date you met. What a way to advertise your love for all the water world to see!

Creative Gifts

A lot of people out there are very creative gift givers. These people enjoy taking their fantasies and making them real. A creative gift is a great way to express your love. In this section, I show you two ways to show your love for your partner: through photography and by making storybook fantasies a reality.

Artistic Love

For centuries, lovers have cherished pictures of their chosen ones. In the past, portraits were drawn or painted, but today, photographs are the medium of choice.

Some photographers can make you look pretty; others can transform you into an exquisite piece of art. As you probably guessed, photography like this is not cheap. Expect to pay several thousand dollars for a professional sitting. The best way to find a great photographer is to look at photos in magazines. If you find a photo that captures your interest, contact that photographer and arrange for a photo shoot. Doing this is easier than you'd think. All you have to do is contact the magazine that you saw the photo in and request the photographer's telephone number.

Artistic love.

Just think of how thrilled your partner would be to see you as a piece of artwork. He'd love it! If you are camera shy because of wrinkles, excess weight, or the loss of youth, you have nothing to worry about. Good photographers have mastered the art of airbrushing, so you'll look just as desirable as any model in the magazines.

Creating Storybook Gifts

Did your partner have a favorite story that he or she loved as a child? If so, you may be able to re-create it as a gift. Sometimes stories make a big impression on a person, and they continue to talk about them in adulthood. If this describes your partner, then you may want to make his or her dreams come true by taking the imaginary and making it real. In this section, you will read about two men who made their partner's storybook fantasies come true with a little creativity and a lot of money.

Cupid's Report

Vladi Private Islands specializes in islands for sale. You can reach this company on the Internet at www.Vladi-Private-Island.com.

The Swiss Family Robinson Gift

Sam's girlfriend had a childhood fantasy of living the experience she had watched on the Disney movie *The Swiss Family Robinson*. Eager to re-create her fantasy, Sam decided to buy an island and propose marriage to her on it. He knew the proposal wouldn't be right unless it could be done in a treehouse. For months, he went to work with an architect who designed and built the most spectacular treehouse ever.

Finally, Sam was ready to propose. He had a ring in his pocket and a treehouse waiting in the South Pacific for his soon-to-be wife. When the day came, she thought they were off on another travel adventure and had no idea what was in store for her. After landing on their own landing strip, they drove by jeep to the treehouse, and Sam proposed marriage after he carried her over the doorway. A month later, their closest family and friends joined them in the most exotic wedding ceremony ever on their island.

The Hansel and Gretel Gift

Brandon's wife had a very demanding sweet tooth. They had been married for 12 years, and he had no idea what to get her for a Valentine's Day gift. Then, one night, a light bulb went off in his head as he overheard his wife reading the story of Hansel and Gretel to their children. Brandon decided that he would build his wife a candy house.

On the morning of Valentine's Day, Brandon served his wife breakfast in bed, complete with a 10-pound bag of assorted hard candies. After breakfast, he suggested that the family take a walk in the woods behind their house. Of course, there was a trail of

Words of the Heart

"The absence of flaw in beauty is itself a flaw."

—Havelock Ellis, 1914

bread crumbs, and Brandon suggested that they follow them and see where they lead. Before long, they came upon 10-foot playhouse made entirely of candy. Painted on the door in red frosting was a heart with the message, "To my sweet wife, Happy Valentine's Day."

When trying to think of something unique to give your mate, you might want to start by learning what cartoons and stories were your partner's favorite. Did he like Speed Racer, the race car driver? If so, a grand prix car and driving lessons would be a great fantasy gift. Throw in his own racetrack to make the present complete.

Whatever the fantasy, if you have the resources and time to be creative, you can come up with a good gift that your partner will love. Just think of how special it will make your partner feel that you care enough to know all about him or her, even his or her childhood dreams.

The Least You Need to Know

➤ Sweep your partner off his or her feet in an extravagant lifestyle. There is no reason to have an ordinary relationship if you can afford to make your romantic dreams come true.

➤ The excitement of a formal party is only enhanced when you make it romantic with long, slow kisses under the night sky and slow dancing to romantic music.

➤ Money gives you the opportunity to spoil your partner with expensive gifts. Make your gifts extra special by adding personal touches to them.

➤ When money is no option, the world is your romantic playground. There is always romantic fun to be had; all you have to do is look for it and pull your partner along to enjoy it with you.

Part 5

Romance Forever

The only way to keep love alive is to keep investing in the relationship you care about. Learning how to be romantic is one thing, but making a choice to devote your life to it is a real commitment. This section shows you how to get out of a rut and enjoy your partner the way two people are supposed to—together with shared activities.

This section brings back the magic of dating. Whether married or single, it takes you from the preliminary concerns of dating, celebrating the love you have, to enjoying the adventure along the way for a life of love and happiness.

FLOWERS ✓
LIMO ✓
RESERVATIONS ✓
TICKETS ✓

Chapter 19

Pre-Date Considerations

In This Chapter

➤ Making time to date

➤ Inviting your date

➤ Greeting your date

➤ Date gifts

➤ Ending the date

Nicki is all dressed up. It's Friday night, and Gary is already 45 minutes late. Just three days earlier, he promised her that he'd be home by 6:30, and they'd have a nice dinner at their favorite restaurant. He said he'd take care of things, including the reservations; all she had to do was look pretty.

She'd heard this a hundred times, but she still believed he'd follow through this time. Finally, at 7:45 the garage door opens, and Nicki is in no mood to go out. Like always, something last-minute came up at work that detained him. To make matters worse, he forgot to make reservations, and when he called from the car, he found out that the restaurant was booked for the evening. With such a bad start to the date, neither person fully recovered, and the evening was far from relaxed and romantic. Instead, Nicki spent the evening feeling angry while Gary felt bad for disappointing her.

If dating is supposed to be fun, why is it that sometimes it seems like so much trouble? This chapter is for the couple who has been dating for awhile and feels like the romance isn't as strong as it used to be. After reading this chapter, you'll learn how to

Words of the Heart

"Spend as much time as possible laughing with your partner. Look for funniness in life and share it with each other, even during difficult times. Shared happiness is the mortar that holds your house together. Mix humor into your relationship as consciously as you mix passion, insight, and judgment. Sometimes the only thing that gets you over a rough spot is a whistle or a smile."

—Toni Sciarra Poynter, from *From This Day Forward: Meditations on the First Years of Marriage*

put the fun back into dating by recharging your relationship batteries. You will learn to behave more like couples who are newly in love. This behavior will put your relationship back into romantic mode and make you look forward to planning times to spend with your partner.

Get Your Relationship on the Right Track

Finding the time to date isn't always easy, but it's important. Think of it this way: If having a strong relationship with your partner is important, then dating needs to be a priority.

Making Dates a Priority

I cannot tell you how many times I have heard couples give excuse after excuse for why they can't date. Here are some of the more common reasons why couples say they don't go out on dates:

➤ "We don't have the money to date."

➤ "We don't have the time."

➤ "If we can't do it right, why bother?"

➤ "We don't have a baby-sitter."

➤ "We don't trust anyone to watch our kids."

All I can say when I hear excuses like these is, if you are able to find time and money for the other things in your life, then you can find time for dating, too. If the young couples with small children who say they don't have the money to date were to look at their spending habits, they might see that they have plenty of money; they are just spending it on other things they consider more important. Does little Bridget really need $100 worth of new clothing each month? Does Mom really need $100 worth of yard sale junk each month? Does Dad really need $100 worth of fast food each month? Probably not. But spending $100 on dating each month would be a wise investment.

When couples have a lot of excuses for not dating, it's time to change things in order to strengthen the relationship. Even if your relationship feels strong, it will weaken if it's neglected long enough. Neglect can happen without your even noticing it. When spending time together as a couple becomes less frequent, you should be concerned. Regardless of how much love you and your partner share, you need to devote quality time to the relationship to keep it strong. Take it from me and from all the couples I have counseled over the years: Keeping a relationship strong is a lot easier than rebuilding one that is neglected.

Spending Time Alone as a Couple

It's time to take some action! If you want to have a relationship that lasts, you need to spend date time alone with your partner. Go on fun dates for a few hours at a time and progress to intimate dates or dates that require extended time together. Chapter 20, "Creative Dating," provides plenty of ideas for three- or four-hour dates that are inexpensive to moderately priced. Chapter 17, "What a Little Extra Money Can Do," also has date ideas; however, they are much more expensive and involve long hours together. My suggestion is to start out slow by picking an idea from Chapter 20. Later on, you'll feel more at ease trying out the suggestions in Chapter 17.

Make a Date and Keep It

The only way to get in the habit of dating your partner is by scheduling a date in advance. Better yet, have a set date night. This night can be the first Saturday of each month, for example, or maybe you want to do it as often as every Wednesday night. It all depends on how much time you are interested in investing in your relationship.

Once you make a date, avoid canceling it at all costs—even if you had a bad day or you are very tired. Once you begin breaking or rescheduling dates, it's just a matter of time before they lose priority all over again, and you're back where you started.

Cupid's Report

Did you know that certain vegetables have messages associated with them just like flowers do? Here is a list of vegetables you might consider giving to your partner (if the message is right):

Vegetables	Message
Cabbage	Gain
Corn	Riches
Pea (sweet)	Lasting pleasure, departure
Mushroom	Suspicion
Rhubarb	Advice
Turnip	Charity

Words of the Heart

"And now good morrow to our waking souls, which watch not one another out of fear; for love, all love of other sights controls, and makes one little room, an everywhere."

—John Donne

Dr. Romance

Like roses, different kinds of daisies mean different things. The next time you send your partner daisies, keep in mind the slight differences in the message behind the types of daisy. In love, everything is so subtle:

Daisy (Michaelmas)	After-thought
Daisy (Ox-eye)	A token
Daisy (Parti-colored)	Beauty
Daisy (White)	Innocent

Words of the Heart

"Love is an endless mystery, for it has nothing else to explain it."

—Rabindranath Tagore

A Must: A "No Cancelation" Policy

Think of a date the same way you view exercising. You may not always feel like going to the gym, but you do it anyway. You know that if you don't go on a regular basis, your body will get out of shape. The same idea applies to dating. Dating is the only way to keep your relationship in shape, so follow the same principle from exercising: Go even when you don't want to, and do it on a regular basis!

In order for you and your partner to enjoy more time together, two factors must be present: desire and opportunity. If you don't have desire, you won't make the opportunity.

Have You Received Your Invitation?

You can ask someone for a date in all sorts of ways. For newer couples, you have the traditional asking over the telephone, the last-minute, "Hey, I've got a great idea," and the asking while you're still on a date. For couples who have been together longer, asking for a date takes a different form. There's the "I have nothing to do; do you want to go do something?" the "I'm going out; you can come along if you want to," and the trusty "We haven't gone out in so long, why don't we plan something?"

When new couples make plans to see each other again, they not only know they want to have another date, but they also schedule a time to ask for it. This is a lot different from couples who have been together longer. In their case, asking for a date seems more like an uneventful afterthought than an opportunity to have a shared adventure.

Of course, there is a difference between new couples and couples who have been together a long time. The biggest difference is that new couples have the initial excitement of just being together to make things romantic. A big part of their excitement comes from the newness of the situation. Couples who have been together longer can create this kind of excitement when they act more like newer couples. This means not only planning dates, but also preparing for just the right time to ask for a date.

Asking for a Date Creatively

Paper invitations were invented for a reason. They serve three primary purposes. First of all, they act as a reminder of an upcoming event. They also make the person accountable for not being able to attend by requesting that the person responds by a certain date. Last, they make the act of inviting someone to do something extra special.

If you want to go the traditional route, you can mail an invitation to your partner. If you want to do something a bit more exciting, try any of the following ideas:

Dr. Romance

Ovid gave advice to lovers over 2,000 years ago. In the following quote, he gets the poignant message across that a suitor needs to show effort if he wants to keep the one he loves. "I liked her looks, wrote promptly for a meeting. 'It's not allowed,' she wrote back nervously. And when I asked why not, she gave the reason that, 'You attend the girl too tiresomely.'"

1. Place the invitation somewhere your partner will see it while you two are riding in the car together. Some places you might put it are: by a stop sign, in the bushes, on the curb, tacked to a telephone pole, taped to a stop light, with a gas station attendant, or on the ground next to a mailbox. You get the idea. All you have to do is point it out when you are driving by. When you get close, stop the car, and ask your partner to pick it up. Tell her that someone must have dropped it, and you need to put it in a mailbox when you see one. The surprise comes when your partner picks up the envelope and sees that it's addressed to her.

2. Put the invitation on her car windshield or inside the car on the driver's seat. You can make the invitation on a piece of paper by hand or on the computer. This will be a different type of invitation, better known as a flyer. Just like above, flyers can be left in all sorts of places for your partner to find.

3. Write an invitation on a piece of fruit and leave it in the refrigerator or have a store employee deliver it while she's grocery shopping.

4. Print out an invitation on a small piece of paper and put it inside a fortune cookie.

5. Tape an invitation to your partner's favorite section of the newspaper for him to find when he reads it.

6. Have a messenger service deliver the invitation in the form of a telegram.

7. Type an invitation on her or his computer screensaver.

8. Send an invitation electronically via fax, pager, or e-mail. To make an e-mail invitation extra special, refer to Chapter 15, "Technology and Romance," for a bunch of ideas.

Words of the Heart

"What you don't know would make a great book."

—Sydney Smith

Dr. Romance

Imagine how you would feel if you had the chance to have your hair cut by someone who cuts hair for celebrities. I bet you think it would either be impossible to get an appointment or too expensive to afford, right? Wrong. If you ever see a hairstyle in a local magazine that you like, contact the magazine and ask who the stylist was. The magazine will give you the salon name and phone number, and you can have your hair done by someone who knows what he or she is doing.

9. Tuck an invitation in his or her book in place of the bookmark.

10. Tuck an invitation under your partner's pillow so that he or she will find it when he or she goes to bed.

What Do You Mean I Have to Look Good?

Part of the fun of dating is seeing your partner's eyes light up when he or she looks at you. Looking attractive and smelling nice not only feels good, it also makes your partner attracted to you. For many couples, the longer they stay together, the less time they devote to primping prior to a date. For some reason, it becomes less important to them. This is probably one of the biggest mistakes couples can make.

You've heard of the expression "The grass is always greener on the other side." This expression can apply to your appearance when dating. Too many couples get comfortable and forget how important it is to keep your side of the grass green! If you don't make yourself look physically attractive, then your partner will naturally look to greener pastures. This is just human nature.

Looking good on a date is very important, even if you have been together for 20 years. Take your time and put the effort into looking your best for date night. For more direction on how to look your best, refer to Chapter 14, "Seducing Your Senses."

Dress You Up in My Love

Dressing for a date does not mean having to wear a tie or heels. It means wearing flattering colors, ironed clothes, and something other than the clothes you wear around the house.

Because date night is special, you'll want to dress a little fancier than you are used to. You might even try wearing something new. A simple rule to follow is to dress as though you are going on your first date.

Primping for a date makes it feel more special. Dates with the one you love are special, so treat them that way. Let your partner know that he or she is special by putting in the extra effort to look nice.

Honey! Your Date Is Here!

One reason dating is exciting is because of the anticipation you feel waiting for your date to arrive. You peek out the window to see if he's there. You hurry to the phone, hoping it will be him telling you he's on the way. When you hear him at the door, you quickly rush to open it and always wonder if he'll have a surprise for you.

The longer a couple is together, the less exciting it is when your partner shows up at the door. Things have become predictable because you have learned your partner's habits. There is nothing less exciting than knowing what will happen.

If you live under the same roof, the beginning of a date usually starts with a holler down the hall letting your partner know that you're ready. This is definitely not a romantic way to begin a date with the one you love.

Ding Dong, Someone's Here

If the start of your date isn't exciting, then something needs to be changed. It's time to bring back the excitement you once felt. Any kind of change adds excitement, regardless of how small a change it is. Learn how to put the thrill back into opening the door for your date again.

The few minutes before a date begins are more exciting if you have had an absence of time from your partner. If you live under the same roof, you don't have this luxury unless you create it. Even if you live with your partner, the only way to make a date seem like a real date is to pick up your date by going to her front door and knocking or ringing the doorbell. All you have to do is sneak out when she isn't looking and surprise her.

Just as the lighting of the torch begins the Olympic Games, the knocking or doorbell ringing does the same for the date. It's the same as the announcer saying, "Let the games begin!" To avoid this becoming predictable for married couples, do it only now and then. This way, your partner will always be surprised to find you at the door before your date.

To make your greeting even more like a real date, show up with one of the love offerings from the next section. This gesture will bring back the

Words of the Heart

"No thing great is created suddenly, any more than a bunch of grapes or a fig. If you tell me that you desire a fig, I answer you that there must be time. Let it first blossom, then bear fruit, then ripen."

—Epictetus (320 B.C.E.)

fond memories from the past and delight her all over again. Fantasies are all about what we create and re-create in our relationships.

Passionate Greetings

Date night is the perfect time to put passion into your relationship. When you open the door and see your partner standing there looking great, greet him the way you did in the beginning of your courtship. Push the door open and throw your arms around him and make him glad he asked you out. Kiss him sensuously, and then take him by the hand and invite him in. Even if you barely touch each other all night, there are two times on your date for warm affection: when he arrives and when he leaves.

Part of date night is pretending to be a new couple with lots of passion. If you don't feel passion, "Fake it until you make it," as the saying goes. With enough love and tenderness, it will become genuine.

Pet names make your partner feel special. Now is the time to use them, especially new terms of endearment. If you need some help coming up with some names, refer to Chapter 9, "Expressing Love Verbally." There you will find plenty of new names to choose from.

Dr. Romance

If you want to make your time together romantic, make sure that you:

➤ Don't bring your pager.

➤ Don't bring your cellular phone.

➤ Don't criticize your partner.

➤ Don't make any phone calls when you are out with your partner.

➤ Don't talk about work or the children.

➤ Don't talk about bills.

Love Offerings

Have you ever given thought to what a date really is? A date is a mini-celebration of the two of you. It's a time to come together because you enjoy spending time with each other. What better way to recognize this occasion than with a trinket of your love? It's a terrific way to show your appreciation for your partner.

A trinket is a token of your affection. It's a small, inexpensive gift to give your partner when you meet for a date. You should always show up with one if you can. This rule applies to both men and women. Giving a trinket is one way of letting your partner know that you think about him or her when you are away. It reassures each of you that the love between you is strong.

In this section, you'll read about different kinds of love offerings to give your partner on date night. Because flowers are the most popular token of love given by people in relationships, I'll start there.

A Flower for My Love

Lovers have always felt the need to communicate their feelings to each other. Before the days of love letters, people sent their feelings back and forth through bouquets of flowers. Each flower was assigned a different message that everyone eventually learned.

For instance, a knight who fell off his horse in the presence of his maiden would send her a pomegranate to say he felt foolish. He would also include a bouquet of flowers to explain why he fell: Province rose (his heart was in flames), red rose (he's passionate over her beauty), and peach blossoms (I am your captive).

Flowers are a traditional date trinket. Flowers communicate the good and the bad in such a gentle way. See what messages you can communicate to your partner by using flowers. Just make sure to attach a note that tells him or her the meaning of your choices. It will flatter your date all the more to know that you put so much energy into expressing your love for him or her by picking out a flower.

Most people know that roses symbolize love and romance. But many people don't know that different roses mean different things, as listed in the following table.

Words of the Heart

"As when a flower secretly springs up in an enclosed garden, unknown to the herd, uncrushed by any plough, which the breezes caress, the sun strengthens and the rain brings out, many boys have desired it and many girls. Yet when the same flower fades, nipped by a sharp hail, no boys and no girls desire it. Such is a virgin while she remains intact and is dear to her own; but when she has lost her chaste flower and her body has been sullied, she no longer remains pleasing to the boys or dear to the girls."

—Catullus, *Gaius Falerius* (84 B.C.E.)

Type of Rose	Message
Austrian	You are lovely
Bridal	Happy love
Campion	Only you deserve my love
Carolina	Love is dangerous
China	Beauty always new
Christmas	Please relieve my anxiety
Daily	I aspire to your smile
Damask	Brilliant complexion; freshness
Dog	Pleasure and pain
May	Precocity
Mundi	Variety
Pompom	Prettiness
Province	My heart is in flames
York	War

Dr. Romance

Take pictures on your date! This night is special, and you'll want at least one picture of the loving couple laughing and having a good time together.

Just think of the things that flowers can do for your relationship. If you have a hard time communicating in words, you can let flowers do it for you.

By the 1600s, flowers offered a powerful communicating tool to say what might be difficult to say in words. Take, for example, a married man who finds a pretty single woman attractive. He could proposition her with flowers by sending her a tuberose (dangerous pleasures). If she were interested in his suggestion, she could send him a moss rosebud (confession of love). If his wife happened to see what was going on, she could send each of them a single lotus (discovery of an illicit affair). However, if the young woman was not interested in the married man's advances, she would send him a pennyroyal (go away).

Flowers can become a creative way to extend a love letter. For instance, you can tell your partner that you are going to be giving her one line of a love letter along with a flower each time the two of you go on a date over the next month. You can tell her that the first line will begin when you pick her up on Saturday in the form of a flower. All month she'll eagerly await a flower, not only for the beauty, but for the message. By the time the month ends, her beautiful message will be complete. Long after the flowers have died, she'll still have your written interpretations of each flower's message to keep for a lifetime.

Flowers Aren't the Only Messengers

Not all bouquets have to come in the form of flowers. If your partner is a cook, you can bring her an arrangement of edible flowers and herbs for her to put in recipes. You can attach a note that says, "To some, the scent of these is beautiful, but the more distinguished know it's the *taste* that's meant to be appreciated."

You do not always have to bring flowers as a token of your love. If your partner loves gardening, you can bring a gift that she can plant and care for. The trees in the following list have a secret message attached to them.

Tree	Message
Almond	Indiscretion
Ash	Grandeur
Bay	Glory
Box	Stoicism
Chestnut	Do me justice
Fern	Sincerity

Tree	*Message*
Judas	Unbelief
Laurel	Glory
Oak	Hospitality
Orange	Generosity
Plane	Genius
Plum	Keep your promises

If you do send a tree, include a note about the special messages that are attached to the blossoms that will grow in the spring on that particular tree.

Blossoms	*Meaning*
Apple	Preference
Cherry	Spiritual
Lemon	Discretion; fidelity in love
Orange	Your purity equals your loveliness
Peach	I am your captive
Pear	Affection

Sweet Tokens for Your Sweetie

For centuries, lovers have given sweet foods to the ones they love. Consider how much chocolate is bought on Valentine's Day alone!

Chocolate is definitely the most given sweet confection. Some believe that chocolate stimulates the love center in the brain and gives people the feelings of being in love when they eat it. This theory alone should be motivation enough to bring your partner chocolate on a date. You can buy chocolate in varying amounts, from an individual piece all the way up to an enormous heart-shaped box.

Cupid's Report

Hershey knows how much lovers like chocolate. It should, because every day it manufactures 33 million Hershey's kisses.

Healthy Gifts

As crazy as it may sound, not everyone wants to be surprised by chocolate. Some may prefer healthier sweets such as fruits. Just make sure to fill your fruit basket wisely, because each fruit has a message that goes along with it.

Fruit	Message
Apple	Temptation (Eve)
Cherry (white)	Deception
Gooseberry	Anticipation
Fig	Argument, longevity
Lemon	Zest
Mulberry	I will not survive you
Orange	Generosity
Peach	Your qualities, like your charms, are unequaled
Pear	Affection
Pineapple	Welcome
Pomegranate	Foolishness
Raspberry	Remorse
Strawberries	Perfect elegance

The Kiss Good Night

Before the date ends, be sure to tell your date that you are looking forward to kissing him or her on the front doorstep. By telling your partner this, it will make him or her excitedly look forward to what kind of kiss you are going to deliver. More than anything, your partner will think it's very romantic. Who knows, your partner may get coy and say, "Maybe I'm not ready to let you kiss me goodnight."

Even if you park the car in the garage, walk to the front door to say goodnight. Stand at the door the way you used to and look deep into your partner's eyes with either your arms around him or her or holding hands. Even if you've been married for 30 years, looking deep into someone's eyes can sends a chill up your spine. My Grandma Brown said she always felt this way about her husband, Grandpa Brown, and they were married 63 years and had eight children!

If you want to make your kiss goodnight extra romantic, follow these tips:

Words of the Heart

"From their eyelids as they glanced dripped love."

—Hesiod, *The Theogony*

➤ Hold your partner's hand as you walk to the door.

➤ Take your time getting to the kiss.

➤ Let your partner know what a good time you had and that you'd like to do it again.

➤ Tell your partner you've been looking forward to this kiss all night. Even if you've kissed all night, this traditional moment is romantic.

➤ Caress your partner's cheek as you look deep into your partner's eyes in a long gaze.

➤ Cup your partner's face in both your hands and tell her how beautiful she is.

➤ Slowly move in for a very long, passionate kiss.

➤ For the sake of romantic drama, if you are holding a sweater, keys, or something nonbreakable, let it drop to the ground in the middle of the kiss. Your date will love this display of a loss of control.

➤ Keep talking to a minimum. Let your eyes and body language talk for you.

The Least You Need to Know

➤ The only way to stay in love with your partner is by going out of your way to spend special time together.

➤ Actions speak louder than words. Stop talking about going out and do it. You'll have so much fun.

➤ You don't need to spend a fortune on a bouquet of flowers—you can communicate a strong message with just one flower that has a special meaning attached to it.

➤ No one ever forgets how to kiss passionately, so if you haven't kissed your partner that way in a while, pucker your lips and get ready for action!

Chapter 20

Creative Dating

<table>
<tr><td align="center">**In This Chapter**</td></tr>
</table>

➤ Matching your date to your mood

➤ Planning the perfect date

➤ The Date Activity Book

➤ Dating at home

At the end of the month, Stuart and Susan were running low on money, so they decided to put off going out on a date until the first of the month. Then Susan had a great idea. "Stuart, we don't have to cancel our plans. Why don't we just go on a date at home?" She explained the details of her plan. "We were going to have dinner and go dancing, so why don't we just do that here?"

They set their date for Saturday night at 7 P.M. and went through the typical routine of preparing for a date: showering, primping, and anticipating the evening. At first Stuart thought it was a little silly to do this, but once he began, he noticed that the preparation made the evening feel just as special as if they were going out. They met by the fireplace, listened to romantic music, and started the evening with a nice glass of wine. Their evening went so well that they planned another date at home for the following month.

Words of the Heart

"Imagination is more important than knowledge."

—Albert Einstein

Dr. Romance

Date night should be reserved for just you and your partner. Use this time to grow closer and learn more about each other. If you want to include others in evening plans, make plans for a night not reserved for the two of you.

As you see, dating can create the same feelings whether you go out on the town or stay at home. In this chapter, you will learn how to figure out an easy way to not only plan dates but also have them meet the changing moods that you experience from date to date. This tactic makes dating something that both partners look forward to doing. This chapter will also broaden your idea of dating at home by supplying plenty of stay-at-home dates for you and your partner to try.

In the Mood

What you choose to do on your date sets a certain mood. These different moods are what give dating such variety. One of the first steps in date planning is to decide what you are in the mood for, emotionally speaking. If you've had a stressful week, for example, think of what kind of evening will make you feel better. If you need a laugh, your date could be dinner and a show at a comedy club.

Of course, you'll want to consider your partner's mood, too. Instead of asking what your partner would like to do, ask your partner what kind of emotional state he or she is in. Dating is for both partners; if both feel their needs are being considered, the time together will be more enjoyable.

Decide what kind of mood you need for your date and then plan accordingly. The following list describes some moods you may be in. Next to each mood, write some date ideas that meet each mood for you. Have your partner do the same.

Mood of Date	Type of Activity to Meet Mood
Relaxing?	_____
Exciting?	_____
Adventurous?	_____
Elegant?	_____
Sexy?	_____
Intellectual?	_____

Romantic?   _____

Other?   _____

When you understand what kind of date will meet your needs and your partner's, figuring out what to do is much easier. If you partner tells you he feels like doing something elegant, you'll know what date ideas will satisfy that need of his. Remember, dating is meant to be enjoyable, so if you have the least bit of hesitation or dread for a date, then you need to consider changing the mood (or your date!).

It's All in the Planning

If you want to plan a date effectively, you have to be organized. Sure, you may not know what your mood will be for your date, but this section will teach you how to plan dates to prepare for the various moods you and your partner may experience.

I'm going to show you how to use a Date Activity Book so that you have ideas jotted down in advance. This way, you won't be stuck with the frustration of coming up with ideas of what to do. But remember, if you want to see how effective this dating aid is, you have to actually use it!

Organizing a Date Activity Book

Coming up with an idea for a date can be stressful, especially if you're a person who doesn't enjoy planning. To make the planning easier, you will need to get a blank notebook, henceforth known as your Date Activity Book. The Date Activity Book will be your resource for the things you would like to do with your partner.

On the top of each page, put the title of all categories that are interesting to you, such as Movies, Plays, Sporting Events, and Music. Just make sure to cover a broad range of interests that will appeal to a variety of moods.

Cupid's Report

Some believe people are connected to each other through a sixth sense. If this sounds like you, you may want to go on a date that appeals to your mystical interests. Here are a few ideas to try: chanting, séance, tarot card reading, palm reading, magic show, or metaphysics.

Words of the Heart

"To cheat oneself out of love is the most terrible deception; it is an eternal loss for which there is no reparation, either in time or in eternity."

—Anonymous

To help you generate some ideas for your Date Activity Book categories, jot down eight categories of things you and your partner enjoy doing:

1. _____
2. _____
3. _____
4. _____
5. _____
6. _____
7. _____
8. _____

Expanding Your Choices

Under each broad category in your Date Activity Book, put several subcategories. For instance, under the Food category, divide restaurants you would like to go to into different groups:

➤ **Price ranges:** Inexpensive, moderately priced, expensive

➤ **Types of food:** Italian, French, Mexican, Chinese, and so on

➤ **Style of establishment:** Small and romantic, formal, modern and fast-paced, and so on

➤ **Best known for:** Sunday brunch, late-night dinners (after 10 P.M.), lunch, dessert, and so on

Dividing each category this way will make dating easier. It will take away almost every pressure you have to come up with an idea at the very last minute. It also helps you to get out of the rut of going to the same place and doing the same thing every time.

Filling in Activities

One way to find date activities is to use what I call "The 5-minute Sunday Homework Habit." This term describes a very effective tool for planning ideas for later dates with your partner. What it entails is spending five minutes with your Sunday newspaper each week.

Each Sunday, look through the newspaper for upcoming events that sound like fun to you. Cut out the announcements and tape them on the corresponding page of your Date Activity Book. That way, when date night rolls around, you can just pop open your Date Activity Book, and you'll have a bunch of choices right in front of you. For instance, if you and your partner are in an excited mood and feel like dancing, you will have a list of places to go dancing. Likewise, if the two of you are in a mood to just relax, flipping to the Music category in your Date Activity Book will list places that have soft music playing.

Lying Low

The staying-in date should not be confused with just hanging out. Hanging out is just two people under the same roof, doing their own separate things. The staying-in date has the same elements as a going-out date: You prepare your activity, dress for the occasion, and give your evening a beginning, middle, and ending. There are so many things to do on a date at home besides lie on the couch and watch television! Keep reading, and you'll catch on very quickly to how much fun staying home on a Saturday night can be.

Cupid's Report

At www.love@aol.com you will find an icon called Date Planner. This program is everyone's dream come true because it takes the frustration out of deciding what to do on a date. The Date Planner takes about five minutes to do.

Board Games Are Not Boring

Games are a wonderful way to nurture intimacy between two people. Just being physically close to your partner while playing a game can stimulate sexual arousal between the two of you. If that isn't enough incentive to play, you'll get even more stimulation if you play games that have a sexual slant. (Keep in mind that you won't find these games at Toys 'R' Us.) Try any of the following games:

➤ "An Enchanting Evening" by Games Partnership, Ltd.

➤ "Dirty Minds" by TDC Games

➤ "Dirty Money—The Game of Indecent Proposals" by TDC Games

➤ "Dirty Words—The Card Game" by Matscot International, Inc.

➤ "The Game—Charades—Fun Through the Art of Communication" by John M. Hansen

➤ "Love Dice" by Schocal

➤ "Love Potion No. 9—A Sensual Massage Game for Two" by The Game Works

➤ "Lovers and Liars" by Ty Wilson, Ltd.

Dr. Romance

If you love the water, consider trying out one of the following activities with your partner: baby pool, dinner cruise, dinner on a gondola, evening swim, hose fight, hot springs, Jacuzzi, king of the raft, picnic on the water, row boat rentals, Slip & Slide, washing the car, water balloon fight, water gun fight, and water park.

Cupid's Report

Sensate focus is a therapeutic technique sex therapists use with patients who have sexual dysfunction. This type of massage helps a couple be close to each other without the fear that it will turn into sex. The main rule to this exercise is that sex is off limits.

➤ "Recipe for Romance" by The Game Works
➤ "Sexual Secrets—The Game of Intimate Confessions" by TDC Games
➤ "Talk Dirty to Me" by TDC Games
➤ "X-Rated Charades" by The Game Works

Not all games are erotic by nature, some are just fun. Many board games can be played with a romantic twist. Take the game Scrabble, for instance. If you play the game with your partner, you can make a rule that only terms that deal with love can be spelled: romance, intimacy, sex, lingerie, kiss, love, hug, and so on. It's a great way to increase your love vocabulary.

Almost all games can be sexual if you apply slightly different rules to them. Do you remember playing the game of Twister when you were a child? Just think of how much more fun the game would be now, especially if you wear something sexy. Or what about card games? You can always suggest a game of strip poker. The games are limitless—all you need is a fun, spirited partner with a sense of adventure.

Rub-a-Dub-Dub, Two in a Tub

One of the most relaxing things you can do with your partner is to either bathe your partner or take a bath with him or her. Bathing your companion is a very loving, intimate act that brings you closer together. When you do this, it's pretty hard not to get into the tub yourself. If you do, it will be twice as much fun.

Because bath time is a fun way to be affectionate with your partner, you will want to create an environment that's conducive to pampering your partner's every need. Try some of the following suggestions:

➤ Body paints were created just for indoor dates. If you haven't tried them, get in the car and pick some up. Consider renting the foreign movie *Pillow Book* to get creative ideas of what to paint on your partner's body.

➤ Pour bath oil in the water and sprinkle the water with rose petals.

➤ For a bubble bath, use soap designed for bubble baths so the bubbles will last as long as your bath does.

➤ Certain items can make the bath very romantic because they give you plenty of options for catering to your partner's needs. Have these supplies on hand for bath time: big sponge, neck pillow, scented bath soap, bath crystals, after-bath lotion, big fluffy towels, bath glove, bath oil, bath beads, pulse-control shower head, bath brush, tub toys.

➤ Have a large empty container to fill with fresh water for rinsing time.

➤ Fresh flowers in a vase near the tub is a nice touch.

➤ Soft music adds the perfect amount of romance.

➤ No bath should ever begin without a candle being burned and the lights either turned off or down.

➤ Make sure you have glasses of wine or champagne on hand.

Words of the Heart

"What is yours is mine, and all mine is yours."

—Titus Maccius Plautus

If you decide to try a bath for two, make sure you complement it with candlelight and romantic music. Wash your partner lovingly from head to toe. By the time you are finished, your partner will feel completely loved and relaxed.

A Question-and-Answer Period

One way to grow closer to your partner is through conversation. Although this may sound easy, many times it isn't. Questions make conversation easy and are a great way to lead into talk about serious subjects. For instance, you and your partner can take turns asking the following questions:

➤ What do you consider romantic?

➤ What is your most romantic fantasy?

➤ What is the most romantic thing you've ever done?

➤ When was the first time you fell in love?

➤ How do you know when you are in love?

➤ Why do you love me?

➤ What makes a partner trustworthy?

➤ What do you consider a violation of trust?

➤ What kinds of foreplay do you like?

➤ Describe what an orgasm is to you.

➤ What is the most daring sexual activity you've ever done?

➤ When were your most uncomfortable and most comfortable sexual situations?

➤ When do you need cuddling the most?

➤ When do you need cuddling the least?

➤ How do you let your partner know when you just need to be held?

Dating in Your Own Backyard

Whoever said you have to stay inside the house for an at-home date? To make the evening portion of your date more adventurous, you can head out to your backyard, patio, lanai, or porch. Lying under the night sky has a way of relaxing even the most tense person and is very romantic. All you need is a sleeping bag or a pile of blankets, pillows, a flashlight, and a little mischievousness! A tent wouldn't quite be the same, but if you lack privacy, it's a good alternative. You may like it so much that you make it a summer habit.

Pseudo Vacations

In the privacy of your own home, you can bring the imaginary to life with a little creativity. Who says you can't go to the beach on a rainy day? If you bring the beach to your home, you can have an incredible day at the beach!

Creating a beach scene or any vacation in your living room is possible if you set it up right. This means having props to give it a convincing feel of whatever theme you want. For a beach scene, for instance, put a big blanket on the floor, have a colorful umbrella opened, and set out a beach ball, a raft, a cooler, and a portable radio on top of the blanket. In place of suntan lotion, you can use hand lotion and rub it on each other's bodies. Even without sun, you won't want to skip this agreeable task. A bonus to beaching inside is that you can't get arrested for sunbathing nude!

The Least You Need to Know

➤ Don't put off dating because you are not in the mood. Instead, make your date meet the mood you are in.

➤ Date night should be reserved for just the two of you. It's not a time to bond to a group of others, but to each other.

➤ The simplest way to plan a date is to paste ideas that you find into your Date Activity Book.

➤ A date at home can be just as great as going out, especially if you have some creative date ideas.

Celebrate the Good Times

With Valentine's Day quickly approaching, symbols of love were everywhere to remind Elizabeth and Raymond that their 10th wedding anniversary would soon be here. It was Raymond who'd insisted on being married on February 14 so that he'd never be the kind of husband who forgot an anniversary. How could he forget when everyone around him would also be celebrating the day? To make their anniversary extra special, they planned to remarry in front of their friends and family in a grand celebration to reaffirm their love to each other. The day came, and what a celebration it was! It proved to the two of them that they loved each other so much that if given the chance to do it all over again, they would (and did).

If you're not celebrating love, why not? Isn't love the most difficult thing to find in this lifetime? Isn't it love that makes you happier than anything else on earth? If you've found love, go forth and celebrate it!

Words of the Heart

"Time is the most valuable thing
a man can spend."

—Theophrastus

In this chapter, you will learn how significant the celebration of love is by valuing the fact you have a partner to share love with. Because celebrations usually involve gift giving, this chapter teaches you simple ways to know what to buy for the various occasions that come up. Last, you'll learn to remember to cherish the one you love when you see the symbols of love all around you.

Cause for Celebration

Love should be celebrated every day of the year. There's no sense in waiting for Valentine's Day to emphasize the importance of your relationship. The fact that you have someone in your life to love is cause for celebration. Besides, it's a lot more touching to celebrate on your own without a forced holiday.

The Rituals of Love

Romantic holidays usually originate around ceremonies and rituals of love. Everything we celebrate related to love begins because of a first meeting, a first kiss, a first everything a couple experiences together. The purpose of these celebrations is having someone to share life with.

Can you remember all of the firsts you had along with your partner? If not, it's time to find out what they are and begin to celebrate them. Fill in the dates for the following firsts:

Dr. Romance

Being romantic may be uncomfortable, but you can do it! Even the man dubbed "The World's Most Romantic Man" by the *St. Petersburg Times*, Michael Webb, said he felt awkward at first, but after a while, romance became natural. The same will happen to you.

First met: _____

First date: _____

First kiss: _____

First I love you: _____

First made love: _____

Why Should I Celebrate?

Some people choose not to celebrate holidays such as Valentine's Day because they think they are only for commercial profit. Unfortunately, the ones who lose out when you don't celebrate along with the masses are you and your partner. If this is the way you feel about romantic holidays, keep one thing in mind: Everything in America is for profit, so stop being a party pooper and celebrate like everyone else!

To Give or Not to Give

There are four occasions for which buying a present is not an option, but a requirement: anniversaries, Valentine's Day, birthdays, and Christmas. You may think that your partner knows you love him or her, but presents confirm it. Remember, your partner is constantly reminded by the symbols of love such as hearts and cupids all around him or her that love is meant to be celebrated.

The price of the present or even what you give isn't important. What's important is the act of giving. You should give because you want to give and because you care about your partner.

Words of the Heart

"The manner of giving shows the character of the giver more than the gift itself."

—Johanna Kaspar Lavater

Anniversaries

Each year you and your mate are together, you will have an anniversary to celebrate. You don't have to be married to celebrate your anniversary; many couples celebrate the anniversary of their first date. As you know, whenever there is a special occasion, you need to think about getting a gift. Anniversary gifts are probably the easiest gifts to buy because there is a gift-giving guide already provided for you to follow.

Anniversary	Traditional Gift	Modern Gift
1	Paper	Clock
2	Cotton	China
3	Leather	Crystal
4	Silk	Appliances
5	Wood	Silverware
6	Candy	Wood
7	Wool	Desk set
8	Bronze	Linens
9	Pottery	Leather
10	Tin	Diamond
11	Steel	Fashion jewelry
12	Linen	Pearls
13	Lace	Textiles
14	Ivory	Gold jewelry
15	Crystal	Watch
20	China	Platinum
25	Silver	Silver
30	Pearl	Pearl
35	Coral	Jade

continues

continued

Anniversary	Traditional Gift	Modern Gift
40	Ruby	Ruby
45	Sapphire	Sapphire
50	Gold	Gold
55	Emerald	Emerald
60	Diamond	Diamond
75	Diamond	Diamond

The only drawback to this table is that it's so general. For instance, wool is the gift to buy on a seventh anniversary. Is a sheep appropriate? To help you out, I've created a list of more specific ideas for the vaguer items suggested.

Traditional Anniversary Gift	Specific Gifts
Aluminum	Fishing rods, cookware, barbecue grill
Bronze	Pots, plant holders, candlesticks
Cotton	Clothing, linens, monogrammed cloth items
Crystal	Set of crystal glasses, vases, wall ornaments, bowls, baking dishes, stained-glass windows
Linens	Linens for any room in the house or clothing
Paper	Stationery, books
Silk	Clothing, flowers, ties
Silver	Silverware, jewelry, and household items
Steel	Kitchen items such as knives or cookware, pocketknife
Textiles	Any gift made of a fabric: clothing, reupholstered furniture or car seats, wall hangings
Tin	Decorative boxes or accessories for your home or office

Traditional Anniversary Gift	Specific Gifts
Wood	Bookends, shelves, jewelry box
Wool	Blankets or clothing
Leather	Belts, wallets, purses, luggage, gloves, clothing

One of the most treasured gifts you should remember to include in every anniversary celebration is a card that tells your partner how you feel about him or her and why he or she is important to you after all the time you've been together. It's a time to reflect on your relationship and why you still want to include your partner in your life.

Give Good Gifts

For holidays such as Valentine's Day, birthdays, and Christmas or Hanukkah, you have to give presents. Instead of viewing gift giving as a chore, think of it as a privilege. Without your partner, you'd have no one to give gifts to.

Finding a gift can sometimes make you so frustrated you want to either pull your hair out or not buy a gift at all. Just remember what Henry Wadsworth Longfellow said: "Give what you have. To someone it may be better than you dare to think."

Can't think of anything? How about a card and dinner? Flowers also are a great present for either sex. If you feel you still need some help choosing a gift, ask a friend who loves to shop.

Cupid's Report

There are all kinds of romantic holidays that you may not be aware of. Here are just a few for lovers to celebrate:

Creative Romance Month

Marriage Proposal Day

An Affair to Remember Month

Pleasure Your Mate Month

National Wedding Month

Pay a Compliment Day

Celebration of Love Week

World Marriage Day

For a complete list of holidays and dates, see the book *Chase's Calendar of Events*.

Friends love to help brainstorm for gift ideas, especially women. If you ever lack ideas or enthusiasm, just call up a woman—she'll be more than glad to help you.

When giving a gift, strive for something personal. Pete, for instance, had no idea what kind of gift to give Angie for their anniversary, which was one day away. Then he thought about the new house they were moving into, which had a huge bathtub that she had fallen in love with. They currently lived in a place that had only a shower, so she was looking forward to pampering herself in the new tub. Ah-ha! He had an idea. He went to the big bath supply store nearby and asked the saleslady to

"We should give as we would receive, cheerfully, quickly, and without hesitation, for there is no grace in a benefit that sticks to the fingers."

—Seneca from *Epistles*

help him out. The next day, he presented Angie with the best-stocked basket of bath supplies she'd ever seen. She was thrilled that he remembered how important the tub was to her.

Think personal in every area of the gift: For instance, in your card, write a personal note. (Chapter 11, "Writing a Love Letter," will give you plenty of sayings to use.)

La La La La La La Give for Today

Just when you thought you knew all of the romantic holidays to celebrate with your partner, here's another list from *Chase's Calendar of Events:*

➤ The first week of March is National Write a Letter of Appreciation Week. Send a letter expressing your gratitude to your mate, acknowledging the goodness that you find in him or her.

➤ March 20 is Smile Rejuvenation Day. Begin spring with a smile. Smiles are a tool for romantic interaction and are a key behavior in nonverbal communication. Show your partner that you care by smiling in his or her direction.

➤ March 21 is Single Parent's Day. This day is dedicated to recognizing and heightening awareness of Americans to the issues related to single-parent households. Dating is a big issue.

The Post-Its of Love

The symbols of love act as reminders of why love is important to you. They prompt you to remember the significance of your partner, kind of like a Post-it note. In this case, the reminder is that the love you share is important and needs to be remembered. Basically, love symbols reinforce the choice you made to be with your partner. If you aren't familiar with some of the more common symbols, keep reading.

With This Ring

According to Greek mythology, Prometheus was the first ring maker. He created them from the fire he stole from the gods. This myth is a pretty powerful image about the significance of a ring worn by lovers.

A ring is symbolic of committed love, whether the ring is a friendship, promise, engagement, or wedding ring. This ring tells you, and the rest of the world, that out of all the others on the planet, the two of you have chosen to be together.

The practice of wearing an engagement ring dates back to 1477, when Emperor Maximilian of Austria proposed to Mary of Burgundy with a gold ring adorned with diamonds. Back then diamonds were extremely rare and could only be afforded by the aristocracy. However, in 1870 large deposits of diamonds were discovered in Africa, and since that time, they have become the gemstone of choice for most brides.

For centuries, engagement and wedding rings have been playing musical chairs on the fingers of men and women. Rings were not always placed on the left ring finger the way they are today. Here is a list of where lovers of the past have worn their rings and why:

➤ The Egyptians wore wedding rings on the middle finger on the left hand because they believed that the vein in this finger ran directly to the heart.

➤ The Puritans disapproved of a ring in the wedding ceremony, but somehow it showed up on the bride's hand afterward.

➤ In some European countries around 1200, rings were worn on the right hand.

➤ Greek women wear their rings on the left hand during the engagement period and switch the rings to the right hand after marriage.

Cupid's Report

Each religion uses a different ceremonial saying during the marriage service when the rings are exchanged and placed on each person's finger. Here is a list of five vows:

Episcopal: "I give you this ring as a symbol of my vow and with all that I am and all that I have. I honor you in the name of the Father and the Son, and the Holy Spirit."

Jewish: "Behold you are consecrated unto me with this ring according to the law of Moses and Israel."

Lutheran: "I give you this ring as a sign of my love and faithfulness."

Presbyterian: "This ring I give you in token and pledge of our constant faith and abiding love."

Protestant: "With this ring I thee wed, with my body I thee worship, and with all my worldly goods, I thee endow."

➤ During a medieval marriage ceremony, the groom first placed the ring on the bride's thumb, then index and middle fingers, and finally on the traditional third finger on the left hand. This ritual was to respect the holy trinity in a sort of prayer.

➤ In the Jewish community, the bride used to wear her ring on her index finger so it would be visible to witnesses during the ceremony.

His and Hers Rings

The double ring ceremony, in which both the bride and groom exchange rings, didn't start until Elizabethan times in northern Europe. Back then, men wore engagement rings, too. During the engagement period, a pair of interlocking rings were purchased for the couple. The man wore one ring, and the other was placed on the woman's finger. On the wedding day, the ring was taken off the man's finger, and both rings were placed on the woman's finger in an interlocking ring pattern.

The main purpose for the dual engagement ring wearing was symbolic. It meant that a couple must stick to their commitment because each partner was wearing half the wedding ring. It also showed that they were worth more together than apart.

Cultural Symbols

Many people are familiar with the dual colored yin-yang circle as a symbol of love. This circle is composed of two conflicting parts: the yin, the black side, and the yang, the white side. The yin side represents femininity, which is made up of soul, wetness, cold, night, the moon, darkness, the Earth, sustenance, and the negative and passive power. The yang is the masculine side and represents spirituality, light, heat, dryness, day, the sun, heaven, creation, dominance, and positive and active power. Together, they create a perfect and complementary balance, which is something to strive for and something to be celebrated.

Rich folklore is associated with precious gemstones. When you give one as a gift, make sure you know the meaning behind it so that you give the appropriate one. Each month is also associated with a certain gemstone, usually referred to as a birthstone. Here is a list of what each stone symbolizes:

Month	Gemstone	Symbolizes
January	Garnet	Faithfulness
February	Amethyst	Peacemaking
March	Bloodstone	Courage
April	Diamond	Innocence
May	Emerald	True Love
June	Pearl	Beauty
July	Ruby	True friendship
August	Sardonyx	Conjugal happiness
September	Sapphire	Repentance
October	Opal	Hope
November	Topaz	Friendship
December	Turquoise	Happiness in love

Living Things

Sometimes romantic symbols are in the form of living things such as animals, sea life, and birds. This section introduces some of the most popular symbols in this category to show you just how broad the symbols of love are:

➤ **Cats.** In the Ancient Egyptian religion, cats were considered sacred to the goddess of love, Bast. She was often depicted as a woman with the head of a cat.

➤ **Sea life.** In the Eastern part of the world, the carp is a symbol of love, courage, dignity, and good fortune. The Japanese word for carp is a homophone of the word for love. The Roman goddess of love, Venus, was said to be created from foam and carried ashore on a scallop shell. This myth is the reason why the shell is a universally positive feminine symbol of love, birth, life, resurrection, and good luck.

➤ **Swans.** Swans represent both masculinity and femininity because they have a rounded body and long neck. The rounded body symbolizes the feminine curves while the neck represents the man's genitalia. Swans are associated with love, light, life, grace, purity, solitude, poetry, music, and sincerity.

➤ **Human signs.** The biological sign for female, the circle with a cross, comes from the Roman goddess of love, Venus. It represents her necklace or mirror. The biological sign for male, the circle with an arrow through it, is the sign for the planet Mars. It was named after the Romans god of war and represents his shield and spear.

Words of the Heart

"Happy Anniversary"
"For thirty-five years we've been together
Both in smooth and stormy weather
But there's never been a test too great
To make me sorry that you're my mate
You've smoothed the way when things got tough
And if that was not enough
You've been the balance in my life
As you've acted as my wife
As the years go by and we get old
Don't forget that you've been told
You're really loved by this proud man
Who so long ago you gave your hand
Keep on being who you are
In our lives you are the star
That shines so bright and lights the road
As we walk together and share the load
When our lives on earth are through
And the angels look at you
They'll see a special jewel in your crown
For the life you lived as Frieda Brown."
—James Dale Brown, 1979

Let all the symbols listed in this chapter demonstrate the importance love has in the human race. They continue to be reminders of the significance we place on love and romance. The next time you see a love symbol, let that be a reminder to you that you have someone you share your life with. And that fact is worth celebrating!

The Least You Need to Know

➤ A true romantic seeks out occasions other than calendar holidays to celebrate and works at making them special for the one he loves.

➤ Gift giving is easier when you remember that the only reason you're giving is because you have someone who loves you. Consider yourself lucky.

➤ These four romantic holidays require presents: anniversaries, Valentine's Day, birthdays, and Christmas (or another significant religious holiday).

➤ Let the symbols of love remind you to celebrate the relationship you have and value it for what it is: precious.

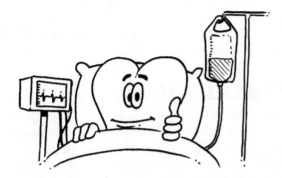

Chapter 22

Keeping Romance Alive

> ### In This Chapter
>
> ➤ Sharing and talking
>
> ➤ The importance of affection
>
> ➤ Your commitment to romance

No two people showed their love more than Jim and Della in the story of *The Gift of the Magi* by O. Henry. If you don't remember the story, it was about a poor couple at Christmas. The only two possessions of value in their home were Della's long, beautiful hair and Jim's watch that had once been his grandfather's. As the story goes, Della sells her hair to buy Jim a chain for his watch, and Jim sells his watch to buy Della combs for her hair. This story is about giving for the sake of love, even if you have to sacrifice the one thing you treasure the most.

The Gift of the Magi illustrates what this entire book is about: romantic gestures. A romantic gesture is a physical way to show your partner you care. The important aspect of the gesture isn't its grandness or cost. The intent behind the gesture is the true present. Romance boils down to making the extra effort, even when you think you don't have the time or the energy to show your love.

In this chapter, you will learn a few final points about how to keep your romance alive by paying attention to the little things. Everyday gestures of love show your partner how much you appreciate him or her and demonstrate that the relationship is a top priority. When you learn how to protect your investment in your relationship, you and your partner will bask in the rewards of a romantic life together.

It's the Little Things

Children are the real experts on how to show their sweethearts they love them. They do it with common-sense innocence. They don't have ulterior motives, and they don't expect anything in return. When they give, it's because they want to please the one they have a crush on.

This advice can work on grown-ups, too. (Yes, that means you.) We all have an understanding about how to please a partner. It never goes away; it's always there for you to use if you decide you want to. All it takes is a desire to tap into this ability.

Make Your Partner a Part of Your Life

One day over lunch, Bridget told her friend that she felt as though she and her husband of 12 years were just strangers living together under the same roof. They got along like two roommates without any problems, but something was missing. Bridget reminisced about how close she and her husband had once been and had no idea when things changed. She missed the closeness and had no idea how to get it back. Her friend sympathized with her because she felt the same way about her husband, too.

These two women share a very common problem in long-term relationships. Fortunately, this problem is easily fixed: Just remember to make your partner a part of your life.

Dr. Romance

Here is some very serious advice given by 10-year-old Brandon Sanchez on how to show a girl you like her:

➤ You have to be nice to her.

➤ Buy presents and flowers.

➤ Give big and little kisses.

➤ Help her with the chores.

➤ It's good to play together like biking, throwing snowballs, swimming, and taking walks.

➤ Talk with her.

➤ Give her attention.

➤ Smile at her.

➤ Laugh with her.

Brandon summed up his advice by saying that "you need to do these things anywhere, anytime, and when you see her."

When a relationship passes the honeymoon stage and into the comfortable stage, people often stop sharing things with their partners. This tendency is a normal process of growing closer. People just get busy in their normal routine and don't take the time to share like they did early in their relationship. The remedy is to devote a certain time every day to share the highs, lows, passions, frustrations, memories, hopes, and everything else you go through every day. Keeping the lines of communication open will keep the romance burning bright in your relationship, and that's the key to feeling close to your partner.

Talk Time

Knowing someone takes a lifetime, so you need to keep the lines of intimate conversation going. These important conversations will prevent the two of you from ever feeling like strangers living together.

Encourage these conversations by reserving nightly time together before you fall asleep to have talk time. You don't have to verbally arrange a time to talk—it's better to keep it casual by creating a habit of talking each night. Talk time isn't a time for serious discussions; it's more a time for relaxed, fun conversation to get to know each other better. The following are some good questions for you to ask your partner at talk time:

➤ Tell me about your favorite pet when you were a child.

➤ Who has been your best friend the longest?

➤ What's a holiday tradition that you like/dislike?

➤ When you are old, what will be the highlight of your life?

➤ If you could be the creator of any invention throughout time, what would it be?

➤ Tell me about your first day in high school.

➤ What are your favorite smells of each season?

Words of the Heart

"Only a life lived for others is a life worthwhile."

—Albert Einstein

Dr. Romance

A great way to communicate how much you love your partner is by giving him or her a love coupon. This piece of paper promises your partner that you will provide a service, such as a foot massage. The company Gentle Persuasions at www.gentleone.com has developed an extensive line of laminated coupons that appear more like a gift because of the size, artwork, and matching colored envelopes.

Words of the Heart

"Pains of love be sweeter far than all other pleasures are."

—John Dryden, 1669

Make Love Last Forever

So far in this book, you've read about how to put romance and passion back into your relationship or use a little romance to start a new relationship. The key to keeping the romance in a relationship is to continue to practice what you've learned in this book.

Like anything new, you will go through the excited phase of the relationship where romance is easy. As time goes on and the realities of life settle in, maintaining romance will be more difficult. At this point, you need to commit to making your relationship your number-one priority.

The longer you keep making romantic gestures, the more they will become a habit you do without thinking. What won't become programmed is your partner's reaction. The more you show your love, the more your partner will show it in return.

Remember, the easiest way to change your partner's behavior is to change your own. If you want to be romanced, all you have to do is try a little romancing yourself. You'll be amazed by how it works.

Keeping Life Balanced

In most couples today, both people have careers. Dual-career couples often experience an increase in relationship stress and a decrease in the amount of time they have for each other. As long as the relationship is well-organized, and nothing unexpected comes up, work and relationships run smoothly. However, life usually doesn't work that way.

Couples must keep their lives in balance. If they don't, their relationships will suffer. You won't fall out of love just because you're a workaholic. But continually putting your other responsibilities ahead of your relationship means that you and your partner will pay in terms of emotional neglect for each other's needs. Get a sitter if you need some time alone. Take a sick day to put your relationship back in good health. Do what's necessary to balance the needs of your life with the needs of your relationship.

An Affair to Remember

Christopher Reeve, best known for his portrayal of Superman, and Dana Morosini met when he was a successful film actor and she was a cabaret singer. Christopher was not looking for love because he had been separated from his wife for only five months. But when Christopher saw Dana performing in a cabaret, he went down, hook, line, and sinker. He asked her out after the show, but she turned him down. Later that night, he ran into her at a party, and he tried again. This time he was successful, and they married just a few months later. Their marriage was a happy one. Years later, he was left quadriplegic after a fall from his horse. But even Kryptonite couldn't weaken this couple. Dana has honored the commitment "in sickness and in health." After the accident, Dana told Christopher, "You're still you, and I love you."

Keep the Lovin' Comin'

Nothing builds a bond between two people like genuine affection and lovemaking. Skin-to-skin touch is very important in romantic relationships. Skin-to-skin touch can be any kind of touch, not necessarily sexual. However, sexual touch is very important to a couple and should be a regular activity. This is sometimes easier said than done.

Although these statistics are for happy couples, the numbers of sexual contacts per week seem low. My recommendation is to double the times you make love and watch how your relationship flourishes. Who wants to stop with one bite? Have the whole thing! It will satisfy both you and your partner.

Words of the Heart

"Grow old along with me! The best is yet to be, The last of life, for which the first was made: Our times are in His hand Who saith, 'a whole I planned,' Youth shows but half; trust God; see all, nor be afraid!"

—Robert Browning

Affection Is a Must

Receiving affection makes you happier and helps you live longer. Not only that, but it also feels really good. It feels good when you touch someone you love, and it feels wonderful when that person touches you, too.

Words of the Heart

"All that you do, it brightens my day,

You fulfill and excite me in a special way,

The things that you do make me want to stay

All that you do, it brightens my day.

All that you need is all that I'll be,

Time to be held or time to be free,

No matter how hard, I hope you will see

All that you need is all that I'll be."

—Ken Daly, 1997

If you notice a decrease in affectionate touching in your relationship, you need to take action. Trying some of the following suggestions will guarantee a quick increase in affection between the two of you:

➤ Sleep naked every night. If you have to, keep your door locked. No one but the two of you will know. If you get cold, snuggle closer to your partner or pull on an extra blanket.

➤ Shower together. It not only saves on the water bill, it also puts a little extra steam between the two of you.

➤ Ask your partner to kiss you, hold you, and caress you.

➤ Sit next to each other when you watch television or read.

➤ Hold your partner when you feel like crying or when you suspect your partner needs to be held.

➤ Stroke your partner's hair or face each time you walk past him or her.

➤ Hold hands when you walk together.

➤ Kick off your shoes and touch your partner's feet during meals.

Making Your Dreams Come True

Too often obligations in life keep you from maintaining the closeness you originally sought in your relationship. You can combat this by focusing on sharing your life with your partner.

Real romance isn't about flowers and candy, it's about daily expressions of love. It's about your commitment to your partner and the actions that prove your commitment. Expressing love is not about the big things you do for your mate, but the small things. These little gestures make your partner feel appreciated, cared for, and special. For those times when you don't feel up to giving, just remember that it's hard to have a vibrant, growing relationship with someone when you are more deeply committed to something else.

Even if you aren't comfortable expressing your love, you still need to do it. Be realistic; it's all right if you start out slow. The point is to start. In a great country song called "Me Too," a husband struggles to tell his wife he loves her, but he can only manage to say, "Me too." Of course, she urges him to say, "I love you," but he can't. To reassure her, he talks about all the things he does to say "I love you," but she misses all of them.

Let this song be a reminder that sometimes your partner may be trying his best to show you he loves you. Sadly, some people find it difficult to express their love verbally. But this difficulty does not mean they do not show their love in other ways. You just have to learn the ways your partner shows you he cares. Just think of how good it will make your partner feel to know you see how he expresses his love for you. Every effort either of you make to be romantic and to show love counts.

Make your relationship a top priority in your life by keeping your full attention on it. Relationships don't stay strong and happy because of mere proximity. Instead, your relationship is happy because you care enough to make it work.

The Least You Need to Know

➤ Having a romantic relationship requires you to consciously decide to be romantic. Romance does not just happen; it requires work.

➤ Being romantic is not something you do twice a year when you celebrate your anniversary and Valentine's Day. Romance is something you work into your life because it's important to you.

➤ The more committed you are to having a happy relationship, the longer and harder you will work toward making it happen.

➤ It's always easier to be romantic during the easy times. The test that proves your commitment to the relationship comes when times are the most difficult. Those are the times that strengthen your relationship the most if you continue to show your love romantically.

Romantic Resources

Aphrodisiacs

Aphrodisiac Cooking by Bruce Carlson. Hearts N Tummies, 1995.

Aphrodisiacs: A Guide to What Really Works by Esmond Choueke. Carol Publishing Group, 1998.

Charms, Potions & Aphrodisiacs by Vera Lee. Mount Ivy Press, 1996.

A Dictionary of Aphrodisiacs by Harry E. Wedeck. M. Evans & Company, Inc., 1991.

Essence of Love: Fragrance, Aphrodisiacs, & Aromatherapy for Lovers by Maggie Tisserand. Harper San Francisco, 1994.

Herbal Love Potions: The Magic & Ritual Use of Aphrodisiacs by W. E. Lee and Lynn Lee. Keats Publishing, Inc., 1991.

Plants of Love: Aphrodisiacs in Myth, History, & the Present by Christian Ratsch. Ten Speed, 1997.

Secrets of Gypsy Love Magic by Raymond Buckman. Llewellyn, 1990.

Sex, Drugs & Aphrodisiacs by Adam Gottlieb. Ronin Publishing, Inc, 1996 (in paperback).

Aromatherapy

Aromatherapy: A Lifetime Guide to Healing with Essential Oils by Valerie Cooksley. Prentice Hall, 1995.

Aromatherapy Book of Applications and Inhalations by Jeanne Rose. Atlantic Books, 1992.

Aromatherapy Workbook by Marcel F. Lavabre and Marcel Levabre. Inner Traditions, 1996.

Illustrated Encyclopedia of Essential Oils by Julia Lawless. Barnes & Noble Books, 1995.

Practical Aromatherapy: How to Use Essential Oils to Restore Vitality by Robyn M. Feller. Harper Collins, 1994.

Lovemaking

101 Nights of Grrreat Sex by Laura Corn. Park Avenue Press, 1995.

101 Grrreat Quickies by Laura Corn. Park Avenue Press, 1997.

The Art of Arousal by Dr. Ruth Westheimer. Abbeville Press Incorporated, 1997.

The Kama Sutra of Vatsyayana translated by Sir Richard Burton and F. F. Arbuthnot. Berkley, 1963.

Soulful Sex: Opening Your Heart, Body, & Spirit to Lifelong Passion by Victoria Lee. MJF Books, 1997.

The Massage Book by George Downing. Random House, 1997.

In the Mood by Doreen Virtue, Ph.D. Harper Paperbacks, 1995.

The Erotic in Literature: A Historical Survey of Pornography as Delightful as It Is Indiscreet by David Loth. Barnes & Noble Books, 1994.

The Art of Kissing by William Cane. St. Martin's Press, 1995.

Relationships

Desirable Men: How to Find Them by Nancy Fagan (a.k.a. Dr. Romance). Prima Publishing, 1997.

A Fine Romance: The Passage of Courtship from Meeting to Marriage by Michael Morgenstern. Ballantine Books, 1988.

Being Intimate: A Guide to Successful Relationships by John Amodeo and Kris Wentworth. JODA, 1994.

Creating Love: The Next Stage of Growth by John Bradshaw. Bantam Doubleday Dell Publishing Group, 1993.

Getting to "I Do": The Secret to Doing Relationships Right by Dr. Pat Allen. Avon Books, 1994.

Intimate Partners: Patterns in Love and Marriage by Maggie Scarf. Ballantine Books, 1988.

Romantic Videos

When Harry Met Sally (1989) Billy Crystal and Meg Ryan prove that men and women can't be just friends.

Brief Encounters (1945) Trevor Howard and Celia Johnson in a wartime romance.

Camille (1936) Greta Garbo, Robert Taylor, and Lionel Barrymore interpret a love tale.

Indecent Proposal (1993) Woody Harrelson, Demi Moore, and Robert Redford deal with the aftermath of a proposal for sex.

The Heiress (1949) Olivia de Havilland is threatened with disinheritance when she falls for Montgomery Clift.

Casablanca (1943) Humphrey Bogart and Ingrid Bergman as star-crossed lovers during wartime.

Overboard (1988) Goldie Hawn and Kurt Russell in a romantic comedy.

The African Queen (1951): Humphrey Bogart and Katharine Hepburn find unlikely love.

Pretty Woman (1991) Richard Gere and Julia Roberts in a love story of a businessman and a prostitute.

Roxanne (1987) Daryl Hannah and Steve Martin find love in spite of his big nose.

Romantic Music CDs

Power of Love by Luthur Vandross

Time, Love, & Tenderness by Michael Bolton

Forever Friends by Justo Almaro

Something of Time by Nightnoise

Livin' Inside Your Love; Breezin' by George Benson

MCMXC A.D. by Enigma

The Colour of My Love by Celine Dion

Heartstrings by Earl Klugh

Shepherd Moons; Watermark by Enya

Keys to Imagination; Optimystique; Out of Silence by Yanni

In the Garden, by Eric Tingstad and Nancy Rumbel

Intimacy by Walter Beasley

Heartsounds; Seasons; Impressions; Pianoscapes by David Lanz

Love Delux by Sade

Romantic Web Sites

Couples	www.friendsandlovers.com
Cupid	www.banzai.neosoft.com/citylink
Cyber Kissing	www.cyberkisses.com
Dating	www.debbieguide
Dating Tips	www.1st-spot.net/topic_Romance.html
Engagements	www.topropose.com
Flirting	www.flirt.com/advice/angel/flirts/index
Kissing	www.homearts.com/kissnet.com
Kissing Tutorials	www.adolescentadulthood.com/kissing
Love Coupons	www.gentleone.com
Love Scopes	www.4yourhoroscope.com/romantic.com
Online Dating	www.love@aol.com
Relationships	www.committment.com
Relationships	www.ivillage.com
Romance Tips	www.theromantic.com
Sex	www.drruth.comSex
Quiz	www.women.com/sex/quiz
Tips for Men	www.mixnmatch.com/match/pub/98/06/16
Virtual Kisses	www.thekiss.com

Love Poetry

In this appendix you'll find additional poetry to help you communicate your feelings of love for your partner. For great ideas on how to use poetry in romance, see Chapters 10, "Romantic Readings," and 11, "Writing a Love Letter."

She Walks in Beauty

> She walks in beauty, like the night
> Of cloudless climes and starry skies;
> And all that's best of dark and bright
> Meet in her aspect and her eyes:
> Thus mellow'd to that tender light
> Which heaven to gaudy day denies.

—Lord Byron

My Love

> My Love
> Is like the grasses
> Hidden in the deep mountain:
> Through its abundance increases
> There is none that knows

—Ono No Yoshiki

Upon Julia's Clothes

> When as in silks my Julia goes,
> Then, then, methinks, how sweetly flows
> That liquefaction of her clothes.
>
> Next, when I cast mine eyes, and see
> That brave vibration each way free,
> O how that glittering taketh me!

—Robert Herrick

from *Paradise Lost*

> Love refines
> The thoughts, and heart enlarges, hath his seat
> In reason, and is judicious, is the scale
> By which to heavenly love thou mayest ascend.

—John Milton

Heart Exchange

> My true love hath my heart, and I have his,
> But just exchange, one for the other giv'n:
> I hold his dear, and mine he cannot miss:
> There never was a bargain better driv'n.
>
> His heart in me keeps me and him in one,
> My heart in him his thoughts and senses guides;
> He loves my heart, for once it was his own;
> I cherish his, because in me it bides.
>
> His heart his wound received from my sight:
> My heart was wounded with his wounded heart.
> For as from me on him his hurt did light:
>
> So still me thought in me his heart did smart.
> Both equal hurt, in his change sought our bliss;
> My true love hath my heart, and I have his.

—Sir Philip Sidney

How Do I Love Thee?

> How do I love thee? Let me count the ways.
> I love thee to the depth and breadth and height
> My soul can reach, when feeling out of sight
> For the ends of being and ideal grace.
> I love thee to the level of every day's
> Most quiet need, by sun and candlelight
> I love thee freely, as men strive for right;
> I love thee purely, as they turn from praise.
> I love three with the passion put to use

In my old griefs, and with my childhood's faith.
I love thee with a love I seemed to lose
With my lost saints—I love thee with the breath,
Smiles, tears, of all my life!—and, if God choose,
I shall but love thee better after death.

—Elizabeth Barrett Browning

Sonnet 116

Let me not to the marriage of true minds
Admit impediments. Love is not love
Which alters when it alteration finds,
Or bends with the remover to remove;
O, no! It is an ever-fixed mark,
That looks on tempests and is never shaken;
It is the star to every wandering bark,
Whose worth's unknown, although his height be taken.
Love's not time's fool, though rosy lips and cheeks
Within his bending sickle's compass come;
Love alters not with his brief hours and weeks,
But bears it out even to the edge of doom.
If this be error, and upon me prov'd,
I never writ, nor no man ever lov'd.

—William Shakespeare

When We Have Loved

When we have loved, my love,
Panting and pale from love,
Then from your cheeks, my love,
Scent of the sweat I love:
And when our bodies love
Now to relax in love
After the stress of love,
Ever still more I love
Our mingled breath of love.

—from the Sanskrit

Desire

Where true love burns desire is love's pure flame;
It is the reflex of our earthly frame,
That takes its meaning from the nobler part,
And but translates the language of the heart.

—Samuel Taylor Coleridge

Love

All thoughts, all passions, all delights,
Whatever stirs this mortal frame,
All are but ministers of love,
And feed his sacred flame.

—Samuel Taylor Coleridge

Drink to Me Only with Thine Eyes

Drink to me only with thine eyes,
And I will pledge with mine;
Or leave a kiss upon the cup,
And I'll not look for wine.
The thirst that from the soul doth rise
Doth ask a drink divine;
But might I of Jove's nectar sup,
I would not change for thine.
I sent thee late a rosy wreath,
Not so much honouring thee,
As giving it a hope that there
It could not wither'd be.

—Ben Jonson, from "The Forest"

First Love

I ne'er was struck before that hour
With love so sudden and so sweet,
Her face it bloomed like a sweet flower
And stole my heart away complete.

My face turned pale as deadly pale,
My legs refused to walk away,
And when she looked, what could I ail?
My life and all seemed turned to clay.

And then my blood rushed to my face
And took my eyesight quite away,
The trees and bushes round the place
Seemed midnight at noonday.
I could not see a single thing,
Words from my eyes did start—
They spoke as chords do from the string,
And blood burnt round my heart.

Are flowers the winter's choice?
Is love's bed always snow?
She seemed to hear my silent voice,
Not love's appeals to know.
I never saw so sweet a face
As that I stood before.
My heart has left its dwelling-place
And can return no more.

—John Clare

Love in Her Sunny Eyes

Love in her sunny eyes does basking play;
Love walks the pleasant mazes of her hair;
Love does on both her lips for ever stray;
And sows and reaps a thousand kisses there.
In all her outward parts love's always seen;
But, oh, he never went within.

—Abraham Cowley, from "The Change"

Index

D

train ride meals, 182
picnics
  essentials, 144
  location suggestions, 143-144
  setting up, 144-145
presentation of food, 141
role in romance, 137
spices, associated meanings, 142
sweets, 209
vegetables
  associated meanings, 209-210
  fertility, 138
forceful kissing, partners' kissing, 83-84
foreign cities, 173
foreign train travel, 176
forties (1940s), 20
fragrances
  appeal of, 155
  aromatherapy, 155
  essential oils, 155
    guidelines for using, 155-156
    types of oils/uses, 156-157
fruits
  associated meanings, 209-210
  fertility, 138

G

Gable, Clark
  actresses who kissed him, 135
  Harlow, Jean, romance with, 60
games, board games (adult), 217-218
Garbo, Greta and John Gilbert, 133
gemstones, associated meanings, 228

gender differences, sexual fantasies, 69-70
gestures
  appropriate, 28
  nonsexual gestures, 24, 26, 28
  Romantic Tools List, 28-29
    cooking dinners, 25
    examples, 26-27
    prior to birth control, 25
    sexually transmitted diseases (STDs), 25
    tattoos, 25
    unresponsiveness to, 27-28
  sexual gestures, 25
  unresponsiveness to, 27-28
getaways. *See* weekend getaways
The Gift of the Magi, 231
gifts
  anniversaries, 223-225
  bringing for dates, 206
    flowers, 207-208
    fruits, 209-210
    plants, 208-209
    sweets, 209
  bringing to dates, 206
    flowers, 207-208
    fruits, 209-210
    plants, 208-209
    sweets, 209
  clothing, 191-192
  considerations, 190-191
  extravagant gifts
    clothing, 191-192
    considerations, 190-191
    jewelry, 192-193
    medical assessments, 193
    photographs, 194
    recreating stories, 195-196
    yachts, 193-194

giving
  essential occasions to give, 223-225
  ideas, 225
  personalizing, 226
  ideas, 225
  jewelry, 192-193
  medical assessments, 193
  online shopping, 162-163
  personalizing, 226
  photographs, 194
  recreating stories, 195-196
  yachts, 193-194
Gilbert, John and Greta Garbo, 133
Goldleaf Train Service, 175
golf courses, extravagant vacations, 188
Gone with the Wind, 34
good girl images vs. bad girl images, 29-30
graham crackers, effect on sexual interest, 16
Great South Pacific, foreign train travel, 176
Greek mythology, 6
  Eros (Cupid)
    affair with Psyche, 9
    goals, 8
  Mount Olympia, influence on romance, 7
green (color), associated moods, 55-56
greeting dates, 206
group sex (cybersex), 166
"Happy Anniversary" poem, 229

H

habits (eating), quiz, 138-140
hairstyles
  copying, 204
  letting go, 150

proper places/times
daytime, 85
nighttime, 84
public displays of affection, 85
romantic readings
reading together
origins, 107
Romeo and Juliet, 108
roses, associated meanings, 207-208
Royal Scots, foreign train travel, 176
rules, unwritten rules, 11-12

S

sadism, 77
saying "I Love You," 97
appropriate time, 97-98
in other languages, 101-102
scents
appeal of, 155
aromatherapy, 155
bedrooms, 53
essential oils
diffusers, 155
guidelines for using, 155-156
types of oils, 156-157
sea life, symbols of love, 229
seduction
assessing seductive behavior, 62
cerebral seduction, 59
empty nest syndrome, 59
goals, 60-61
media ads, 59
process, 60
common behaviors, 61-62
conversational skills
assessing, 63
essentials, 64

flirting
emotionally attractive people, 66
flirting, 64, 68
body language, 65-66
essentials, 65
eye contact, 67
importance, 64-65
Reading People, 65
touching, 68
verbal flirting, 67
improving, 62-63
myths
attractive individuals, 58
media, 58
proper timing, 58
wealthy people, 58
weight, 58
negative connotations, 57-58
stress reduction, 63
value of, 63
selfish partners, 40
Sentara center, 193
serenades
common songs, 131-132
considerations, 131
serenading, 185
seventies (1970s), 20
sex
alternative terms, 89
aphrodisiacs
Spanish flies, 89
spices, 84
attitudes about, 30-31
birth control pills
prior to birth control, 25
widespread use, 21
exhibitionism, 78
fantasies
assessing, 85-86
discussing with partners, 71-73
dressing up, 76
encouraging, 73
fetishism, 79

gender differences, 69-70
masochism, 78
men's fantasies, 70
plan of action, 86
sadism, 77
sample characters, 76-77
sample scenes to act out, 74-76
voyeurism, 78
writing down, 72-73
fetishism, 79
masochism, 78
on airplanes, 172
positions, from Kama Sutra, 88
premarital sex, increase, 25
problems
alernative treaments, 88-89
sadism, 77
societal views of, 24
Victorian era, 29
World War II, 24
Victorian era
sexual interest, 17-18
societal views of, 29
voyeurism, 78
women
perceptions of women, 29-30
sexual love, movie themes, 135
sexuality
societal view, 71-72
Victorian era views, 29
sexually transmitted diseases (STDs)
Civil War, 18
nonsexual gestures, 25
Shakespeare, William "Sonnet 17," 120
Shaw, George Bernard, love letters, 120
shopping
online shopping, 163
shopping together, 184

Y–Z